Ultimate AWS Certified Cloud Practitioner (CLF-C02) Certification Guide (2nd Edition)

A Beginner's Guide to AWS Concepts, Core Services, Security, and Architecture to Crack the CLF-C02 Exam with Ease

Gaurav H Kankaria

www.orangeava.com

First Published: Feburary 2026

Published By: Orange Education Pvt Ltd, AVA®

Address: 9, Daryaganj, Delhi, 110002, India

275 New North Road Islington Suite 1314 London,

N1 7AA, United Kingdom

ISBN (PBK): 978-93-49887-31-2

ISBN (E-BOOK): 978-93-49887-59-6

Scan the QR code to explore our entire catalogue

www.orangeava.com

Get a Free eBook

We hope you're enjoying your recent book purchase! Your feedback is incredibly valuable to us and helps other readers discover books that truly make a difference.

If you found this book useful or enjoyable, we'd greatly appreciate it if you could leave a short review with a 5-star rating on Amazon. Your review supports our work and allows us to reach more learners worldwide.

As a thank-you, we're happy to offer you a **free digital copy of this book** plus a **30% discount code** for your next purchase on our official websites:

www.orangeava.com

www.orangeava.in (For the Indian Subcontinent).

☑ **How it works:**

Leave your review on Amazon, take a screenshot of the confirmation or use the following link to submit the claim and email it to **info@orangeava.com.** Once received the required detail, we will send your rewards within 24 hours, **along with one month free subcription to the book on AVA SkillShelf!**

Claim Form
https://rebrand.ly/4d2477

Thank you for your support—it truly means a lot to us.

Enjoy 1 Month of Free Access to AVA SkillShelf!

The future belongs to lifelong learners. With AVA SkillShelf, you go beyond reading books and start building real, job-ready skills curated by industry experts.

Your membership unlocks **200+ learning products** covering AI, Cloud, Python, Cybersecurity, Data Science, DevOps, and more—all in one platform. Our bestselling technical books are transformed into structured courses designed for practical, real-world application.

Learn directly from experienced professionals and published authors, with no filler—just actionable insights. Earn **verified digital certifications** to strengthen your CV, LinkedIn profile, and professional credibility.

Learn anytime, anywhere, on any device, at your own pace. Ideal for students, professionals, career switchers, and tech leaders.

For full access to all current and future courses, choose our **Annual Membership**. Simply scan the QR to get started!

For 1 month Free access, simply refer to the steps on the previous page titled: Get a Free ebook!

https://www.avaskillshelf.com/

Colored Images

Please follow the links or scan the QR codes to download the ***Images*** of the book:

You can find code bundles of our books on our official Github Repository. Go to the following link to and QR code to explore the further:

https://github.com/orgs/ava-orange-education/repositories

The code bundles and images of the book are also hosted on ***https://rebrand.ly/7ac100***

In case there's an update to the code, it will be updated on the existing GitHub repository.

Errata

We take immense pride in our work at **Orange Education Pvt Ltd,** and follow best practices to ensure the accuracy of our content to provide an indulging reading experience to our subscribers. Our readers are our mirrors, and we use their inputs to reflect and improve upon human errors, if any, that may have occurred during the publishing processes involved. To let us maintain the quality and help us reach out to any readers who might be having difficulties due to any unforeseen errors, please write to us at :

errata@orangeava.com

Your support, suggestions, and feedback are highly appreciated.

Dedicated to

My Grandparents,

Shri Manohar Raj Kankaria and Smt. Kamala Bai Kankaria.

And

My Parents,

Shri Harish Kumar Kankaria and Smt. Indra Kankaria.

My Wife, Pooja as well as My Daughters, Vridhi and Aanya.

About the Author

Gaurav H Kankaria is a passionate technologist with more than a decade of experience in Data and Analytics. He specializes in driving business growth for retail and financial clients, leveraging his expertise in architecting data-intensive solutions, and utilizing AI/ML technologies to solve complex challenges.

Gaurav's proven track record includes designing scalable data architectures, implementing predictive analytics solutions, and leading projects that have delivered significant top-line and bottom-line improvements for diverse clients across the retail and financial sectors.

Recognized for his contributions to the AWS community, Gaurav served as an AWS Partner Ambassador. This designation reflects his deep understanding of cloud technologies, and his commitment to sharing his expertise with others. Gaurav's certifications further solidify his credentials such as AWS Cloud Practitioner, AWS Solutions Architect - Professional, AWS Data Analytics - Specialty, AWS Security - Specialty, AWS AI Practitioner, and AWS Machine Learning Specialty.

This combination of real-world experience, in-depth technical knowledge, and industry recognition positions Gaurav as a trusted guide for readers seeking to navigate the exciting world of AWS cloud computing!

About the Technical Reviewer

Sriram Kuravi has over 16 years of experience designing and engineering data-intense enterprise applications on AWS. He has worked with global technology solution companies to drive Cloud Migrations and Modernizations, transforming existing workloads on AWS. Sriram has extensive working experience with Startups in education space, universities, and public sector organizations, helping them with their cloud transformation journeys.

Currently, Sriram works as a Senior Solutions Architect at AWS India, where he assists System Integrator Partners build new technology practices on AWS. He is passionate about data-driven transformations, and building as well as nurturing teams of experts to support such transformations.

Acknowledgments

Writing a book—especially a second edition—is a journey of reflection, learning, and rediscovery. Coming back to this work has been both humbling and incredibly rewarding. With this edition, I set out not only to update the content with the latest advancements in AWS, but also to go a step further by including ideas that are slightly ahead of the exam syllabus. This is to enable readers gain a deeper, more intuitive understanding of how cloud technologies are evolving. I have also added clearer explanations, real-world scenarios, and richer references which I wish I had when I first began exploring the cloud.

While I have thanked many wonderful people in the first edition, this time, I want to focus on what it felt like to revisit and rebuild this book. Rewriting a second edition is not simply about editing chapters—it is about re-immersing yourself in a subject and asking, "How can this be even more meaningful for someone starting from scratch?" This thought guided every paragraph. It has been incredibly fulfilling to rethink explanations, rework examples, and redesign the flow so that beginners can approach AWS with confidence, rather than intimidation.

To everyone who will read this book—whether you are a student, a working professional, or someone simply curious—I am truly grateful knowing that this book may play even a small role in your learning journey, and make my late nights and every re-write worth it! Thank you for giving me the reason to return to these chapters, rethink them, and rebuild them with even more clarity and purpose.

Preface

Welcome to your starting point in the world of AWS Cloud Computing, and your roadmap to the AWS Certified Cloud Practitioner certification. Hence, whether you are an experienced IT professional or someone stepping into the cloud for the first time, this book aims to be your complete companion on the journey ahead.

Connecting Concepts with Real-World Applications

Cloud computing can feel overwhelming at first, especially when you are preparing for a certification. That is why this guide walks you through the essentials in a way that blends clear explanations with practical insights. You will not only learn the foundational ideas behind AWS services—you will also understand how to apply them in real scenarios, and how to approach the Cloud Practitioner exam with confidence.

A Learning Path Designed with You in Mind

Every learner absorbs information differently, so this book is structured to be accessible to all. Each chapter focuses on a specific pillar of AWS, breaking down the core services, pricing models, security principles, architectural best practices, and deployment strategies. Interactive elements such as hands-on exercises, practice questions, and relatable examples are woven throughout to reinforce what you learn and help it stick.

Here is a quick look at what lies ahead:

Chapter 1: Introduction to AWS Cloud Practitioner Exam

A clear overview of the exam, why it matters, and what you can expect—along with helpful strategies to begin your preparation.

Chapter 2: Understanding Cloud Computing

A beginner-friendly explanation of core cloud concepts such as scalability, elasticity, and the pay-as-you-go model, along with an introduction to the major cloud service models.

Chapter 3: Introduction to AWS and Global Infrastructure

A tour through AWS's origin, global footprint, and the fundamental services that form the backbone of the platform.

Chapter 4: AWS Well-Architected Framework and Shared Responsibility Model

An essential guide to designing secure, efficient, and cost-effective cloud architectures as well as clarifying what AWS handles versus what you are responsible for.

Chapter 5: AWS Core Services – Part 1

A deep dive into the services you will encounter most often such as virtual servers, serverless computers, storage solutions, and managed databases.

Chapter 6: AWS Core Services – Part 2

Learn how AWS supports seamless migration, efficient networking, and streamlined development workflows.

Chapter 7: AWS Core Services – Part 3

A detailed look at AWS's security ecosystem, and the governance tools that help you operate safely and responsibly in the cloud.

Chapter 8: Other AWS Services

A broad exploration of analytics, machine learning, IoT, frontend tools, and emerging AI-powered services.

Chapter 9: Billing and Pricing

A breakdown of AWS's pricing models and cost-management tools because the cloud should empower you, not overwhelm your budget.

Chapter 10: Preparing for Exam

Practical tips, revision strategies, and mock exam insights to help you feel fully prepared on the test day.

Chapter 11: AWS Hands-on Guide for Beginners

Alongside the theory, you will find a dedicated hands-on section that walks you through setting up your AWS account, configuring permissions, and working with the vital services like EC2 and S3. So, think of it as a guided practice to build your confidence!

A Book for Everyone

No technical background? No problem. This book explains every concept in simple, approachable language. Thus, if you are new to cloud, you will find the clarity you need to move forward without hesitation, and if you are a seasoned professional, you will gain a refreshed understanding of the fundamentals and the validation of earning a globally recognized certification.

By the time you turn the final page, you will be well-prepared to:

- Grasp vital AWS services and cloud computing fundamentals.
- Confidently approach and clear the AWS Certified Cloud Practitioner exam.
- Apply your knowledge to build and deploy applications in the cloud.
- Navigate through the rapidly evolving cloud ecosystem with clarity and competence.

So, welcome to your AWS journey, and let us begin...

DID YOU KNOW

Did you know that Orange Education Pvt Ltd offers eBook versions of every book published, with PDF and ePub files available? You can upgrade to the eBook version at **www.orangeava.com** and as a print book customer, you are entitled to a discount on the eBook copy. Get in touch with us at: **info@orangeava.com** for more details.

At **www.orangeava.com**, you can also read a collection of free technical articles, sign up for a range of free newsletters, and receive exclusive discounts and offers on Print Books and eBooks.

PIRACY

If you come across any illegal copies of our works in any form on the internet, we would be grateful if you would provide us with the location address or website name. Please contact us at **info@orangeava.com** with a link to the material.

ARE YOU INTERESTED IN AUTHORING WITH US?

If there is a topic that you have expertise in, and you are interested in either writing or contributing to a book, please write to us at **business@orangeava.com**. We are on a journey to help developers and tech professionals to gain insights on the present technological advancements and innovations happening across the globe and build a community that believes Knowledge is best acquired by sharing and learning with others. Please reach out to us to learn what our audience demands and how you can be part of this educational reform. We also welcome ideas from tech experts and help them build learning and development content for their domains.

REVIEWS

Please leave a review. Once you have read and used this book, why not leave a review on the site that you purchased it from? Potential readers can then see and use your unbiased opinion to make purchase decisions. We at Orange Education would love to know what you think about our products, and our authors can learn from your feedback. Thank you!

For more information about Orange Education, please visit **www.orangeava.com**.

Table of Contents

CHAPTER 1

Introduction to AWS Cloud Practitioner Exam

Introduction

Welcome aboard, future cloud practitioner! If you are here, you are likely pondering about embarking on the journey of becoming an AWS Certified Cloud Practitioner (CLF-C02). This exam is not just another qualification on your resume—it is your ticket to showcasing your overall knowledge of the AWS Cloud, independent of a specific job role. But what exactly does that entail? Well, buckle up because we are about to delve into the nitty-gritty of this examination.

The AWS Certified Cloud Practitioner exam is designed for individuals who can effectively demonstrate their understanding of AWS Cloud's value proposition, the shared responsibility model, security best practices, and the economics of cloud computing. It is not just about memorizing facts; it is about understanding the core principles that drive the AWS Cloud and being able to apply them in real-world scenarios.

This exam is designed for anyone who wants to validate their knowledge of the AWS, regardless of their professional background. According to AWS, the typical candidate has **up to six months of exposure** to AWS concepts, design, or operations. But do not worry if you are starting fresh—you do not need prior hands-on experience to succeed.

If you are a seasoned IT professional, this certification will broaden your skill set and validate your cloud expertise. However, if you are new to technology or coming from a non-IT background, this book will guide you through the fundamentals step by step. With consistent study, practice, and hands-on exploration using the AWS Free Tier, even complete beginners can build the knowledge and confidence that is needed to clear the exam.

Now, let us talk about preparation. We recommend dedicating a good 30-45 days to focused study, with 1-2 hours of dedicated preparation each day. Of course, everyone's schedule and learning pace are different, so feel free to adjust accordingly. If you are looking to shorten your preparation time, you are smart enough to calculate the hours required to meet your goal. Remember, it is not just about the time you put in—it is about how you use that time. That is why this book is structured to guide you through each concept, providing clear explanations, real-world examples, and hands-on exercises to help you develop muscle memory on key AWS services. While the exam does not require you to work on the services, practicing with hands-on examples will help you recall answers intuitively and confidently tackle exam questions.

So, if you are ready to take your AWS Cloud journey to the next level, if you are ready to unlock new opportunities and advance your career, then let us dive in and get started!

Structure

In this chapter, we will cover the following topics:

- Career Impact of the AWS Certification
- Overview of AWS Cloud Practitioner Certification Exam
- Content, Technology, and Domains Tested in AWS Cloud Practitioner Certification Exam
- Step by Step Guide to Register for the AWS Cloud Practitioner Exam

Career Impact of the AWS Certification

Now that we have covered the basics, let us delve into why pursuing the AWS Certified Cloud Practitioner certification can be a game-changer for your career. Hence, whether you are a seasoned coder, a budding developer, a savvy salesperson, a forward-thinking product manager, or a decision-maker navigating the ever-changing tech landscape, this certification holds immense value.

For coders and developers, mastering AWS opens doors to a world of possibilities. It is not just about writing code anymore; it is about leveraging the power of cloud computing to build scalable, resilient, and cost-effective solutions. By obtaining the AWS certification, you will be able to demonstrate your ability to harness the full potential of AWS services, from computing and storage to databases and beyond. This not only enhances your technical prowess, but also makes you an asset to any team or project.

Sales professionals, listen up! Understanding AWS is no longer a mere nice-to-have feature—it is a must-have in today's tech-driven world. By earning the AWS Certified Cloud Practitioner certification, you can gain a competitive edge in the market. Thus, you are not just selling products or services; you are selling solutions that can leverage the unparalleled capabilities of AWS. Your in-depth knowledge of AWS will equip you to better understand customer needs, address pain points, and drive business growth.

Product managers should also pay attention to this aspect. The AWS Certified Cloud Practitioner certification is not just about adding another credential to your resume—it is about gaining a deeper understanding of the technology that powers the products and services you manage. By mastering AWS, you are better equipped to make informed decisions, drive product innovation, and deliver exceptional value to your customers. Whether you are designing new features, optimizing workflows, or shaping product roadmaps, your AWS expertise will set you apart in the competitive tech landscape.

And finally, decision-makers, this one is for you. Whether you are a CTO, a CEO, or a team leader, having a solid grasp of AWS is essential for driving business success. By earning the AWS Certified Cloud Practitioner certification, you can demonstrate your commitment to staying ahead of the curve and embracing innovation. You are not just leading your team; you are paving the way for digital transformation and future growth. With your newfound AWS expertise, you will be better equipped to make strategic decisions, allocate resources effectively, and drive organizational change.

In short, regardless of your role or industry, the AWS Certified Cloud Practitioner certification is your ticket to unlocking new opportunities, advancing your career, and making a lasting impact in the ever-evolving tech landscape.

Overview of the AWS Certified Cloud Practitioner Exam

As you embark on your journey towards becoming an AWS Certified Cloud Practitioner, it is crucial to gain a comprehensive understanding of the exam structure, scoring, and content. So, let us delve into the details to ensure that you are fully prepared to ace the exam, and advance your career in the cloud computing domain.

Exam Structure and Question Types

The AWS Certified Cloud Practitioner exam features a diverse range of question types designed to evaluate your knowledge and skills effectively. Understanding the question formats and how they contribute to your overall score is key to your success.

Question Types

A **total of 65 questions** will be asked in the exam which would be required to be completed in **90 minutes**. Out of 65 only 50 questions would affect your score (the remaining 15 unscored questions will not affect your score. Please note that these unscored questions are not identified in the exam).

Multiple Choice: These questions present you with one correct response and three distractors. It is therefore essential to carefully analyze each option to identify the correct answer.

Multiple Response: In these questions, you must select two or more correct responses from a list of five or more options. Pay close attention to all possible correct answers to ensure accuracy.

Scoring and Results: Your performance on the AWS Certified Cloud Practitioner exam is evaluated based on a scaled scoring system that assigns scores from 100 to 1,000. Achieving a minimum passing score of 700 is necessary to earn the certification.

Scoring Breakdown:

- **Scaled Score:** Your exam results are reported as a scaled score, while providing a comprehensive overview of your performance.
- **Pass or Fail Designation:** The exam follows industry best practices and guidelines to determine whether you meet the minimum standard for the certification. The results of the exam will be shared as soon as you complete your exam.

Content Outline and Domains

The exam content is organized into four distinct domains, each focusing on specific knowledge areas and skills that are essential for cloud practitioners. Familiarizing yourself with the content outline and domain weightings is hence crucial for effective exam preparation.

Domain Overview

The following is a list of domains that AWS uses to assess candidates during the examination:

S.No	Domain	% Scored Content
1	**Cloud Concepts**	**24%**
2	**Security & Compliance**	**30%**
3	**Cloud Technology & Services**	**34%**
4	**Billing, Pricing and Support**	**12%**

Table 1.1: *Domains and Percentage-Wise Weightage for Scores in the Certification Exam*

Preparing for Success

Thorough preparation is essential to excel on the AWS Certified Cloud Practitioner exam. Utilize a variety of study materials, practice exams, and hands-on exercises to reinforce your understanding of key concepts and topics.

Study Resources

- **Practice Exams:** Familiarize yourself with the exam format and question types by taking practice exams.
- **Hands-on Exercises:** Gain practical experience with AWS services by completing hands-on exercises and labs.
- **Additional Reading:** Supplement your studies with relevant AWS documentation, whitepapers, and online resources.

By mastering the exam structure, scoring methodology, and content domains, you will be well-equipped to succeed on the AWS Certified Cloud Practitioner exam and take the next step in your cloud computing journey.

Let us now deep dive into each domain to understand what exactly AWS is looking for by evaluating its candidates for this certification.

Domain 1: Cloud Concepts

In this domain, we will explore the foundational concepts of AWS. It is all about understanding why the cloud matters, how it works, and the benefits it offers.

Defining the Benefits of AWS

- **Understanding the Value:** Let us talk about why AWS is such a big deal. It is not just about storing data somewhere else; it is about the cool things you can do with it. Think of it like renting a space in a super high-tech storage facility, but in a unique way.
- **Saving Money:** One of the best things about the cloud is that it can save you a ton of cash. Since AWS has so many customers, they can spread out the costs, which means that you will pay less. It is like buying in bulk at the grocery store, and you getting a better deal.
- **Going Global:** Another unique feature about the cloud is that it is everywhere. AWS has data centers all over the world, so no matter where you are, you can access your data at your convenience. It is like having your own personal assistant who can teleport your files wherever you need them.

Identifying the Design Principles of AWS

- **Building for Success:** When you are working with the AWS Cloud, it is essential to follow some basic rules to make sure everything runs smoothly. Think of it like building a house – you need a solid foundation and a good plan to make sure it does not fall.
- **Well-Architected Framework:** AWS has this fancy framework called the Well-Architected Framework, which is like a blueprint for building unique architectures on the cloud. It covers things like making sure your data is secure, reliable, high performing, sustainable and cost-effective.

Understanding the Benefits of and Strategies for Migration to AWS

- **Moving to the Cloud:** So, you have decided to make the move to the cloud—congratulations! However, you might be wondering about the next steps. There are diverse ways to migrate your stuff to AWS, depending on what you are trying to do.
- **Cloud Adoption Framework:** AWS has defined a Cloud Adoption Framework (CAF), which is like a roadmap for moving to the cloud. It helps you figure out the best way to get from where you are now to where you want to be. The framework also helps organizations align cloud adoption with wider business and compliance outcomes such as Environmental and Sustainability Goals (ESG).
- AWS also describes common migration strategies often called the 6 R's—rehost, replatform, repurchase, refactor, retire, and retain. These strategies provide businesses different paths to move their applications to the cloud, depending on speed, cost, and modernization needs.

Understanding the Concepts of Cloud Economics

- **Saving Money:** One of the biggest reasons people love the cloud is that it can save them a ton of money. With the cloud, you only pay for what you use, so you do not have to worry about spending a fortune on expensive hardware that you might not even need. In some cases, customers can also **Bring Your Own License (BYOL)** for software such as Windows or databases, while others may choose AWS's license-included options, whichever reduces cost and complexity
- **Automation and Managed Services:** A unique aspect about the cloud is that it can do a lot of work for you. With things like automation and managed services, you can set things up once and then forget about them, which frees up your time to focus on more important stuff. Another key idea is **rightsizing**, which refers to making sure resources are matched to actual demand instead of being over-provisioned.

Since AWS serves millions of customers worldwide, you also stand to benefit from the provider's **economies of scale**, where costs go down as usage grows across the platform.

Understanding these fundamental concepts of AWS is essential for your success in the certification exam and beyond.

Domain 2: Security and Compliance

This domain is all about keeping things safe and secure in AWS. We will explore how AWS ensures that your data and resources are protected and how you can play your part in keeping everything secure.

Understanding the AWS Shared Responsibility Model

- **Teamwork Makes the Dream Work:** When it comes to security in AWS, it is a team effort. AWS and the customer, both are responsible for ensuring that everything stays safe and secure.

- **Shared Responsibility:** AWS takes care of the security of the cloud infrastructure, like the data centers and networks, while you are responsible for securing your own stuff, like your applications and data. It is important to note that the split of responsibilities can vary depending on the service used. For example, with Amazon EC2 customers manage the operating system; Amazon RDS AWS takes care of patching, and serverless services such as AWS Lambda, AWS are used to handle nearly everything behind the scenes.

Understanding AWS Cloud Security, Governance, and Compliance Concepts

- **Staying Compliant:** Compliance is extremely important when it comes to security in the cloud. AWS provides a bunch of tools and resources to help you ensure that your structures meet all the necessary regulations and standards.
- **Locking Things Down:** AWS gives you a bunch of tools to help you keep your data safe and secure. From encryption to access controls, you have got everything you need to make sure that only the right people can access your data.

To help with audits and governance, AWS provides services like **AWS Artifact** for compliance reports and **AWS Audit Manager** for continuous audit readiness.

Identifying AWS Access Management Capabilities

- **Who Has Got Access:** Managing access permissions for your data is crucial for security. With AWS Identity and Access Management (IAM, which is also called AWS Single Sign-on), you can control who can do what in your AWS account and make sure that only the right people have access to your data.
- **Locking Down the Root User:** The root user is like the master key to your AWS account, which is why you would want to make sure that it is super secure. With IAM, you can set up strong passwords, enable multi-factor authentication, and limit what the root user can do.

Identifying the Components and Resources for Security

- **Building a Fort:** When it comes to security in the AWS Cloud, you will have several tools at your disposal. From firewalls to monitoring services, AWS will offer you everything you might need to build a fortress around your data.
- **Stay Informed:** AWS provides a bunch of resources to help you stay on top of security best practices and keep your data safe. From whitepapers to webinars, there is always something new to learn about keeping your data secure.

With a solid understanding of security and compliance in the AWS Cloud, you will be well-equipped to protect your data and resources, and pass the certification exam with flying colors.

Domain 3: Cloud Technology and Services

In this domain, we will dive into the exciting world of AWS services and technologies. You will learn about the numerous services available on AWS, and how to use them to build powerful and scalable solutions.

Defining Methods of Deploying and Operating in the AWS Cloud

- **Getting Started:** So, you have decided to build something awesome on AWS—great choice! But how do you get started? There are many different ways to deploy and operate your applications in the cloud, depending on what you are trying to do.
- **Choosing Your Tools:** When it comes to deploying and operating in AWS, you have a ton of tools at your disposal. From APIs and SDKs to the AWS Management Console, you can pick the tools that work best for you and your team.

Defining the AWS Global Infrastructure

- **Around the World in Seconds:** AWS has data centers all over the world, so no matter where you are, you are never far from the cloud. This global infrastructure means you can build applications that are fast, reliable, and scalable, regardless of where your users are located.
- **High Availability:** One of the coolest things about the AWS global infrastructure is its high availability. By spreading your applications across multiple availability zones, you can ensure that your users always have access to your services even if something goes wrong in one region.

Identifying AWS Compute Services

- **Powering Your Applications:** When it comes to running your applications on AWS, you have a bunch of options to choose from. From virtual servers to serverless computing, you can pick the compute service that best fits your needs and budget.
- **Scaling Up and Down:** One of the best things about AWS compute services is their scalability. With features like auto-scaling, you can automatically add or remove resources based on demand to ensure that your applications always have the right amount of compute power.

Identifying AWS Database Services

- **Storing Your Data:** Every great application needs a place to store its data and AWS has you covered. From relational databases to NoSQL databases, you can pick the database service that best fits your needs and scale as your data grows.
- **Migration Made Easy:** Moving your existing databases to the cloud is easy with AWS. With tools like the AWS Database Migration Service (DMS), you can quickly and securely migrate your databases to AWS with minimal downtime.

Identifying AWS Network Services

- **Connecting Your Services:** Networking is a crucial part of any cloud architecture, and AWS provides a bunch of services to help you connect your resources securely and reliably. From virtual private clouds to content delivery networks, you have everything you will need to build a robust network infrastructure.
- **Speed and Performance**: With AWS network services, you can ensure that your applications are fast and responsive, no matter where your users are located. By using features like Amazon Route 53 and AWS Global Accelerator, you can minimize latency and improve the user experience.

Identifying AWS Storage Services

- **Storing Your Data:** When it comes to storing your stuff in the cloud, AWS has a wide range of storage services to choose from. Whether you need object storage, block storage, or file storage, you can find the perfect solution for your needs on the AWS platform.
- **Backup and Recovery:** Keeping your data safe and secure is crucial, and AWS provides a bunch of tools to help you do just that. From automated backups to disaster recovery solutions, you can ensure that your data is always protected and accessible when you need it.

Identifying AWS Artificial Intelligence and Machine Learning (AI/ML) Services and Analytics Services

- **Unlocking the Power of AI:** AI and machine learning are revolutionizing the way we build and deploy applications, and AWS provides a wide range of AI and ML services to help you harness the power of these technologies. From image recognition to natural language processing, you can build intelligent applications that can see, hear, and understand the world around them.
- A newer area within AWS's AI/ML portfolio is **Generative AI**, powered by services like **Amazon Bedrock and Amazon Q**. It lets you build and scale applications using Foundation Models (FMs) without having to manage the underlying ML infrastructure
- **Gaining Insights:** In addition to AI and ML services, AWS also provides a bunch of analytics services to help you gain insights from your data. Whether you are analyzing customer behavior or predicting future trends, you can use AWS analytics services to turn your data into actionable insights.

With a solid understanding of AWS technology and services, you will be well-equipped to build powerful and scalable solutions.

Domain 4: Billing, Pricing, and Support

In this domain, we will explore the financial aspects of using AWS, including how to understand your bill, manage costs, and get support when you need it. Understanding billing, pricing, and support is essential for optimizing your AWS usage and getting the most value out of the platform.

Comparing AWS Pricing Models

- **Understanding Your Options:** AWS offers a variety of pricing models to fit your needs and budget. From pay-as-you-go to reserved instances, you can choose the pricing model that works best for your workload and usage patterns.

- **Getting the Best Deal:** By understanding the different pricing options available, you can optimize your costs and ensure that you are getting the best possible deal on your AWS usage. Whether you are running a small startup or a large enterprise, there is a pricing model that is made for you.

Understanding Resources for Billing, Budget, and Cost Management

- **Keeping Costs in Check:** Managing costs is a crucial part of using AWS effectively. With tools like AWS Budgets and AWS Cost Explorer, you can track your spending, set budgets, and get alerts when you are approaching your limits. For organizations managing costs across multiple accounts, **AWS Billing Conductor** can customize and share billing data, while **allocation tags** help track and assign costs to specific teams or projects.

- **Planning for the Future:** By effectively managing your costs and budgets, you can plan for future growth and ensure that you are getting the most value out of your AWS investment. Through careful planning and monitoring, you can avoid unexpected costs and maximize your ROI.

Identifying AWS Technical Resources and AWS Support Options

- **Getting Help When You Need It:** AWS offers a variety of support options to help you get the assistance you need when you encounter issues or have questions about using the platform. From basic support to enterprise-level assistance, there is a support option that is right for you.

- **Accessing Resources:** In addition to support options, AWS provides a wealth of technical resources to help you learn more about using the platform and troubleshoot issues on your own. From documentation and whitepapers to forums and training courses, you can access the information you need to be successful on AWS.

Understanding billing, pricing, and support is essential for effectively managing your AWS usage and getting the most value out of the platform. By mastering these aspects of AWS, you will be able to optimize your costs, plan for the future, and get the help you need whenever necessary.

Key Concepts and Technology for the Exam

In this section, we have mentioned the key concepts and technologies which the AWS Certification tests candidate on.

- **Cloud Fundamentals:** Understanding the foundational concepts and advantages of migrating to AWS includes the following components:
  - Benefits of Migrating to AWS
  - AWS Global Infrastructure (for example, Regions, Availability Zones)
  - Infrastructure as Code (IaC)
  - Migration and Data Transfer
- **Compute Services:** This includes exploring the diverse options for computational resources, including virtual servers and instance types mentioned as follows:
  - Compute
  - Amazon EC2 Instance Types (for example, Reserved, On-Demand, Spot)
- **Storage Solutions:** This includes examining the following storage options available on AWS:
  - Storage
  - Databases
- **Networking:** You must learn about network services to connect resources securely and efficiently within the AWS environment.
- **Security and Compliance:** Ensuring data protection and regulatory compliance through robust security measures and the shared responsibility model includes the following:
  - Security
  - AWS Compliance
  - AWS Shared Responsibility Model
- **Management and Governance:** This includes managing costs effectively, implementing best practices, and optimizing AWS resources using frameworks like the Well-Architected Framework. Its components are:
  - Cost Management
  - Management and Governance
  - AWS Well-Architected Framework
- **Developer Tools and Support:** Accessing tools, support, and resources for developers to build, deploy, and manage applications on AWS is essential for developers. Some of them are mentioned as follows:

- APIs
- AWS SDKs
- AWS Partner Network
- AWS Support Plans
- AWS Support Center
- AWS Professional Services
- AWS Prescriptive Guidance
- AWS Knowledge Center
- AWS Pricing Calculator
- AWS re:Post
- AWS Solutions Architects
- AWS Security Blog

- **Advanced Topics:** Delving into advanced topics to develop innovative solutions on the AWS platform is essential for prospective developers. These concepts are:
    - Machine Learning (ML)
    - Analytics

Services That are Beyond the Scope of the Examination:

The following list contains the AWS services and features that are beyond the scope of the examination. This list is non-exhaustive and is subject to change.

- **Game Tech:** Amazon GameLift, Amazon Lumberyard
- **Media Services:** AWS Elemental Appliances and Software, AWS Elemental MediaConnect, AWS Elemental MediaConvert, AWS Elemental MediaLive, AWS Elemental MediaPackage, AWS Elemental MediaStore, AWS Elemental MediaTailor, Amazon Interactive Video Service (Amazon IVS)
- **Robotics:** AWS RoboMaker
- **Storage:** Amazon FSx for Lustre
- **Security, Identity, and Compliance:** Amazon Cloud Directory, AWS Network Firewall
- **Networking and Content Delivery:** AWS Cloud Map, AWS Network Access Analyzer, AWS Ground Station, Amazon VPC Lattice
- **Migration and Transfer:** AWS Migration Hub Refactor Spaces, AWS Transfer Family
- **Management and Governance:** AWS Chatbot, Amazon Data Lifecycle Manager, Amazon Elastic Transcoder, AWS Launch Wizard
- **Machine Learning (ML):** Amazon Fraud Detector, Amazon Lookout for Metrics, Amazon Mechanical Turk, AWS Panorama, Amazon Personalize

- **Internet of Things (IoT):** AWS IoT Device Defender, AWS IoT Greengrass, Amazon Monitron
- **Analytics:** Amazon AppFlow, AWS Clean Rooms, AWS Data Exchange, Amazon DataZone, Amazon Managed Streaming for Apache Kafka (Amazon MSK), Amazon Timestream for LiveAnalytics
- **Application Integration:** AWS AppFabric, Amazon Simple Workflow Service
- **Business Applications:** Amazon WorkDocs, Amazon WorkMail
- **Compute:** AWS App Runner, AWS Copilot, AWS Wavelength
- **Customer Enablement:** AWS Activate, AWS IQ, Amazon Managed Services (AMS)
- **Database:** Amazon Keyspaces (for Apache Cassandra), Amazon MemoryDB for Redis OSS, AWS AppConfig
- **Developer Tools:** AWS Application Composer, AWS CodeArtifact, AWS CodeDeploy, Amazon CodeGuru, AWS CloudShell, AWS Device Farm

Registering for the AWS Cloud Practitioner Exam

When it comes to scheduling your AWS Certification exam, you have two primary options that are mentioned as follows:

Online Proctoring:

Experience the convenience of taking your AWS exam from the comfort of your home or office. Online proctoring offers flexibility, and allows you to select a time that suits your schedule. This option is available for all AWS Certification exams and is facilitated by Pearson VUE.

With online proctoring, you will be connected to a live proctor who ensures your exam environment adheres to AWS security standards and remains tamper-free. Should you encounter any technical glitches during your exam, be rest assured that the proctor will promptly assist you in resolving them.

While online proctoring appointments are accessible 24/7, it is advisable to schedule your exam in advance to secure a time slot that aligns with your time zone.

Testing Centers:

If you prefer a more traditional approach, you can also take the exam at a physical testing center. This option suits individuals who require specific technical equipment such as a computer that meets system and security requirements. Keep in mind that choosing this option involves factoring in travel time and expenses, as you will need to visit a designated testing center.

To find a testing center near you, simply search for availability by ZIP Code through Pearson VUE.

Be mindful that testing center availability may vary depending on your location and some centers may still be closed due to local health guidance. Therefore, it is advisable to check the availability of testing centers before initiating the booking process.

The next section details the step-by step process on how to register for the AWS Cloud practitioner exam for Online Proctoring.

Step 1: Creation of AWS Training and Certification Account

1. Visit the webpage https://www.aws.training/Certification to create the AWS certification account.
2. Click **Sign In**.

Figure 1.1: *AWS Training and Certification Page*

3. Post clicking the **Sign In** button, you will be directed to the Login page, which will have the following options:
   a. **Login with the "AWS Builder ID":** This is the most preferred option; if you do not have a builder ID, use your personal email to register for it.
   b. **Login with "Organization SSO":** This option is available for select companies only.
   c. **Login through "AWS Partner Network":** This option is only for AWS partners; check with your organization if they are a registered AWS partner.

d. **Login using "`Amazon employee single sign-on`"**: This option is for Amazon employees only.

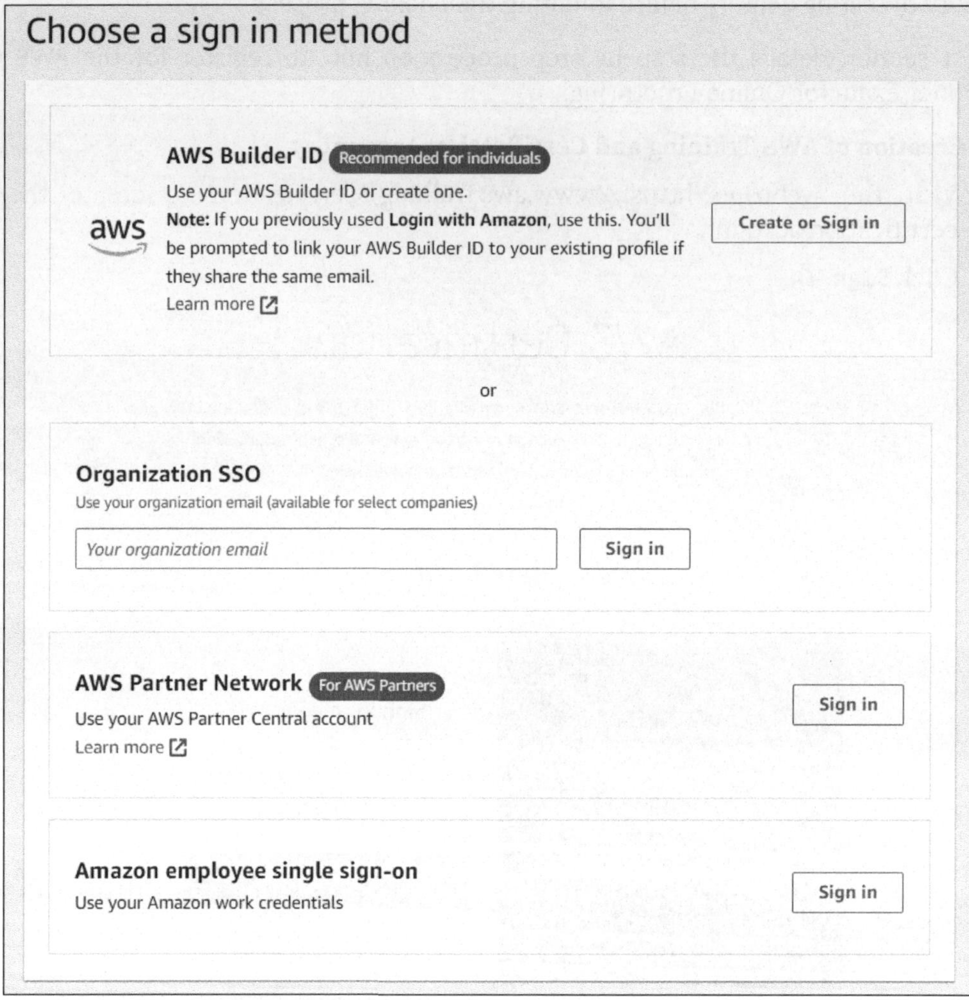

Figure 1.2: *Sign in Page for the Certification Exam*

In the AWS Builder ID section, you can use your Amazon account to login or you can create a new one by following the guidelines provided on the webpage:

4. Once you sign in (post MFA), you will be present on the cp.certmetrics.com webpage and the front page would consist of the word **`Dashboard`**. You can click the highlighted portion on the image to begin your registration for the exam.

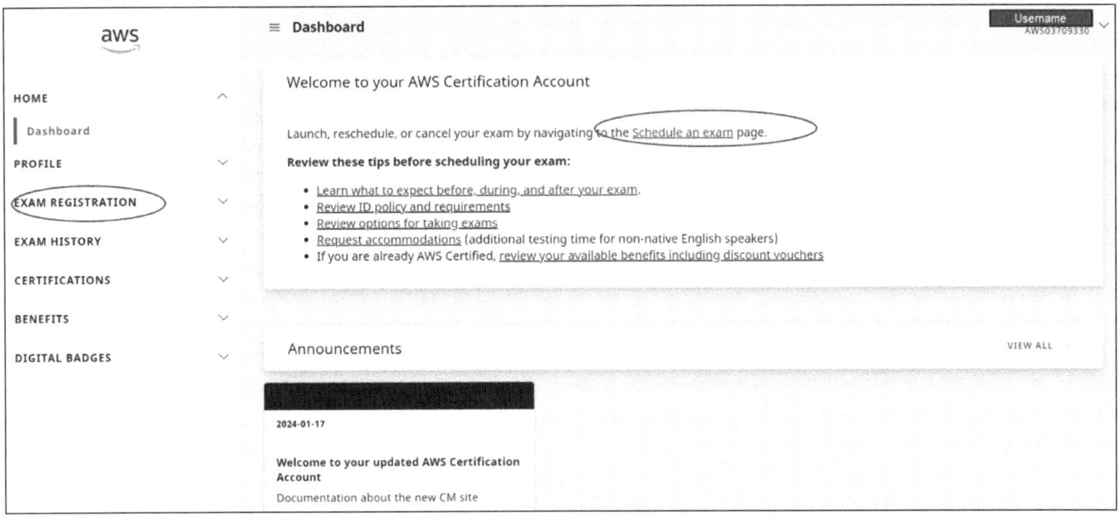

Figure 1.3: *Cert Metrics Homepage*

5. Search for the Cloud Practitioner exam in the Search Page in the Schedule exam page, and click the "**`Schedule`**" Button.

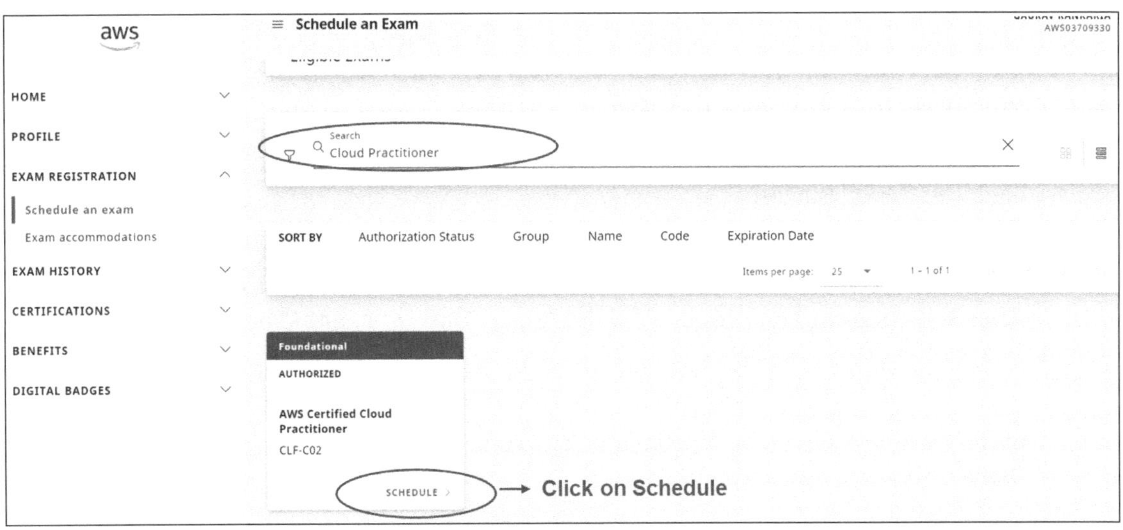

Figure 1.4: *Schedule Exam Page on the Cert Metric Webpage*

6. You will be directed to a webpage starting with **`wsr.pearsonvue.com/`** where you would need to choose your preferred mode of examination. In our case here, we will be choosing the Online with **`OneVUE`** option.

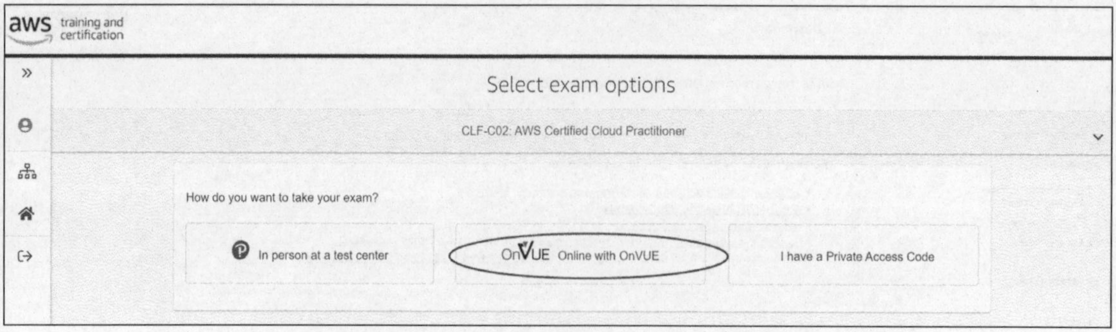

Figure 1.5: *Selecting the Mode of Examination*

7. On the next page, you will be asked to run some tests on your computer to ensure that your system is compatible with exam requirements. Make sure that the guidelines are followed exactly as mentioned on the webpage. Once all the compliances are checked, click the "`Next`" button.

8. Select your preferred language for the exam. In our case, we will choose "`English`" and then to click the "`Next`" Button.

9. Go through the exam policy and click the checkboxes once you have read the policy. Please note that failing to adhere to any of the guidelines present in the policy would lead to termination from the exam. This can happen during the exam as well. Once you have read the policy, click the "`Agree`" button.

10. Select the preferred language of the proctor. Here, we will select "`English`" and then click the "`Next`" Button.

11. Next, you need to select your time zone to find an appointment for the exam. Select your preferred time zone. In the case demonstrated here, it is "`Asia/Calcutta - IST`". After selecting the time zone, click the "`Yes, That's right!`" button.

12. Select the date when you want to give the exam from the calendar present on the screen, post that the webpage will display the available dates for the exam. You can modify the available slot by clicking "`Explore more time`", or can proceed with the "`Book this appointment`" button.

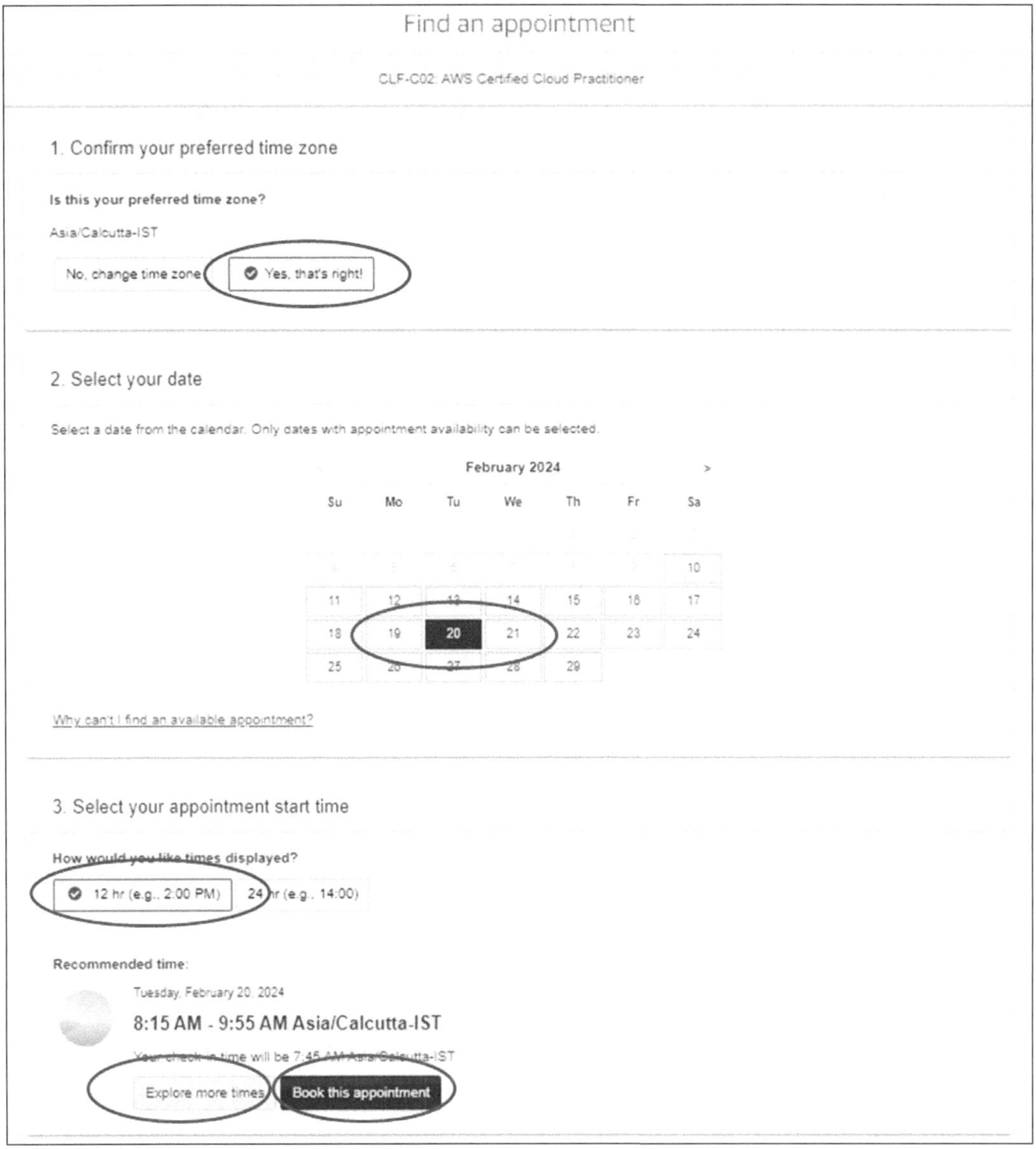

Figure 1.6: *Scheduling the AWS Cloud Practitioner Exam*

13. The webpage will now re-direct you to the "**`Cart`**" page where you can re-confirm the exam details (Exam, date, time, and so on) and then click the "**`Proceed to Checkout`**" button on the screen. In certain cases, you may have a coupon code/exam voucher which you can punch in the "**`Billing Page`**". Please note, the tax on certification exams is applicable based on the respective government norms of a region.

14. Make the payment for the exam. Once done, you will receive a confirmation mail which includes the exam details, bill invoice, and other necessary links for the exam.

Conclusion

Armed with the knowledge gleaned from this chapter, including insights into the exam structure, content domains, and registration process, you will be well-equipped to take the next step in your AWS journey. In the upcoming chapters, we will continue to build upon this foundation and explore the core principles of cloud computing and diving into essential concepts that underpin AWS services. So, gear up and stay tuned as we delve deeper into the dynamic world of cloud technology, while empowering you to excel in your AWS Certification journey.

In the next chapter, we will learn about the concepts of cloud, its advantages, and various cloud computing models present in the market today.

Points to Remember

- The AWS Certification validates broad AWS Cloud knowledge for various roles.
- Eligible candidates include those with limited AWS experience, even non-IT backgrounds.
- The exam covers AWS value, shared responsibility, security, costs, and core services.
- Out-of-scope tasks for the exam may include coding, architecture design, and troubleshooting.
- Exam Format: 65 questions to be answered in 90 minutes, multiple-choice and multiple-response questions, out of which 50 are scored and 15 are unscored (these are assigned by AWS randomly).
- Pass/fail result will be immediate; the exam uses a scaled score from 100-1000, where the minimum passing score is 700.
- Exam Preparation: Hands-on practice is recommended for effective learning.

References

- https://d1.awsstatic.com/training-and-certification/docs-cloud-practitioner/AWS-Certified-Cloud-Practitioner_Exam-Guide.pdf

CHAPTER 2

Understanding Cloud Computing

Introduction

Welcome to the world of cloud computing, where sky is the limit when it comes to accessing computing resources. In this chapter, we will explore the fascinating concept of cloud computing, its evolution, and why it has become the go-to solution for businesses worldwide.

Structure

In this chapter, we will discuss the following topics:

- Introduction to Cloud Computing
- Key Concepts (Elasticity, Scalability, Pay-As-You-Go, and so on.)
- Cloud Service Models (IaaS, PaaS, SaaS, FaaS)

Introduction to Cloud Computing

Cloud computing revolutionizes the way businesses access and utilize computer system resources such as data storage and computing power. It eliminates the need for users to actively manage these resources, while offering them on-demand availability without the hassle of direct oversight. In essence, cloud computing operates like a virtualized ecosystem, where large-scale functions are distributed across multiple locations, with each acting as an individual data center.

Figure 2.1: *Cloud Computing*

Let us understand why and how cloud computing plays an important role in any organization through an example.

Before Cloud Computing: The Story of TechSolutions Inc.

TechSolutions Inc., a mid-sized technology consulting and software company, was thriving but constantly running into challenges with its traditional IT setup. Their applications were hosted on in-house servers and sat in a small but costly data center at their headquarters.

As their business grew, so did their pain points, which are mentioned as follows:

- **Remote Work and Collaboration:** With teams spread across different cities after the pandemic, accessing on-premises systems became slow and unreliable. VPN bottlenecks and hardware limits frustrated employees.
- **Customer Expectations:** Clients expected faster delivery cycles, mobile-ready applications, and seamless global access. These were demands that the legacy infrastructure could not keep up with.

- **AI and Data Growth:** TechSolutions wanted to experiment with Machine Learning (ML) for analytics and customer insights, but provisioning the required compute power on-premises was expensive and slow.
- **Sustainability Goals:** Like many modern businesses, TechSolutions had a sustainability initiative. Running power-hungry servers on-site did not align with their "green IT" commitments.

The result was equally disturbing. The organization saw constant firefighting by their IT team, spending an exorbitant amount on hardware refreshes, and the emergence of frequent scalability bottlenecks.

Overcoming Challenges with AWS Cloud: The Transformation of TechSolutions Inc.

To overcome these barriers, TechSolutions migrated to **AWS**. The impact was immediate and bore the following results:

- **Cost Reduction and Flexibility:** Instead of buying new servers every year, they adopted AWS's **pay-as-you-go** model. This freed up capital for R&D and innovation.
- **Global Reach:** By deploying applications across multiple **AWS Regions**, TechSolutions delivered faster, low-latency experiences to its international clients.
- **Remote-First Productivity:** Through services like **Amazon WorkSpaces** and **Amazon Chime**, employees could collaborate securely from anywhere without depending on office-bound servers.
- **Innovation with AI/ML:** With **Amazon SageMaker**, TechSolutions quickly prototyped machine learning models for client projects—something that would have taken months on-premises.
- **Resilience and Security:** By leveraging **multi-AZ deployments** and **automated backups** with Amazon RDS and Amazon S3, downtime became a thing of the past.
- **Sustainability:** Shifting workloads to AWS allowed TechSolutions to benefit from Amazon's investments in renewable energy and aligned their IT with corporate sustainability goals.

Advantages of Cloud Computing

Now that we have seen an example of how TechSolutions solved their infra problems using the cloud, let us expand on each of the advantages of cloud computing for further understanding as follows:

- **Cost-Efficiency:** One of the most immediate advantages of cloud computing is its impact on cost. In the traditional IT model, companies had to invest heavily in physical servers, networking gear, and data center space. These upfront **Capital Expenditures (CapEx)** often ran into millions of dollars and much of hardware sat underutilized most of the time.

Cloud computing flips this model on its head. With AWS, businesses move from CapEx to **Operational Expenditure (OpEx)**, paying only for what they actually consume. This **pay-as-you-go** model eliminates the need for large upfront investments and allows organizations to align costs directly with usage. A small startup can experiment with new ideas at minimal cost, while a global enterprise can take advantage of **volume discounts, savings plans, and spot instances** to optimize long-term workloads.

AWS also provides additional savings through its **Bring Your Own License (BYOL)** program. Many companies have made significant investments in software licenses for platforms like Microsoft Windows Server, SQL Server, or Oracle databases. With BYOL, these existing licenses can be reused in AWS environments to reduce duplication of costs. For example, financial institutions migrating to **Amazon RDS for SQL Server** often bring their current licenses with them, cutting licensing costs while gaining the operational benefits of a managed database service.

Real Life Example:

A powerful real-world example of cloud cost efficiency is **Airbnb**. As the platform grew rapidly to serve millions of hosts and guests worldwide, it had to scale its infrastructure without sinking massive amounts into physical data centers. Instead, Airbnb migrated nearly all of its infrastructure to AWS early in its journey, while leveraging services like **Amazon S3** for cost-effective storage and **EC2** for elastic compute capacity. This strategy allowed them to scale globally, pay only for what they used, and stay agile in response to unpredictable demand.

- **Scalability/Elasticity:** One of the most compelling features of cloud computing is its ability to scale resources on-demand to meet changing workload requirements. Traditional IT infrastructure was often over-provisioned to accommodate peak demand, resulting in wasted resources and higher costs. In contrast, cloud computing allows businesses to scale their infrastructure up or down dynamically in response to fluctuations in demand, ensuring optimal resource utilization and cost-efficiency.

Whether it is handling a sudden spike in website traffic, processing large volumes of data, or launching a new application, businesses can provision additional resources in minutes with just a few clicks. This elasticity of cloud computing enables businesses to respond rapidly to changing market conditions, seize new opportunities, and stay ahead of the competition.

Moreover, cloud computing provides unlimited scalability, allowing businesses to scale their infrastructure seamlessly as their needs evolve over time. Whether it is expanding into new markets, adding new product lines or accommodating seasonal fluctuations in demand, businesses can rely on the virtually unlimited capacity of the cloud to support their growth without constraints.

Real Life Example:

A well-known example of scalability and elasticity in action is **Netflix**, which runs almost all of its infrastructure on AWS. Netflix serves more than 200 million members worldwide. Due to its immense popularity, usage can spike dramatically during evenings or when popular shows are released. Instead of building massive data centers to handle peak demand, Netflix uses **AWS Auto Scaling** and **Amazon EC2** to automatically add capacity when viewership surges and scale back down during off-peak hours. This elasticity ensures a seamless viewing experience for customers while keeping costs optimized.

- **Flexibility**: Cloud computing offers unparalleled flexibility, which empowers businesses to work anytime, anywhere, and on any device. Traditional IT infrastructure was often limited by physical constraints and required employees to be tethered to office-based systems and networks. With cloud computing, employees can access data, applications, and resources over the internet from any location with an internet connection, which enabled remote work, collaboration and productivity on the go.

Furthermore, cloud computing supports a wide range of deployment models including public, private, and hybrid clouds. This allowed businesses to choose the approach that best aligned with their needs and preferences. Whether it is leveraging the scalability and cost-efficiency of the public cloud, the security and control of a private cloud, or the flexibility and agility of a hybrid cloud, businesses can tailor their cloud strategy to meet their unique requirements and objectives.

Additionally, cloud computing enables businesses to adopt modern work practices and technologies, such as Virtual Desktop Infrastructure (VDI), cloud-based collaboration tools, and Bring-Your-Own-Device (BYOD) policies. By embracing these innovations, businesses can enhance employee satisfaction, improve collaboration, and drive innovation, which helps them gain a competitive edge in the digital economy.

Real Life Example:

A compelling real-world case is **Capital One**, which is one of the largest banks in the United States. By migrating entirely to AWS, Capital One transformed how its employees and agents operate. With services like **Amazon Connect**, Capital One enabled tens of thousands of contact center agents to work securely from anywhere and allowd them to scale their operations without relying on physical call-center infrastructure. This cloud-first approach gave them the flexibility to adapt quickly to changing customer demands while maintaining high levels of security and compliance.

- **Reliability**: Reliability is a cornerstone of cloud computing, as cloud service providers invest heavily in infrastructure, redundancy, and security to ensure high availability and data protection. In the traditional model, businesses were responsible for managing and maintaining their own IT infrastructure. These operations included backups, disaster recovery, and security, which often resulted in gaps, vulnerabilities, and downtime.

With cloud computing, businesses can rely on the expertise and resources of cloud service providers to deliver enterprise-grade reliability and security. Cloud providers operate state-of-the-art data centers with redundant systems, failover mechanisms, and geographic diversity to ensure continuous uptime and data availability. Additionally, cloud providers implement robust security measures, including encryption, access controls, and threat detection to protect data from unauthorized access, breaches, and cyberattacks.

Real Life Example:

A powerful demonstration of cloud reliability is **Nasdaq**, one of the world's largest stock exchange operators. Nasdaq migrated critical market systems to AWS to improve performance, scalability, and resilience. By leveraging AWS's multi-AZ and multi-region architecture, Nasdaq ensures that its trading and data platforms remain available even in the face of hardware failures or unexpected demand surges. This level of reliability is essential when handling **billions of dollars in transactions every day**, where even seconds of downtime could have major financial implications. AWS's resilient infrastructure gives Nasdaq the confidence to innovate while maintaining continuous operations.

- **Security and Compliance:** Security is often the top concern for businesses moving to the cloud and AWS addresses this with a comprehensive set of security features and compliance certifications. In the traditional IT model, companies had to build their own security stack, implement firewalls, manage encryption, and keep up with evolving threats, which was a costly and resource-intensive task.

With AWS, security becomes a **shared responsibility**. AWS secures the cloud infrastructure itself, while customers control and secure their applications and data within it. AWS provides built-in features such as **encryption at rest and in transit, Identity and Access Management (IAM), Key Management Service (KMS), and network isolation through VPCs**. In addition, AWS maintains compliance with a wide range of global standards, including **PCI DSS, HIPAA, GDPR, and ISO certifications**, which gives customers confidence that their workloads meet regulatory requirements.

Real Life Example:

A strong example of security and compliance in the cloud is **Intuit**, the financial software company behind TurboTax, QuickBooks, and Mint. Intuit manages sensitive financial data for millions of customers and must comply with strict regulatory standards. By migrating to AWS, Intuit gained access to advanced security tools such as **AWS KMS for encryption** and **CloudTrail for audit logging**, which ensures transparency and accountability. At the same time, AWS's compliance certifications allowed Intuit to meet industry regulations more efficiently. The result is a secure, compliant, and highly resilient platform that enables Intuit to protect customer trust while continuing to innovate.

- **Sustainability:** In recent years, sustainability has become a major factor in how organizations approach their IT strategy. Traditional on-premises data centers consume vast amounts of power for servers, cooling, and operations, often without the efficiency gains that are possible at scale. Companies are under increasing pressure to reduce their carbon footprint, not only for compliance reasons but also to meet customer and shareholder expectations.

Cloud computing enables businesses to align with these goals by shifting workloads to providers like AWS, which are committed to operating more sustainably. AWS has pledged to power its operations with **100% renewable energy by 2025** and is already the world's largest corporate buyer of renewable energy. For customers, this means that simply moving workloads to AWS can immediately reduce the carbon intensity of their IT operations compared to running on-premises.

Real Life Example:

A great demonstration of sustainability in action is **Volkswagen Group**. As one of the world's largest automakers, Volkswagen is using AWS to build its **Industrial Cloud to connect** factories, supply chains, and partners worldwide. By running these workloads on AWS, Volkswagen not only gains scalability and efficiency, but also benefits from AWS's renewable energy commitments. This cloud-first strategy helps Volkswagen advance its ambitious goal of becoming a carbon-neutral company by 2050. The collaboration shows how cloud adoption can reduce environmental impact while driving innovation in one of the most complex global industries.

Exercise 1: Test Your Cloud Knowledge

1. Which term describes the ability of cloud computing to rapidly provision and release resources to meet fluctuating demands?
    a. Scalability
    b. Elasticity
    c. Affordability
    d. Flexibility
2. Which value proposition of cloud computing converts Capital Expenditures (CapEx) into Operational Expenditures (OpEx), and provides greater financial flexibility?
    a. Scalability
    b. Flexibility
    c. Cost Reduction
    d. Device Independence

3. Which term describes the ability of cloud computing to handle sudden spikes in workload by dynamically provisioning additional resources?
    a. Scalability
    b. Elasticity
    c. Cost Savings
    d. Reliability

Answers

1. b
2. c
3. b

Types of Cloud Computing

In the realm of cloud computing, there are four primary categories that are mentioned as follows:

- Infrastructure as a Service (IaaS)
- Platform as a Service (PaaS)
- Software as a Service (SaaS)
- Function as a Service (FaaS)

These categories offer varying degrees of control, flexibility, and management, while empowering you to choose the suite of services that aligns best with your requirements. Let us consider each one of them in detail.

Infrastructure as a Service (IaaS)

Infrastructure as a Service (IaaS) is a cloud computing model that provides virtualized computing resources over the internet. With IaaS, cloud providers offer scalable and on-demand access to essential IT infrastructure components such as Virtual Machines (VMs), storage, and networking resources, without the need for businesses to invest in physical hardware.

Figure 2.2: *Examples of Companies Providing IaaS*

Here is a more detailed explanation of IaaS along with real-life examples:

Virtual Machines (VMs): IaaS providers offer virtualized computing instances, known as virtual machines, which emulate physical servers. Users can deploy and manage VMs on-demand, while scaling compute resources up or down based on workload requirements. For example, a software development team can use IaaS to provision multiple VMs with different operating systems and configurations to test their applications across diverse environments.

Examples: Amazon Elastic Compute Cloud (Amazon EC2) and Microsoft Azure Virtual Machines are popular examples of IaaS VM services.

Storage: IaaS includes scalable and durable storage solutions that allow businesses to store and retrieve data over the internet. Users can provision storage resources based on their storage needs, with options for object storage, block storage, and file storage. For instance, a media streaming service can leverage IaaS storage to store and deliver large volumes of video content to users globally.

Examples: Amazon Simple Storage Service (Amazon S3) and Google Cloud Storage are leading IaaS storage services.

Networking: IaaS providers offer virtualized networking infrastructure that enables businesses to build and manage complex network architectures in the cloud. Users can create virtual networks, subnets, load balancers, and VPN connections to connect their cloud resources securely. For example, a multinational corporation can use IaaS networking to establish a secure and high-performance network backbone connecting its offices worldwide.

Examples: Amazon Virtual Private Cloud (Amazon VPC) and Azure Virtual Network are examples of IaaS networking services.

Scalability and Flexibility: One of the key benefits of IaaS is its ability to scale resources dynamically to accommodate changing workload demands. Users can easily scale compute, storage, and networking resources up or down in real-time to ensure optimal performance and cost-efficiency.

For example, an e-commerce website can automatically scale its compute capacity during peak shopping seasons to handle increased traffic without experiencing downtime. This scalability and flexibility enable businesses to adapt quickly to fluctuating demand and scale their infrastructure as needed.

Cost Savings: IaaS allows businesses to reduce IT infrastructure costs by eliminating the need for upfront hardware investments and ongoing maintenance. Users pay only for the resources they consume on a pay-as-you-go basis and avoid the costs associated with overprovisioning and underutilization of hardware. Additionally, IaaS eliminates the need for physical data centers, which reduces operational expenses related to power, cooling, and physical space. As a result, businesses can achieve significant cost savings and improve their overall IT cost management.

In summary, Infrastructure as a Service (IaaS) offers businesses the flexibility, scalability, and cost-effectiveness to build and manage their IT infrastructure in the cloud. By leveraging IaaS solutions from providers like Amazon Web Services (AWS), Microsoft Azure, and Google Cloud Platform (GCP), businesses can focus on innovation, agility, and growth without being encumbered by the complexities of managing physical hardware.

IaaS (Infrastructure as a Service): Provides virtualized computing resources over the internet, while allowing users to rent infrastructure components like virtual machines, storage, and networking. It also reduces the need for physical hardware maintenance.

Platform as a Service (PaaS)

Platform as a Service (PaaS) is a category of cloud computing that provides a platform allowing customers to develop, run, and manage applications without encountering the complexity of building and maintaining the underlying infrastructure. In other words, PaaS offers a ready-made environment for developers to focus solely on coding and deploying applications rather than worrying about hardware provisioning, operating system updates, or network configuration.

One of the key benefits of PaaS is its ability to streamline the application development process, enabling developers to rapidly build and deploy applications with minimal overhead. PaaS platforms typically provide a range of development tools, middleware, and runtime environments and allow developers to choose the tools and technologies that best suit their needs. This abstraction of infrastructure complexities accelerates the development lifecycle, while reducing the time to market, and promotes innovation.

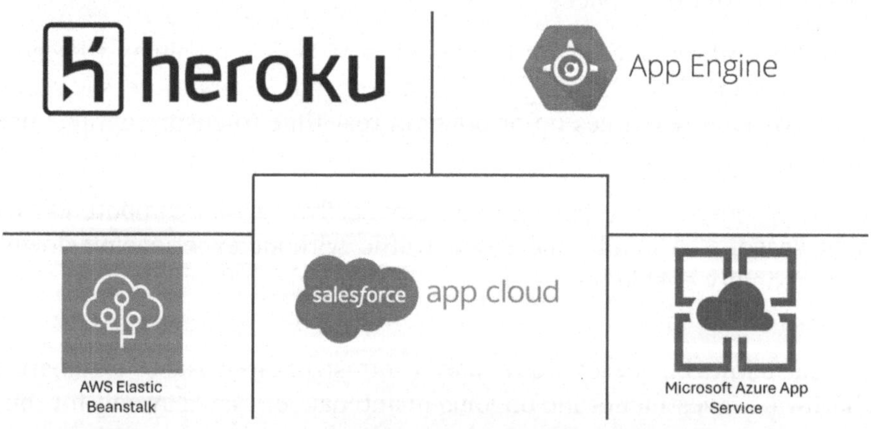

Figure 2.3: *Examples of Companies Providing PaaS*

Real-life Examples of PaaS Include:

- **Google App Engine:** Google's PaaS offering allows developers to build and deploy scalable web applications on Google's infrastructure without managing servers or runtime environments. Developers can write applications in popular programming languages such as Java, Python, and Node.js, and Google handles the deployment, scaling, and monitoring aspects.
- **Microsoft Azure App Service:** Azure App Service is Microsoft's PaaS offering that enables developers to build, deploy, and scale web, mobile, and API applications seamlessly. Developers can choose from various development frameworks, such as .NET, Java, Node.js, and Python, and leverage integrated DevOps tools for continuous integration and delivery.
- **Heroku:** Heroku is a cloud platform that simplifies the deployment and management of web applications, particularly those built using Ruby on Rails, Node.js, Python, and other popular frameworks. Heroku abstracts away infrastructure concerns, which allows developers to focus on writing code and deploying applications with ease.
- **AWS Elastic Beanstalk:** Amazon Web Services (AWS) offers Elastic Beanstalk as a PaaS solution for deploying and managing web applications and services. With Elastic Beanstalk, developers can upload their application code, and AWS automatically handles the deployment, scaling, load balancing, and monitoring aspects, which simplifies the deployment process.
- **Salesforce App Cloud:** Salesforce's PaaS offering, known as App Cloud, provides a suite of tools and services for building, deploying, and managing enterprise applications and integrations. Developers can leverage Salesforce's platform to create custom applications, extend existing Salesforce functionality, and integrate with third-party systems with declarative and programmatic tools.

PaaS (Platform as a Service): Offers a comprehensive platform that includes development tools, services, and infrastructure to streamline the application development process. It enables developers to focus on coding without managing underlying complexities.

Software as a Service (SaaS)

Software as a Service (SaaS) is a cloud computing model that delivers software applications over the internet on a subscription basis. In the SaaS model, the software is hosted and maintained by a third-party provider, which eliminates the need for users to install, manage, or update the software locally on their devices. Instead, users can access the software through a web browser or application interface, typically paying a monthly or annual fee for usage.

One of the primary advantages of SaaS is its accessibility and ease of use. Users can access SaaS applications from any device with an internet connection, while enabling seamless collaboration and productivity across geographically dispersed teams. Moreover, SaaS providers handle all aspects of software maintenance such as updates, patches, and security enhancements, while relieving users of the burden of software management.

Figure 2.4: *Examples of Companies Providing SaaS*

Real-life examples of SaaS include:

- **Google Workspace (formerly G Suite):** Google Workspace is a suite of cloud-based productivity tools that includes Gmail, Google Drive, Google Docs, Google Sheets, Google Slides, and more. Users can collaborate in real-time on documents, spreadsheets, and presentations, while storing their files securely in the cloud and accessing them from any device.

- **Microsoft 365 (formerly Office 365):** Microsoft 365 offers a range of cloud-based productivity applications, including Microsoft Word, Excel, PowerPoint, Outlook, and Teams. Users can create, edit, and share documents, spreadsheets, and presentations online, while collaborating with colleagues in real-time and accessing their files from anywhere.

- **Salesforce:** Salesforce is a leading provider of cloud-based Customer Relationship Management (CRM) software. Salesforce's SaaS platform enables businesses to manage customer relationships, track sales leads, automate marketing campaigns, and analyze business performance from a centralized dashboard.

- **Zoom:** Zoom is a cloud-based video conferencing platform that has gained widespread popularity for remote meetings, webinars, and virtual events. With Zoom, users can host high-definition video conferences, share screens, and collaborate with colleagues and clients in real-time, all from a web browser or mobile app.

- **Slack:** Slack is a cloud-based messaging and collaboration platform designed to streamline communication and collaboration within teams and organizations. Slack enables users to create channels for different projects or topics, share files, integrate with other productivity tools, and communicate via text, voice, and video.

- **Adobe Creative Cloud:** Adobe Creative Cloud offers a suite of cloud-based creative software applications for graphic design, video editing, photography, and web development. Users can access industry-standard tools such as Photoshop, Illustrator, Premiere Pro, and Dreamweaver from any device, while collaborating with team members and clients on creative projects in real-time.

These examples illustrate how SaaS applications empower users to access powerful software tools and services without the need for complex installations or maintenance, which enables greater efficiency, collaboration, and innovation in various industries and use cases.

SaaS (Software as a Service): Delivers software applications over the internet, eliminating the need for local installations and maintenance. Users can access applications on a subscription basis, which promotes accessibility, collaboration, and seamless updates.

Function as a Service (FaaS)

Function as a Service (FaaS), commonly known as **serverless computing**, is a model where developers focus entirely on writing code, while the cloud provider automatically handles the underlying infrastructure, scaling, and availability. With FaaS, you deploy individual functions that are triggered by events such as a file upload, a database update, or an API call.

Key benefits of FaaS include:

- **No Server Management:** You never have to provision or manage servers.
- **Automatic Scaling:** Functions scale instantly in response to workload.
- **Cost Efficiency:** You pay only for the compute time your functions consume, which is measured down to milliseconds.

Real Life Example:

A common example of FaaS is **AWS Lambda**. Many companies use Lambda to run background tasks like image processing, log analysis, or chatbot integrations without maintaining servers. For instance, when a photo is uploaded to an S3 bucket, a Lambda function can automatically resize it for different device types. This event-driven model allows developers to build scalable, highly responsive applications with minimal operational overhead.

Function as a Service (FaaS) – A serverless model where developers run code in response to events without managing servers, paying only for the compute time used.

Conclusion

In conclusion, cloud computing revolutionizes the way businesses operate by offering scalability, flexibility, and cost-effectiveness. Its four main models—Infrastructure as a Service (IAAS), Platform as a Service (PAAS), Software as a Service (SAAS) and Function as a Service

(FaaS) cater to different needs, from basic infrastructure provision to full-fledged software applications. For instance, Dropbox is a SAAS example, which offers file storage and sharing services. Next, we will delve into AWS cloud, its inception, and key services, followed by an exploration of AWS's global infrastructure, including regions and availability zones.

Keep practicing the end-of-chapter questions to strengthen your understanding and prepare for the upcoming chapters.

Points to Remember

- Cloud computing offers cost-efficiency, scalability, flexibility, reliability, security, and sustainability, transforming the traditional IT landscape.
- The four main cloud service models—IaaS, PaaS, SaaS, and FaaS (serverless)—provide varying levels of control and management, while catering to diverse business needs.
- Essential cloud computing features include on-demand self-service, broad network access, resource pooling, rapid elasticity, and measured service.
- Businesses benefit from cloud computing's agility, device independence, maintenance ease, multitenancy, enhanced performance, productivity gains, compliance readiness, and availability improvements.

Multiple Choice Questions

1. Which cloud computing advantage allows organizations to replace large upfront capital expenses with usage-based operational expenses?
    a. Scalability
    b. Cost Efficiency
    c. Elasticity
    d. Reliability
2. A retail application experiences a sudden surge in traffic during a holiday sale. Which cloud feature provisions additional resources automatically to meet demand?
    a. Resource Pooling
    b. Elasticity
    c. Flexibility
    d. Broad Network Access

3. Which advantage of cloud computing allows employees to securely access applications and data from any device and location?
    a. Flexibility
    b. Agility
    c. Reliability
    d. Multitenancy
4. A financial services company requires continuous availability and automatic failover across multiple availability zones. Which cloud advantage does this represent?
    a. Reliability
    b. Security
    c. Elasticity
    d. Flexibility
5. Which cloud service model allows developers to deploy code in response to events without managing servers?
    a. IaaS
    b. SaaS
    c. PaaS
    d. FaaS
6. Which of the following is an example of the **shared responsibility model** in AWS?
    a. AWS manages data encryption keys.
    b. The customer configures IAM roles and permissions.
    c. AWS ensures availability of global infrastructure.
    d. AWS patches the underlying hypervisor.
7. An organization wants to reduce its carbon footprint, and align IT operations with sustainability goals. Which advantage of cloud computing supports this objective?
    a. Agility
    b. Reliability
    c. Sustainability
    d. Compliance

Answers

1. b
2. b
3. a
4. a
5. d
6. b
7. c

References

- https://aws.amazon.com/what-is-cloud-computing/
- https://web.archive.org/web/20100722074526/http://blogs.idc.com/ie/?p=190
- https://en.wikipedia.org/wiki/Cloud_computing#Service_models
- https://aws.amazon.com/solutions/case-studies/innovators/airbnb/
- https://aws.amazon.com/solutions/case-studies/innovators/netflix/
- https://aws.amazon.com/solutions/case-studies/capital-one-all-in-on-aws/
- https://aws.amazon.com/solutions/case-studies/nasdaq-case-study/
- https://aws.amazon.com/solutions/case-studies/innovators/intuit/
- https://aws.amazon.com/solutions/case-studies/innovators/volkswagen-group/

CHAPTER 3

Introduction to AWS and Global Infrastructure

Introduction

Now that we have a clear understanding of cloud computing and its service models—**IaaS, PaaS, SaaS, and FaaS**—the next logical step is to see how these concepts are implemented in a real-world cloud platform. This is where **Amazon Web Services (AWS)** comes into focus. AWS takes the foundational ideas of scalability, elasticity, and pay-as-you-go pricing discussed in the previous chapter and delivers them through a practical, service-driven cloud ecosystem used by organizations worldwide.

AWS is more than a collection of services; it is a globally distributed cloud architecture designed to deliver high availability, fault tolerance, and low latency. Its infrastructure is built around Regions, Availability Zones, and edge locations, which together allow applications to run closer to users while remaining resilient to failures. Understanding this architecture is critical, as it explains how AWS supports everything from simple web applications to large-scale, enterprise-grade workloads.

In this chapter, we will explore the origins of AWS, gain a high-level view of its core services, and then examine AWS's global infrastructure in detail. This knowledge will not only help you understand how applications are designed and deployed on AWS but will also form an essential foundation for the **AWS Cloud Practitioner Certification Exam** and the chapters that follow.

Structure

In this chapter, we will be exploring the following:

- About Amazon Web Services and Its Origins
- A Brief Overview of Core Services Offered by AWS along with Real Life Examples
- Detailed Introduction to AWS Global Infrastructure

Amazon Web Services (AWS)

Amazon Web Services (AWS) is the top choice for cloud computing worldwide. With over 200 services available globally, AWS serves a wide range of customers, from startups to big companies and government agencies. Businesses use AWS to save money, improve security, and innovate faster.

AWS offers a comprehensive suite of tools and resources for businesses. It covers everything from computing power to storing data, managing networks, and even using Artificial Intelligence (AI). These services are designed to meet the needs of different types of businesses.

One of the best things about AWS is its flexibility. You can easily adjust your cloud setup to fit your needs. Whether you need more computing power for busy times or extra storage space, AWS lets you make changes quickly without breaking the bank.

AWS has data centers all around the world. This network helps keep things running smoothly and makes it easy to follow rules that detail where data is stored.

Security is a big deal with AWS. They have lots of security features, and follow strict rules to keep your data safe from cyber threats.

In short, AWS is the go-to choice for cloud computing. It offers a wide range of services and solutions to help businesses grow and succeed in the digital age. Recently, AWS has also expanded heavily into generative AI. It is offering services like Amazon Bedrock that let businesses quickly build AI-driven applications without managing complex infrastructure. At the same time, AWS continues to work towards sustainability, with initiatives to power its global infrastructure with renewable energy, and help customers reduce their own carbon footprint.

Origins of Amazon Web Services (AWS)

Amazon Web Services (AWS) has an interesting backstory that includes iconic moments, many of which are rooted in Seattle. Seattle played a crucial role in the evolution of AWS because it was home to Amazon's headquarters and a deep pool of engineering talent with expertise in large-scale distributed systems. The region's strong technology ecosystem and culture of innovation enabled Amazon to experiment, iterate, and eventually transform its internal infrastructure challenges into AWS, which later grew into a global cloud platform.

In the early 2000s, Amazon found itself facing a dilemma. Its talented software engineers were spending endless hours grappling with the complexities of digital infrastructure. They felt like they were reinventing the wheel with every project, while struggling to keep up with the demands of scaling up computing power and offering internet-based services.

Amidst these challenges, a pivotal moment occurred during a casual gathering at McMenamins Six Arms on Capitol Hill in 2005. It was here that AWS senior technologist Allan Vermeulen sketched the initial design principles for a groundbreaking cloud-computing service on the back of a napkin, all while sipping on a Hammerhead ale. Little did he know this napkin would lay the foundation for one of the most revolutionary innovations of the digital age.

However, the seeds of AWS had been planted long before. Amazon had already begun exploring the potential of offering digital infrastructure as a service, recognizing its strengths in building reliable data centers, and providing services like database management. Engineers complained about spending too much time on infrastructure, which diverted their focus from designing innovative products to attract consumers to Amazon.com.

Recognizing the need for greater efficiency and scalability, Amazon centralized the development of its digital infrastructure and made these capabilities available not only to internal teams but also to external developers. This initiative led to the creation of Amazon Web Services (AWS), under the leadership of Andy Jassy. With a strong focus on building scalable, reliable platforms and expanding access to cloud technology, AWS set out to simplify infrastructure management and enable organizations to innovate and reach customers more effectively.

In March 2006, AWS unveiled its first mass-market product, Simple Storage Service (S3), to much fanfare. This groundbreaking service allowed developers to store and retrieve vast amounts of data from anywhere on the web and set the stage for a new era of innovation. Soon after, Elastic Compute Cloud (EC2) was introduced to grant developers access to on-demand computing power like never before.

As the years passed, AWS continued to innovate and expand its offerings, while rolling out hundreds of services and tools to cater to the diverse needs of its customers. From database management to machine learning, AWS has become the go-to destination for businesses that want to harness the power of the cloud.

Today, AWS stands as the foremost and extensively embraced cloud platform worldwide, with millions of customers ranging from startups to enterprises and government agencies. Its impact on the digital landscape is undeniable as it has empowered businesses to lower costs, increase security, become more agile, and innovate faster than ever before.

In the ever-evolving saga of technology, AWS remains at the forefront, driving unprecedented levels of efficiency, agility, and growth in the modern era of computing. And as the journey continues, one thing is certain–the story of AWS is far from over.

Overview of Core AWS Services

As we venture deeper into the realm of Amazon Web Services (AWS), it is time to acquaint ourselves with the cornerstone of AWS's offerings: its core services. Just as a sturdy foundation supports a towering skyscraper, these core services provide the bedrock upon which countless innovative solutions are built. Let us embark on this exploration of AWS's core services, each designed to address specific needs and challenges faced by businesses in the digital age.

In the world of AWS, core services are the building blocks that empower organizations to harness the full potential of cloud computing. These services span a wide spectrum, ranging from computing and storage to databases, analytics, networking, and beyond. With AWS, businesses gain access to a comprehensive suite of tools and infrastructure, which allows them to innovate, scale, and thrive in today's dynamic landscape.

Throughout this journey, we will unravel the capabilities and functionalities of each core service, exploring how they enable businesses to run applications, process data, manage resources, and secure infrastructure with unparalleled flexibility and efficiency. So, let us dive into the world of AWS's core services and unlock the key to discovering endless possibilities in the cloud.

Compute Services: AWS offers a suite of compute services designed to provide scalable and flexible computing resources for running applications of any size and complexity. From virtual servers in the cloud to serverless computing platforms, AWS provides the tools and infrastructure needed to deploy and manage applications efficiently, handle varying workloads seamlessly, and optimize performance for enhanced user experiences. Whether you require traditional virtual servers for full control or prefer the simplicity and scalability of serverless architectures, AWS offers a comprehensive range of compute services to meet your specific requirements and drive innovation in your business.

Companies like **Netflix** use **Amazon EC2** to dynamically scale their computing capacity based on demand, while ensuring seamless streaming experiences for millions of users worldwide.

Storage Services: Storage lies at the heart of modern data-driven applications, and AWS delivers a comprehensive range of storage services to meet the demands of diverse workloads. Whether it is storing mission-critical data, archiving historical records or serving multimedia content to global audiences, AWS offers highly durable, scalable, and cost-effective storage solutions tailored to every need.

Airbnb leverages **Amazon S3** to store and serve billions of images uploaded by hosts and travelers, which ensures fast and reliable access to photos across its platform.

Database Services: AWS provides a variety of managed database services to handle the growing volumes of data generated by today's applications. From traditional relational databases to NoSQL databases and data warehouses, AWS offers fully managed, highly available, and scalable database solutions that enable organizations to store, retrieve, and analyze data efficiently.

Expedia relies on **Amazon RDS** to manage its vast database of travel information, enabling efficient booking processes and personalized recommendations for users.

Analytics Services: Unlocking the value of data is paramount in today's data-driven world, and AWS offers a suite of analytics services to help organizations derive insights from their data. Whether it is real-time streaming analytics, batch processing, or interactive query analysis, AWS provides the tools and infrastructure needed to process, analyze, and visualize data at scale.

Lyft utilizes **Amazon Redshift** to analyze large volumes of ride data, while gaining insights into user preferences, driver performance, and traffic patterns to optimize its service pricing strategies.

Networking Services: Networking is the backbone of modern cloud architectures. Hence, AWS offers a comprehensive set of networking services to connect resources securely and reliably. From virtual private clouds to content delivery networks, AWS provides the networking capabilities that are required to build resilient and scalable architectures in the cloud.

Pfizer uses Amazon VPC to securely connect its on-premises infrastructure with AWS resources, which enables seamless communication between internal systems and cloud-based applications.

Developer Tools: Empowering developers is a core tenet of AWS and the platform offers a range of developer tools to streamline the software development lifecycle. From continuous integration and delivery pipelines to code repositories and collaboration tools, AWS provides the tools and services needed to build, test, and deploy applications with speed and agility.

Capital One utilizes **AWS CodeDeploy** to automate the deployment of software updates, while enabling faster release cycles and improving the overall reliability of its banking applications.

Management Tools: Managing cloud resources effectively is essential for optimizing costs, ensuring security, and maintaining reliability. AWS offers a suite of management tools to help organizations monitor, automate, and optimize their cloud infrastructure, which allows them to operate more efficiently and effectively in the cloud.

airbnb

Airbnb relies on **AWS CloudWatch** to monitor its AWS infrastructure in real-time to proactively identify, and resolve performance issues to ensure optimal uptime and user experience.

Exercise 3.1: Test Your Cloud Knowledge

1. If a company needs to store and retrieve large amounts of data for analytics purposes, which AWS core service would be most suitable for the task?
    a. Amazon S3 (Simple Storage Service)
    b. Amazon RDS (Relational Database Service)
    c. Amazon Redshift (Data Warehouse Service)
    d. Amazon EC2 (Elastic Compute Cloud)
2. Which AWS core service is ideal for deploying virtual servers to run applications with varying computational requirements?
    a. Amazon EC2 (Elastic Compute Cloud)
    b. Amazon S3 (Simple Storage Service)
    c. Amazon DynamoDB (NoSQL Database Service)
    d. Amazon VPC (Virtual Private Cloud)

Answers

1. a
2. a

AWS Global Infrastructure

Now that we have delved into the world of AWS, exploring its origins and core services, let us take a closer look at one of its most critical aspects: the AWS Global Infrastructure. This expansive network forms the backbone of AWS's cloud computing services, and enables businesses to harness the power of the cloud on a global scale.

Amazon Web Services (AWS) operates one of the most extensive and robust cloud infrastructures in the world, spanning across multiple geographic regions and availability zones. The AWS Global Infrastructure is the backbone of the cloud computing services provided by AWS, as it enables customers to build, deploy, and scale their applications with unparalleled reliability, performance, and scalability.

At its core, the AWS Global Infrastructure is designed to provide customers with low-latency access to a comprehensive suite of cloud services, regardless of their location. With data centers strategically located in key regions around the globe, AWS ensures that customers can leverage cloud resources closer to their end-users, which results in improved application performance and user experience.

The key components of the AWS Global Infrastructure include:

- Regions
- Availability Zones
- Edge Location

So, let us look at each of the infrastructure components in detail.

Regions

When we talk about AWS regions, we refer to the global infrastructure backbone of Amazon Web Services. These regions are essentially separate geographical areas where AWS operates multiple data centers, known as availability zones. Each region operates independently and provides a diverse array of cloud services and resources to cater to the needs of businesses and organizations around the world.

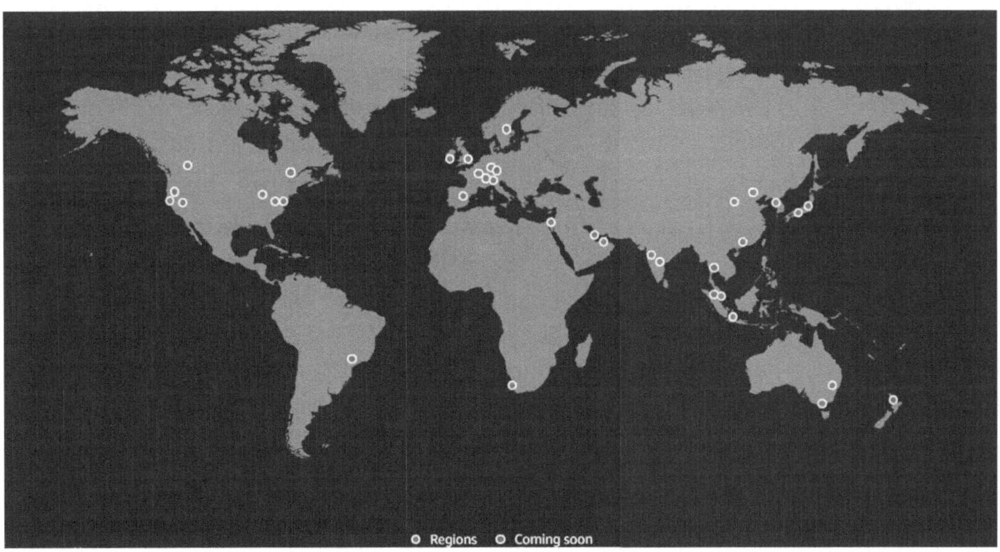

Figure 3.1: *Global Map of All AWS Regions*

The significance of AWS regions cannot be overstated. They play a crucial role in ensuring that businesses can deploy their applications and data closer to their users, thereby reducing latency and improving overall performance. Imagine you are running an online store. With AWS regions, you can choose to host your website and databases in a region that is geographically closer to your customers, while ensuring faster load times and contributing to a better user experience. Additionally, AWS Regions provide redundancy and fault tolerance, which means that even if one availability zone within a region experiences issues, your applications and data can seamlessly failover to another availability zone within the same region, while minimizing downtime and ensuring high availability.

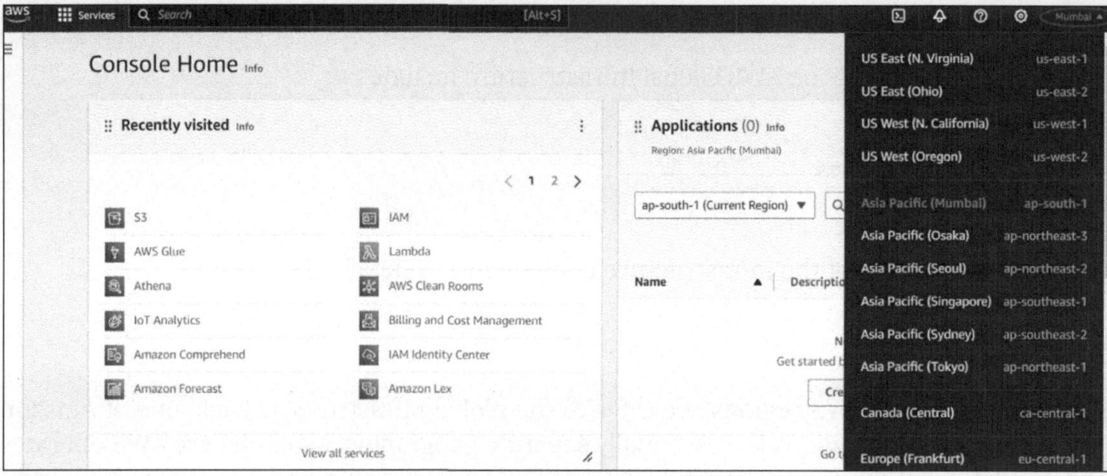

***Figure 3.2:** Selecting Regions in the AWS Homepage*

Currently, **AWS operates 38 geographic regions globally**, spanning across various continents such as North America, Europe, Asia Pacific, and South America. Its growth does not stop there. AWS is constantly expanding its global footprint by adding new regions (including Kingdom of Saudi Arabia, Chile, and the AWS European Sovereign Cloud) to better serve its ever-growing customer base. This expansion allows AWS to reach more customers in different parts of the world and provide them with access to the full suite of AWS services and resources.

It is important to note that resources and pricing can vary between AWS Regions. Factors such as local infrastructure costs, taxes, and regulations can influence the cost of operating in different regions, which leads to differences in pricing for AWS services. Additionally, the availability of certain services may vary between regions based on customer demand and regional requirements. For example, a specific AWS service may be available in one region but not in another due to regulatory restrictions or resource constraints. As a result, AWS adjusts pricing and resource availability accordingly to reflect these differences, while ensuring that customers have access to the services they need at competitive prices, regardless of their location.

In summary, AWS regions form the backbone of AWS, as they provide businesses and organizations with the infrastructure required to deploy their applications and services globally. With over 38 regions and counting, AWS continues to expand its global footprint, while allowing customers to leverage the power of the cloud to innovate and grow their businesses, regardless of where they are located.

AWS Hyderabad, the second AWS Region in India after Mumbai, was launched in 2022, further expanding AWS's presence in the country, and providing businesses with enhanced cloud services and resources.

AWS Availability Zones

AWS availability zones are distinct data centers within a single AWS region. Each region has its own infrastructure and services which is designed to provide fault tolerance and high availability. These zones are interconnected through low-latency links, while enabling redundancy and resilience for applications and data hosted in the cloud.

Availability zones are strategically located to mitigate the risk of service interruptions due to natural disasters, power outages, or other localized issues. They allow businesses to distribute their applications and data across multiple physical locations to reduce the impact of potential disruptions and facilitating continuous operation.

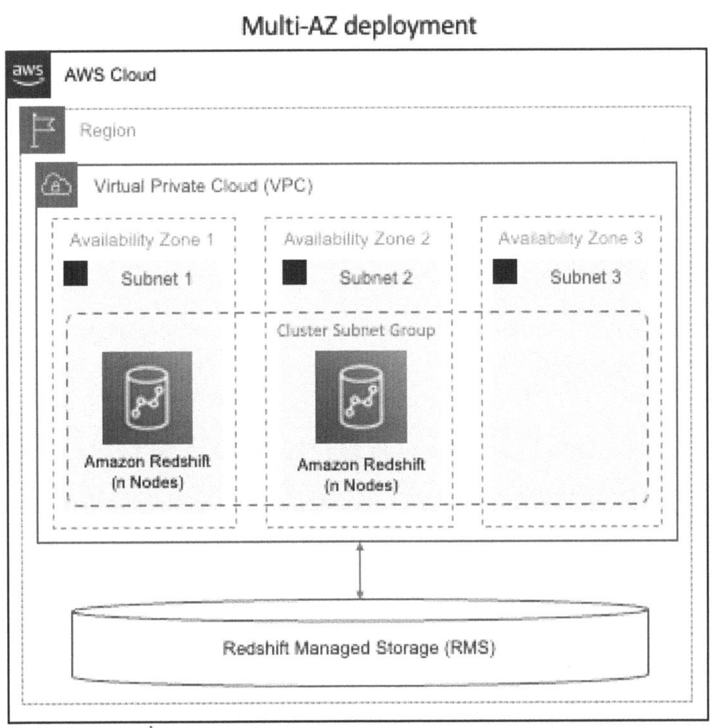

Figure 3.3: *A Diagram of Multi-AZ Deployment of Production System on AWS Cloud*

Each **AWS region is composed of a minimum of three availability zones that are isolated and physically separate zones within a geographic area** to provide customers with options for deploying highly available and fault-tolerant applications. Furthermore, each **availability zone comprises one or more data centers**, which further enhances redundancy and ensures the durability and scalability of AWS infrastructure.

Currently, **AWS operates 120 availability zones** in total which are spread across multiple global regions, with plans for further expansion (13 more zones) to meet the growing demands and enhance the reliability of its cloud services.

AWS Edge Locations

AWS edge locations are endpoints for AWS services that are specifically optimized for content delivery to users at a global scale. They serve as entry points for accessing AWS services and are strategically positioned to reduce latency, and improve performance for end users.

With over **700 edge locations worldwide**, AWS ensures that content is delivered quickly and reliably to users, regardless of their geographic location. These locations cache frequently accessed content closer to end users, which reduces the need for round trips to origin servers and improves the overall user experience.

In addition to edge locations, AWS **operates 11 regional edge caches**, which are larger cache clusters located in major metropolitan areas around the world. These caches further enhance the performance of content delivery by caching and serving frequently accessed content at a regional level, thereby reducing latency and improving scalability for applications with a global user base.

By leveraging edge locations and regional edge caches, AWS customers can deliver content and applications with low latency and high throughput, while providing a seamless user experience and ensuring optimal performance for their web applications, video streaming, gaming, and other content delivery needs.

Note: *Always refer to the AWS global infrastructure site for updated region, availability zone and edge locations prior to the exam.*

Other Infrastructure Components of AWS

Here is a brief explanation of all other AWS infrastructure components.

AWS Local Zones

AWS local zones bring the power of AWS infrastructure closer to end users in metropolitan areas, enabling low-latency access to compute, storage, and other AWS services. Currently, there are **43 local zones** globally that provide customers with the ability to run applications and workloads with single-digit millisecond latency.

These local zones extend the reach of AWS regions and offer a complement to AWS's existing infrastructure, particularly for applications that require ultra-low latency or access to specialized services near end users. By deploying resources in local zones, customers can deliver high-performance, latency-sensitive applications while still benefiting from the scalability, security, and reliability of the AWS Cloud.

With local zones, customers can address use cases such as real-time gaming, media and entertainment content delivery, ML inference at the edge, and interactive streaming services. By leveraging local zones, customers can achieve the performance and responsiveness required for their applications while maintaining the flexibility and agility of the AWS Cloud platform.

AWS Direct Connect

AWS Direct Connect is a dedicated network connection service that provides private connectivity between an organization's on-premises data center or corporate network and the AWS Cloud. This service enables customers to establish a high-speed, low-latency connection to AWS, while bypassing the public internet and ensuring consistent network performance and increased security for mission-critical workloads.

With AWS Direct Connect, organizations can extend their on-premises infrastructure seamlessly into the AWS Cloud and enable hybrid cloud deployments, disaster recovery solutions, and data center migrations. By establishing a dedicated connection, customers can transfer large volumes of data more efficiently, reduce network costs, and meet stringent compliance requirements.

One key distinction between AWS local zones and AWS Direct Connect is their respective purposes and capabilities. AWS local zones are designed to bring AWS infrastructure closer to end users in metropolitan areas, offering low-latency access to compute, storage, and other AWS services. In contrast, AWS Direct Connect focuses on providing dedicated network connectivity between on-premises environments and the AWS Cloud, while ensuring secure and reliable data transfer without traversing the public internet.

Currently, there are **115 Direct Connect locations globally** that offer customers a wide range of options for establishing private connections to AWS. These Direct Connect locations are strategically located in major metropolitan areas around the world, which provide organizations with flexibility and scalability in extending their network infrastructure into the cloud.

AWS Outposts

AWS Outposts extend the AWS infrastructure and services directly into a customer's on-premises data center or co-location facility. They bring the same hardware, services, APIs, and management tools that run in AWS Regions, but are delivered and operated locally by AWS. With Outposts, organizations can run services such as Amazon EC2, EBS, RDS, ECS, EKS, and even S3 right within their own facilities, while still connecting seamlessly to the nearest AWS Region for broader service integration.

This capability is especially valuable for workloads that require **ultra-low latency, local data processing, or strict data residency compliance**. For example, financial institutions can process transactions within national borders while still leveraging AWS for analytics, or manufacturers can run real-time factory floor applications with millisecond latency. In short, Outposts enable a true **hybrid cloud model**, which grants businesses the flexibility of the AWS cloud while meeting the operational realities of on-premises infrastructure.

Naming Convention for AWS Regions and Availability Zones

AWS follows a consistent naming nomenclature for its regions and Availability Zones (AZs) for clarity and uniformity across its global infrastructure. These conventions are explained as follows:

- **Regions:** Each AWS region is identified by a unique name, typically comprising a geographical location followed by a code denoting the region. For example, "us-west-2" represents the US West (Oregon) region, while "ap-southeast-1" corresponds to the Asia Pacific (Singapore) region. This naming convention helps users easily identify and select the region closest to their users or data centers.
- **Availability Zones (AZs):** Within each AWS region, there are multiple availability zones, each identified by a distinct letter. For instance, in the US West (Oregon) region, availability zones may be labeled as "us-west-2a," "us-west-2b," and so on. These letters denote separate and isolated data centers within the same region, while offering redundancy and fault tolerance.

AWS continues to follow the same naming convention for instances (family + generation + size), but newer families now include suffixes like 'g' for Graviton processors, 'a' for AMD-based instances, or 'i' for Intel. This helps customers easily identify the underlying processor or special capabilities of the instance.

By adhering to this naming convention, AWS ensures consistency and clarity in identifying regions and availability zones across its global infrastructure, which allows users to make informed decisions when they are deploying their applications and services.

Conclusion

As we conclude our exploration into Amazon Web Services (AWS), we have delved into its origins and understood how it emerged from the fertile grounds of Seattle, driven by the need to optimize digital infrastructure and revolutionize cloud computing. We have uncovered the core services of AWS, which act as the building blocks for a wide array of applications, from the most basic to the most sophisticated. Venturing further, we have traversed the vast expanse of AWS global infrastructure, while navigating through the intricate network of regions, availability zones, edge locations, local zones, Direct Connect locations, and Outposts, with each contributing to the unparalleled scale, resilience, and performance of the AWS ecosystem. As AWS continues to innovate and expand its footprint across the globe, it remains at the forefront of digital transformation, while empowering organizations of all sizes and industries to unleash their full potential in the cloud-powered world.

In the next chapter, we will delve into the AWS Well-Architected framework and the Shared Responsibility model. We will explore how these foundational principles guide organizations in designing, building, and maintaining secure, high-performing, resilient, and efficient cloud architectures on AWS. By understanding the Well-Architected framework, readers will learn best practices for optimizing their workloads across key architectural pillars like operational excellence, security, reliability, performance efficiency, and cost optimization. Additionally, we will unravel the nuances of the Shared Responsibility Model, while exploring the division of responsibilities between AWS and its customers in ensuring the security and compliance of cloud-based solutions. With practical insights and actionable recommendations, the chapter will equip readers with the knowledge and tools to architect robust and compliant cloud environments on AWS, which will set the stage for success in their cloud journey.

Points to Remember

- AWS, the world's leading cloud platform, offers over **200 services** to cater to diverse business needs.
- With **38 regions globally**, AWS provides high availability and low-latency services to users worldwide.
- Each region consists of minimum **3 availability zones (120 AZ's in total)**, ensuring fault tolerance and redundancy.
- AWS Edge Locations, comprising **700+ Points of Presence** and **11 Regional Edge Caches**, optimize content delivery and enhance user experiences.
- Direct Connect offers secure, low-latency connections to AWS services from **115 locations worldwide.**
- Local Zones (**43 in number**) extend AWS infrastructure to metropolitan areas, facilitating proximity to end-users and low-latency applications.
- Understanding the naming nomenclature of AWS regions and availability zones aids in navigating the global infrastructure efficiently.

Multiple Choice Questions

1. A financial services company wants to set up a secure, logically isolated private network within AWS to run its applications and databases. Which AWS core service should they use?
   a. Amazon VPC (Virtual Private Cloud)
   b. Amazon S3 (Simple Storage Service)
   c. Amazon Redshift (Data Warehouse Service)
   d. Amazon CloudWatch (Monitoring and Management Service)
2. Which AWS core service would be best suited for monitoring the performance and health of various AWS resources in real-time?
   a. Amazon CloudFront (Content Delivery Network)
   b. Amazon CloudWatch (Monitoring and Management Service)
   c. Amazon SQS (Simple Queue Service)
   d. Amazon Elastic Beanstalk (Application Deployment Service)
3. Which of the following accurately describes AWS Regions? (Select all that applies)
   a. Independent geographical areas with multiple Availability Zones
   b. A single data center in a specific location
   c. Each region has a unique name (for example, us-east-1, ap-southeast-2)
   d. Geographically dispersed for redundancy and fault tolerance
4. A healthcare provider wants to deploy a critical application that must remain available even if one data center fails. Which AWS feature should they leverage?
   a. Local Zones
   b. Direct Connect
   c. Edge Locations
   d. Availability Zones
5. In which scenario would you recommend using AWS Direct Connect? (Select all that applies)
   a. When low-latency connections are required for mission-critical applications
   b. When deploying Content Delivery Networks (CDNs)
   c. When extending your on-premises data center to the cloud
   d. When deploying applications with high-frequency trading requirements

6. What is the primary purpose of AWS Edge Locations?
    a. To provide high-speed connections between AWS Regions
    b. To host AWS Direct Connect locations
    c. To cache content for faster delivery to end-users
    d. To facilitate inter-region communication
7. How does AWS ensure high availability within a Region?
    a. By deploying multiple Local Zones within each Region
    b. By ensuring each Region has at least two Availability Zones
    c. By replicating data across all Edge Locations
    d. By leveraging Direct Connect for redundant connections
8. Which statement accurately describes AWS Local Zones?
    a. They are standalone AWS Regions with their own set of services.
    b. They extend AWS infrastructure to metropolitan areas for low-latency applications.
    c. They are primarily used for content caching and distribution.
    d. They provide direct connections to AWS services from on-premises data centers.
9. How does AWS's Global Infrastructure contribute to scalability? (Choose as applicable)
    a. By limiting the number of Regions and AZs
    b. By providing hundreds of Edge Locations for global content delivery
    c. By allowing customers to deploy resources close to end-users worldwide
    d. By focusing only on densely populated metro areas
10. Which AWS feature provides **high-speed, private connectivity** between on-premises data centers and AWS services?
    a. AWS Wavelength
    b. AWS Direct Connect
    c. AWS Edge Locations
    d. AWS Local Zones

Answers

1. a
2. b
3. a, c, d
4. d
5. a, b, c
6. c
7. b
8. b
9. b, c
10. b

References

- https://www.aboutamazon.com/what-we-do/amazon-web-services
- https://www.aboutamazon.com/news/aws/the-deceptively-simple-origins-of-aws
- https://www.seattletimes.com/business/amazon/in-the-15-years-since-its-launch- amazon-web-services-has-transformed-how-companies-do-business/
- https://aws.amazon.com/solutions/case-studies/innovators/netflix/
- https://aws.amazon.com/solutions/case-studies/airbnb-optimizes-usage-and-costs-case-study/
- https://aws.amazon.com/solutions/case-studies/expedia/
- https://aws.amazon.com/solutions/case-studies/lyft/
- https://www.iotone.com/case-study/case-study-pfizer/c18
- https://www.capitalone.com/tech/cloud/serverless-first-strategy/
- https://aws.amazon.com/solutions/case-studies/airbnb-case-study/
- https://aws.amazon.com/about-aws/global-infrastructure/

Chapter 4
AWS Well Architected Framework and Shared Responsibility Model

Introduction

Now that we have delved into the basics of AWS and have explored its origins, core services, and global infrastructure, it is time to explore a crucial concept for the AWS Cloud Practitioner exam: The Well-Architected Framework. This framework serves as a guiding principle for designing and evaluating cloud architectures, while ensuring that they are secure, efficient, and cost-effective. Understanding the Well-Architected Framework is essential for aspiring cloud practitioners as it provides a structured approach to building reliable and scalable cloud solutions. In this chapter, we will explore the key pillars of the Well-Architected Framework and discuss why they are vital for success in the cloud computing landscape.

Structure

In this chapter, we will explore the following topics:

- AWS Well Architected Framework and Its Key Components
- Key Pillars of Well Architected Framework
- Shared Responsibility Model
- Different Ways to Ensure High Security Compliance on AWS Cloud Environment

AWS Well Architected Framework

The Well-Architected Framework is a set of best practices and guidelines developed by AWS to help cloud architects build secure, high-performing, resilient, and efficient infrastructure for their applications. Think of it as a blueprint or roadmap that architects can follow to ensure that their cloud environments are designed in a way that meets the specific needs of their applications and business goals.

For example, imagine that you are building a house. Before you start construction, you consult with an architect to create a blueprint that outlines every detail, from the layout of each room to the materials used for construction. The architect considers factors like the building's location, the local climate, and your lifestyle preferences to design a house that is both functional and aesthetically pleasing. Similarly, the Well-Architected Framework provides cloud architects with a structured approach to designing cloud architectures that consider factors like security, performance, reliability, cost optimization, and operational excellence. By following the guidelines outlined in the framework, architects can ensure that their cloud environments are well-designed and can support their applications' needs.

Significance of AWS Well Architected Framework

The AWS Well-Architected Framework is crucial for practitioners because it provides a structured approach to building and maintaining cloud architectures that align with best practices. By following the principles outlined in the framework, practitioners can ensure that their infrastructure is optimized for performance, reliability, security, and cost-effectiveness.

Firstly, the framework helps in building secure infrastructure by guiding practitioners to implement security best practices at every layer of their architecture. This includes configuring robust Identity and Access Management (IAM) policies, encrypting data at rest and in transit, and implementing network security measures such as firewalls and intrusion detection systems. By adhering to these security principles, practitioners can protect their applications and data from unauthorized access, data breaches, and other security threats.

Additionally, the Well-Architected Framework emphasizes the importance of designing for high performance. Practitioners are encouraged to optimize their infrastructure for speed and efficiency, while leveraging scalable compute resources, caching mechanisms, and strengthening Content Delivery Networks (CDNs) to minimize latency and improve responsiveness. By designing their applications with performance in mind, practitioners can deliver a seamless user experience and meet the demands of modern, data-intensive workloads.

Moreover, the framework focuses on building resilient infrastructure that can withstand failures and disruptions. Practitioners are advised to design for fault tolerance by deploying redundant components, implementing automated failover mechanisms, and regularly testing their disaster recovery procedures. By following these resilience principles, practitioners can ensure that their applications remain available and operational even in the face of hardware failures, natural disasters, or other unforeseen events.

Finally, the Well-Architected Framework helps practitioners optimize their infrastructure for cost-effectiveness. By analyzing their resource utilization, identifying areas of inefficiency, and implementing cost-saving strategies such as rightsizing instances, leveraging spot instances, and optimizing storage usage, practitioners can minimize their cloud spending while maximizing the value they derive from AWS services. By adopting a cost-conscious approach to infrastructure design and management, practitioners can achieve their business goals while staying within budget constraints.

Real Life Example:

One such example is the case study for Well-Architected Framework is of FINRA (Financial Industry Regulatory Authority), a private sector regulator responsible for overseeing the securities industry in the United States.

FINRA implemented the AWS Well-Architected Framework to optimize their cloud infrastructure for performance, security, reliability, and cost-efficiency. By conducting regular reviews of their architecture against the Well-Architected Framework pillars, FINRA was able to identify areas for improvement and implement best practices to address them.

As a result, FINRA achieved significant improvements in their infrastructure's reliability and scalability, which allowed them to handle increased workloads and spikes in demand more effectively. They also enhanced their security posture by implementing robust security controls and monitoring mechanisms to protect sensitive data and ensure compliance with regulatory requirements.

Furthermore, by optimizing their cloud resources based on the Well-Architected Framework principles, FINRA was able to reduce their operational costs while maintaining high performance and reliability levels. This enabled them to allocate resources more efficiently and invest in innovation initiatives to drive business growth.

Overall, the implementation of the AWS Well-Architected Framework enabled FINRA to build a more resilient, secure, and cost-effective cloud infrastructure, which ultimately supported their mission to protect investors and promote market integrity in the financial industry.

Key Pillars of the Well Architected Framework

Now that we have grasped the concept of AWS Well-Architected Framework and explored a real-life application, it is time to dive deeper into its foundation: the six key pillars. These pillars serve as guiding principles for architects and developers and ensure that cloud solutions are built to be secure, efficient, and reliable. Let us begin by providing an overview of each pillar, followed by a detailed examination of their significance and implementation within the framework.

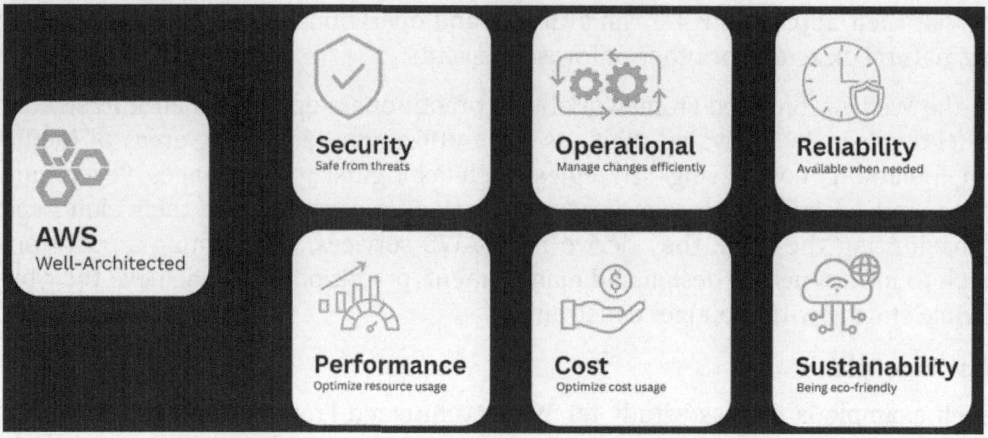

***Figure 4.1**: Pillars of the AWS Well Architected Framework*

Here is a summary of all the key pillars of AWS Well-Architected Framework:

Key Pillar	Description
Operational Excellence	This pillar focuses on supporting the effective development and operation of workloads, gaining insights into operations, and continuously improving processes and procedures to deliver business value efficiently.
Security	The security pillar guides organizations in leveraging cloud technologies to protect data, systems, and assets, thereby enhancing their overall security posture.
Reliability	This pillar encompasses the ability of a workload to perform its intended function correctly and consistently, including the capability to operate and test the workload throughout its lifecycle.
Performance Efficiency	The performance efficiency pillar emphasizes using computing resources efficiently to meet system requirements, maintaining efficiency as demand changes, and leveraging evolving technologies.
Cost Optimization	Cost optimization involves running systems to deliver business value at the lowest price point possible, while optimizing resource utilization, and maximizing return on investment.
Sustainability	The sustainability pillar focuses on continually improving sustainability impacts by reducing energy consumption, thus increasing efficiency across all workload components, and minimizing total resource requirements.

***Table 4.1:** Description of Six Pillars of AWS Well Architected Frame*

You must also review the basic terms and guidelines before we consider a detailed explanation of these key pillars.

In the AWS Well-Architected Framework, we use specific terms to describe the components and structure of cloud solutions such as:

- **Component:** This refers to the code, configuration, and AWS Resources working together to fulfill a requirement. It is often managed as a distinct unit of technical ownership, independent of other components.
- **Workload:** A workload encompasses a set of components collaborating to deliver business value. It is the level of detail typically communicated between business and technology leaders.
- **Architecture:** Architecture focuses on how components within a workload interact and communicate. Architecture diagrams illustrate these relationships.
- **Milestones:** These are significant points marking changes in your architecture's evolution, from design and implementation to testing, deployment, and production.
- **Technology Portfolio:** The technology portfolio comprises the collection of workloads essential for business operations within an organization.
- **Level of Effort:** This categorizes the time, effort, and complexity required for task implementation. It is crucial to consider team size, expertise, and workload complexity for context. These levels are as follows:
  - **High:** Tasks may span weeks or months, often requiring multiple stories, releases, and tasks.
  - **Medium:** Tasks are typically completed within days or weeks, possibly across multiple releases.
  - **Low:** Tasks are generally finished in hours or days, possibly involving multiple smaller tasks.

When architecting workloads, there are several trade-offs between pillars based on business context. These decisions influence engineering priorities, such as optimizing sustainability and cost over reliability in development environments or prioritizing reliability at higher costs for mission-critical solutions. In ecommerce, performance directly impacts revenue and customer engagement. However, security and operational excellence are pillars that are generally non-negotiable and should not be compromised for the sake of others.

General Design Principles

The Well-Architected Framework outlines several key design principles to guide effective cloud design, which are:

- **Capacity Planning:** Avoid guesswork by leveraging the flexibility of cloud computing. With on-demand scalability, you can adjust capacity dynamically to match workload demands, while eliminating the need to over-provision or suffer from resource shortages.
- **Production-Scale Testing:** Cloud environments enable the creation of realistic test environments on demand. By simulating production conditions, you can conduct

thorough testing without incurring the high costs associated with maintaining dedicated testing infrastructure.

- **Automation:** Embrace automation to streamline workload management and reduce manual effort. Automated processes facilitate the creation, replication, and monitoring of workloads, allowing for efficient resource utilization and rapid response to changing requirements.
- **Evolutionary Architectures:** Traditional architectures often struggle to adapt to evolving business needs due to their static nature. Cloud environments support the evolution of architectures through automation and on-demand testing, while enabling continuous refinement and adaptation to meet evolving demands.
- **Data-Driven Design:** Leverage data to inform architectural decisions and optimize workload performance. By collecting and analyzing data on workload behavior, you can identify areas for improvement and make informed decisions to enhance overall efficiency and effectiveness.

Key Pillars of AWS Well Architected Framework

Let us explore the key pillars of AWS Well-Architected Framework in detail here:

Operational Excellence

Operational excellence in AWS encompasses a commitment to building software/solution effectively while ensuring a seamless customer experience. It revolves around implementing best practices to organize teams, design workloads, operate at scale, and evolve over time. By focusing on operational excellence, teams can dedicate more effort to developing new features and less on maintenance and troubleshooting, ultimately leading to enhanced customer satisfaction.

The goal of operational excellence is to deliver new features and bug fixes to customers quickly and reliably. Organizations that prioritize operational excellence consistently delight customers while managing changes, updates, and handling failures. This approach fosters Continuous Integration and Continuous Delivery (CI/CD), which allows developers to consistently deliver high-quality results.

Key Design Principles

The following is list of key design principles:

- **Perform Operations as Code**: Apply engineering principles to automate operations by defining the entire workload as code. Scripting operations procedures and automating responses to events minimize human errors, and ensure consistent outcomes.

- **Make Frequent Small, Reversible Changes**: Design workloads that allow for regular updates through scalable and loosely coupled components. Implementing automated deployment techniques and incremental changes reduces the impact of failures and facilitates faster recovery.
- **Refine Operations Procedures Frequently:** Continuously improve operations procedures as workloads evolve. Regular reviews, updates, and communication of procedural changes ensure effectiveness and familiarity among teams.
- **Anticipate Failure:** Conduct pre-mortem exercises to identify potential failure points and mitigate risks. Test failure scenarios and response procedures regularly to validate effectiveness and readiness.
- **Learn from Operational Failures:** Drive improvement by analyzing and sharing insights from operational events and failures across teams and the organization.
- **Use Managed Services:** Reduce operational overhead by leveraging AWS managed services whenever possible. Building operational procedures around these services streamlines operations and enhances efficiency.
- **Implement Observability for Actionable Insights:** Gain a comprehensive understanding of workload performance, reliability, and cost through observability telemetry. Establishing Key Performance Indicators (KPIs), and leveraging actionable data enables informed decision-making and proactive improvement.

Best Practice Areas

- **Organization:** Define business objectives and organize work to support these outcomes. Implement services for integration, deployment, and delivery to facilitate automated processes.
- **Prepare:** Understand and mitigate inherent risks in workload operation. Ensure that teams are equipped to support the workload and establish metrics to monitor workload health and operational activities.
- **Operate:** Continuously monitor workload performance and respond to incidents promptly. Use business priorities as feedback to drive continual improvement.
- **Evolve:** Adapt operations and priorities based on changing business needs and environmental factors. Utilize feedback loops to drive ongoing improvement in workload operation and organizational processes.

Operational excellence in AWS involves designing systems for efficiency, resilience, and continuous improvement, emphasizing automation, frequent iterations, and proactive risk management to deliver a superior customer experience.

Security

The security pillar within AWS emphasizes the utilization of cloud technologies to bolster the protection of data, systems, and assets, thereby enhancing the overall security posture of workloads. To achieve this, several design principles are employed:

- **Implement a Strong Identity Foundation:** This involves adopting the principle of least privilege and enforcing separation of duties, which ensures that each interaction with AWS resources is appropriately authorized. Identity management is centralized, thereby reducing reliance on long-term static credentials.

- **Maintain Traceability:** Real-time monitoring, alerting, and auditing of actions and changes in the environment are essential. Integration of log and metric collection with systems allows for automatic investigation and action-taking.

- **Apply Security at All Layers:** Employ a defense-in-depth approach with multiple security controls across various layers including the edge of the network, VPC, load balancing, instances, operating systems, applications, and code.

- **Automate Security Best Practices:** Automation of software-based security mechanisms enables more rapid and cost-effective scalability, while ensuring that secure architectures are consistently implemented. Controls are defined and managed as code in version-controlled templates.

- **Protect Data in Transit and at Rest:** Data is classified into sensitivity levels, and appropriate mechanisms such as encryption, tokenization, and access control are applied to safeguard data both during transmission and storage.

- **Keep People Away from Data:** Mechanisms and tools are employed to minimize or eliminate direct access or manual processing of data, which reduces the risk of mishandling, modification, or human error.

- **Prepare for Security Events:** Incident management and investigation policies and processes are established to align with organizational requirements. Incident response simulations are conducted, and automation tools are utilized to enhance speed in detection, investigation, and recovery during security incidents.

These principles collectively contribute to building a robust security posture within AWS workloads, mitigating risks, and ensuring the protection of critical assets and data.

AWS ensures data protection and compliance through a combination of security measures, encryption, and compliance certifications.

- **Encryption:** AWS offers encryption capabilities to protect data both in transit and at rest. Customers can use AWS Key Management Service (KMS) to create and manage encryption keys for their data stored in AWS services. This ensures that sensitive data remains secure and inaccessible to unauthorized users.

- **Compliance Certifications**: AWS adheres to various industry standards and regulations to ensure data protection and compliance. AWS services comply with certifications such as ISO 27001/22301, SOC 1/2/3, PCI DSS, HIPAA, and GDPR, among others. These certifications provide customers with assurance that their data is handled in a secure and compliant manner.

- **Access Controls:** AWS provides robust access controls to restrict access to data based on user roles and permissions. Identity and Access Management (IAM) allows customers to manage user identities and control access to AWS resources, while ensuring that only authorized users can access sensitive data.

- **Data Residency and Privacy:** AWS offers services and features to help customers comply with data residency requirements and privacy regulations. Customers can choose the AWS region where their data is stored to comply with specific data sovereignty laws. Additionally, AWS provides features such as AWS Artifact, which allows customers to access compliance reports and documentation to support their own compliance efforts.

Overall, AWS employs a comprehensive approach to data protection and compliance, while leveraging encryption, compliance certifications, access controls, and other security measures to ensure that customer data is secure and compliant with relevant regulations and standards.

Security pillar of AWS focuses on leveraging cloud technologies to safeguard data, systems, and assets, enhancing overall security posture. It emphasizes principles like strong identity management, automated security practices, and proactive incident preparation to mitigate risks effectively.

Reliability

The reliability pillar of the AWS Well-Architected Framework focuses on ensuring that workloads perform their intended functions correctly and consistently. Here are some key principles and best practices to increase reliability in the cloud:

- **Automatically Recover from Failure:** Monitor workloads for Key Performance Indicators (KPIs) and automate recovery processes to detect and remediate failures in real-time. This proactive approach helps anticipate and address issues before they impact performance.

- **Test Recovery Procedures:** Unlike traditional on-premises environments, cloud platforms allow you to simulate failure scenarios and validate recovery procedures through automation. This testing helps identify and fix potential failure pathways, thereby reducing the risk of downtime during actual incidents.

- **Scale Horizontally:** Increase aggregate workload availability by distributing requests across multiple smaller resources instead of relying on a single large resource. This approach minimizes the impact of a single failure on the overall workload and improves resilience.

- **Stop Guessing Capacity:** Monitor workload demand and utilization in real time to dynamically adjust resource allocation and maintain optimal performance levels. Automation helps manage resource provisioning to meet demand without over or under-provisioning.

- **Manage Change through Automation:** Implement changes to infrastructure using automation to ensure consistency and reliability. Track and review changes to automation processes to maintain a reliable and stable environment over time.

AWS ensures that systems can recover from failures through various mechanisms and best practices that are mentioned as follows:

- **Automated Recovery:** AWS provides tools and services that enable automated recovery from failures. Customers can set up monitoring and alarms using Amazon CloudWatch to detect anomalies or performance issues in their systems. When an issue is detected, AWS Lambda functions or AWS Auto Scaling can automatically respond to the event by triggering recovery processes such as restarting failed instances or scaling out resources to handle increased demand.

- **Multi-AZ Deployments:** AWS offers services with built-in redundancy and failover capabilities across multiple Availability Zones (AZs). For example, Amazon RDS databases can be configured to automatically failover to standby replicas in different AZs in the event of a failure. Similarly, Amazon EC2 instances deployed in an Auto Scaling group can be distributed across multiple AZs to ensure high availability and resilience to failures.

- **Disaster Recovery Solutions:** AWS provides disaster recovery solutions, such as AWS Backup and AWS Disaster Recovery to help customers replicate and recover their data and workloads in the event of a disaster. By using these services, customers can create backup copies of their data and applications in different regions or AZs, while ensuring business continuity and minimizing downtime in case of a catastrophic failure.

- **Fault-Tolerant Architecture:** AWS encourages customers to design fault-tolerant architectures that can withstand failures without impacting the overall system performance. This includes implementing redundant components, designing for graceful degradation, and using distributed systems patterns such as retries and circuit breakers to handle failures gracefully.

Overall, AWS offers a range of tools, services, and best practices to help customers build resilient and recoverable systems that can withstand failures and maintain high availability and performance.

Reliability pillar focuses on ensuring that workloads consistently perform their intended functions correctly, emphasizing automated recovery, testing of recovery procedures, horizontal scaling for increased availability, and capacity management through automation.

Performance Efficiency

Performance efficiency in AWS Well-Architected Framework is achieved through of the following design principles aimed at optimizing workload performance and resource utilization:

- **Democratize Advanced Technologies**: AWS Well-Architected Framework allows organizations to leverage advanced technologies without the need for specialized expertise. By consuming services such as NoSQL databases, media transcoding, and ML as managed services, teams can focus on product development rather than infrastructure provisioning and management.
- **Go Global in Minutes**: Deploying workloads in multiple AWS regions worldwide enables organizations to provide lower latency and a better user experience for customers. With AWS Well-Architected Framework, organizations can easily expand their global footprint and scale their services to meet growing demand.
- **Use Serverless Architectures:** Serverless architectures eliminate the need to manage physical servers for compute activities. AWS Well-Architected Framework provides serverless storage services and event services, which allows organizations to host code without the operational burden of server management. This approach reduces costs and increases scalability by leveraging managed services at cloud scale.
- **Experiment More Often**: With virtual and automatable resources in AWS Well-Architected Framework, organizations can conduct comparative testing using different types of instances, storage, or configurations. This enables organizations to iterate and optimize their workloads more frequently, while improving performance and efficiency over time.
- **Consider Mechanical Sympathy**: AWS Well-Architected Framework encourages organizations to align technology approaches with workload goals. By understanding data access patterns and selecting appropriate database or storage approaches, organizations can optimize performance and efficiency based on workload requirements.

By adhering to these design principles, organizations can enhance the performance efficiency of their workloads in AWS Well-Architected Framework, while delivering faster and more responsive services to their users and optimizing resource utilization and cost-effectiveness.

AWS enables efficient resource scaling through several mechanisms which are mentioned as follows:

- **Auto Scaling:** AWS Auto Scaling automatically adjusts the number of instances in a workload based on demand. It allows organizations to define scaling policies that dynamically add or remove instances in response to changes in traffic patterns, while ensuring optimal performance and cost-efficiency.

- **Elastic Load Balancing:** AWS Elastic Load Balancing distributes incoming traffic across multiple instances to ensure workload availability and scalability. By automatically scaling the load balancer based on traffic volume, organizations can handle sudden spikes in demand without manual intervention.
- **Elasticity:** AWS provides on-demand access to a wide range of compute, storage, and networking resources, which allows organizations to scale resources up or down as needed. This elasticity enables organizations to efficiently allocate resources based on workload requirements, and adjust capacity in real time.
- **Serverless Computing:** AWS offers serverless computing services such as AWS Lambda, which automatically scales resources based on workload demand. With serverless architectures, organizations can focus on application logic without managing underlying infrastructure, leading to efficient resource utilization and cost savings.
- **Global Infrastructure**: AWS regions and availability zones are strategically located around the world, enabling organizations to deploy resources closer to their users for lower latency and improved performance. Thus, by leveraging AWS's global infrastructure, organizations can scale resources efficiently to meet the needs of their global user base.

Performance efficiency in AWS involves optimizing resource usage, leveraging advanced technologies, and adopting serverless architectures to ensure high-performing, cost-effective workloads.

Cost Optimization

Cost optimization in the cloud is crucial for maximizing the value of your investments and achieving financial success. To effectively optimize costs, AWS offers five design principles which are mentioned as follows:

- **Implement Cloud Financial Management:** Building capability in Cloud Financial Management and Cost Optimization is essential for accelerating business value realization in the cloud. This involves dedicating resources and efforts to understand and manage cloud spending effectively. Like other areas like security and operational excellence, organizations should invest in building expertise, processes, and resources for cost efficiency.
- **Adopt a Consumption Model:** With AWS, you only pay for the computing resources you use, which allows you to scale usage based on business requirements without the need for extensive forecasting. For example, you can stop non-production environments when they are not in use, leading to significant cost savings.
- **Measure Overall Efficiency:** It is important to measure both the business output of your workloads and the costs associated with delivering them. This enables you to understand the relationship between increasing output and reducing costs, which will help you optimize efficiency effectively.

- **Stop Spending on Undifferentiated Heavy Lifting:** AWS takes care of the heavy lifting involved in traditional data center operations, such as server management and infrastructure maintenance. Hence, by leveraging managed services, you can offload these operational tasks to AWS and focus on delivering value to your customers and business projects.
- **Analyze and Attribute Expenditure:** AWS provides tools and features that allow you to accurately identify and analyze the usage and costs of your systems. This transparency enables you to attribute IT costs to individual workload owners, measure ROI, and optimize resources accordingly to achieve cost savings.

AWS services offer several ways to manage and reduce expenses, which are mentioned as follows:

- **Right Sizing:** AWS provides tools to analyze resource usage and identify opportunities to adjust resources to match workload demands. By optimizing the size of your resources, you can avoid over-provisioning and reduce costs.
- **Reserved Instances:** AWS offers Reserved Instances, which allow you to commit to a certain amount of usage in exchange for discounted rates. By purchasing Reserved Instances for predictable workloads, you can save money compared to paying on-demand prices.
- **Spot Instances:** Spot Instances allow you to bid for unused EC2 capacity at discounted rates. By using Spot Instances for fault-tolerant or flexible workloads, you can achieve significant cost savings compared to on-demand prices.
- **Auto Scaling:** Auto Scaling automatically adjusts the number of EC2 instances in response to changes in demand. By dynamically scaling your resources up or down based on workload requirements, you can optimize resource utilization and reduce costs.
- **Cost Explorer:** AWS Cost Explorer provides tools for analyzing your AWS spending and identifying cost-saving opportunities. By monitoring your usage and identifying areas of overspending, you can make informed decisions to reduce expenses.
- **Budgets and Alerts:** AWS Budgets allows you to set custom cost and usage budgets with alerts to notify you when you exceed predefined thresholds. By setting budgets and receiving alerts, you can proactively manage expenses and avoid unexpected costs.

Overall, AWS services offer a variety of tools and strategies to help you effectively manage and reduce expenses, allowing you to optimize your cloud spending and maximize value.

With the rapid growth of AI and GenAI workloads, cost optimization has become even more critical. Training and running inference on large models often requires specialized GPU or accelerator instances, which can quickly drive up costs. Applying cost design principles such as Savings Plans, managed AI services like Amazon SageMaker or Bedrock, and right-sizing accelerator usage ensures that organizations can experiment with AI responsibly while keeping expenses predictable. Sustainability also ties closely here, as optimizing AI resource usage reduces both cost and environmental impact.

Cost optimization in AWS involves using various strategies and tools to efficiently manage resources and minimize expenses, ensuring maximum value for your cloud investment.

Sustainability

Sustainability in the cloud involves adopting practices that minimize the environmental impact of your cloud workloads, while maximizing efficiency. Here are the six key principles for achieving sustainability:

- **Understand Your Impact:** Measure and model the environmental impact of your cloud workloads, while considering factors such as resource consumption and emissions. Establish the Key Performance Indicators (KPIs) to evaluate and improve productivity, as well as reduce environmental impact over time.
- **Establish Sustainability Goals:** Set long-term sustainability goals for each workload, aiming to reduce resource consumption per transaction and overall environmental impact. Plan for growth and design workloads to scale efficiently, while minimizing impact intensity as they expand.
- **Maximize Utilization:** Right-size workloads and design them for high utilization to maximize energy efficiency. Reduce idle resources and minimize processing as well as storage to lower overall energy consumption.
- **Adopt New, Efficient Technologies:** Stay updated on advancements in hardware and software offerings that can help reduce the environmental impact of your workloads. Design for flexibility to quickly adopt new technologies that offer improved efficiency.
- **Use Managed Services:** Leverage managed services provided by AWS to maximize resource utilization and minimize infrastructure requirements. Shared services help reduce the environmental impact by optimizing resource usage across multiple customers.
- **Reduce Downstream Impact:** Minimize the energy and resources required for customers to use your services, which reduces the need for device upgrades, and optimizing service delivery. Test and assess the environmental impact of your services to make informed decisions on reducing downstream impact.

Therefore, by implementing these sustainability principles, organizations can contribute to environmental conservation while operating efficiently in the cloud.

Here are some best practices for increasing sustainability across different areas:

- **Region Selection:** Opt for AWS Regions powered by renewable energy sources and consider the proximity to sustainable infrastructure and renewable energy sources when selecting regions.

- **Alignment to Demand:** Ensure that resource provisioning aligns with demand patterns by optimizing resource usage and implementing automated scaling to adjust resources dynamically based on workload requirements.
- **Software and Architecture**: Design energy-efficient architectures prioritizing performance and scalability. Utilize serverless computing and managed services to reduce resource consumption.
- **Data:** Implement data lifecycle management strategies to minimize storage and processing requirements. Utilize compression and efficient data transfer protocols to reduce data transfer costs as well as energy consumption.
- **Hardware and Services:** Choose energy-efficient hardware and services to minimize power consumption. Leverage AWS's commitment to sustainability by utilizing services that prioritize energy efficiency.
- **Process and Culture**: Foster a culture of sustainability within the organization by integrating sustainability considerations into development processes, and encouraging environmentally conscious practices among team members.

AI and GenAI workloads are especially resource intensive, which makes sustainability practices vital. By choosing carbon-aware Regions, leveraging managed services, and optimizing model training cycles, organizations can minimize the environmental footprint of their AI initiatives. This reflects the growing importance of balancing innovation in AI with responsible energy use.

Thus, by implementing these best practices, organizations can make significant strides towards increasing sustainability in their AWS workloads while optimizing resource usage and reducing environmental impact.

Sustainability in the cloud involves optimizing resource usage and minimizing environmental impact through efficient practices, aligning with AWS's commitment to reducing energy consumption and promoting eco-friendly solutions.

Exercise 4.1: Test Your Cloud Knowledge

1. Which pillar of the AWS Well-Architected Framework is emphasized when implementing AWS WAF?
    a. Performance Efficiency
    b. Cost Optimization
    c. Reliability
    d. Security

2. What is the primary function of AWS WAF?
    a. Scaling resources automatically
    b. Monitoring network traffic
    c. Protecting web applications from common web exploits
    d. Optimizing cost usage
3. Which design principle does AWS Well-Architected Framework align with?
    a. Maximizing utilization
    b. Implementing cloud financial management
    c. Democratizing advanced technologies
    d. Applying security at all layers

Answers

1. d
2. c
3. d

AWS Shared Responsibility Model

The AWS Shared Responsibility Model is a crucial concept for understanding how security responsibilities are divided between AWS (the cloud service provider) and its customers (the users of AWS services). It delineates which security aspects AWS manages and which aspects customers are responsible for when using AWS cloud services.

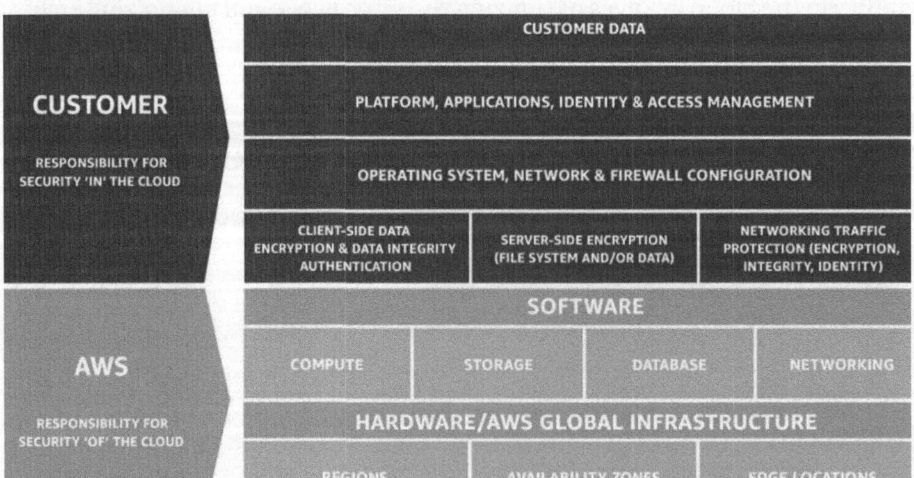

Figure 4.2: *Representation of AWS Shared Responsibility Model*

In essence, AWS is responsible for the security of the cloud. In other words, it is responsible for the smooth functioning of the underlying infrastructure and global network that AWS provides to its customers. This includes the physical security of data centers, hardware, software, and the infrastructure that runs AWS services. AWS also manages the security configuration of its services, while ensuring they are designed to be resilient and secure.

On the other hand, customers are responsible for security in the cloud, which means that they are responsible for securing the data, applications, identity and access management, network configurations, and other resources they deploy or store on AWS services. This includes setting up appropriate access controls, configuring security groups and network ACLs, encrypting data, managing user access and permissions, and implementing security best practices within their applications and workloads.

With the rise of GenAI services such as Amazon Bedrock and CodeWhisperer, the Shared Responsibility Model extends into the realm of "responsible AI." While AWS manages the infrastructure and base models, customers remain accountable for how data is used, stored, and shared in prompts, fine-tuning, or outputs. This includes ensuring compliance with privacy regulations, preventing sensitive data leaks, and embedding responsible AI practices into their workflows.

The division of responsibilities is often depicted as a Shared Responsibility Model, with AWS responsible for security "of" the cloud and customers responsible for security "in" the cloud. This model helps clarify the respective roles and responsibilities of AWS and its customers in ensuring the overall security posture of applications and data hosted on AWS services.

By clearly defining these responsibilities, the AWS Shared Responsibility Model helps organizations understand their obligations regarding security when using AWS cloud services. It also underscores the importance of collaboration between AWS and its customers to maintain a secure environment in the cloud.

Security Responsibility of AWS

AWS is responsible for securing the underlying infrastructure of its cloud services.

This includes:

- Physical security of data centers
- Network infrastructure
- Hypervisor and virtualization infrastructure
- Managed services, such as AWS Identity and Access Management (IAM) and AWS Key Management Service (KMS)

Example: AWS ensures the physical security of its data centers by implementing strict access controls, surveillance systems, and environmental controls. For instance, only authorized personnel with biometric access can enter the data center premises.

AWS manages the security of its network infrastructure by deploying firewalls, intrusion detection systems, and Distributed Denial of Service (DDoS) protection mechanisms to safeguard against cyber threats targeting its network.

AWS also provides managed services like AWS IAM, which allows customers to control user access to AWS resources through permissions and policies.

Security Responsibility of Customers

AWS customers are responsible for securing their data, applications, and configurations within the AWS environment. This includes:

- **Data Protection:** Encrypting sensitive data stored in AWS services like Amazon S3 or Amazon RDS
- **Access Management:** Setting up appropriate IAM policies and roles to control access to AWS resources
- **Configuration Management:** Configuring security settings for EC2 instances, RDS databases, and other services based on best practices
- **Network Security:** Implementing security groups, network ACLs, and VPC configurations to control traffic flow

Example:

- A company hosting its web application on Amazon EC2 instances is responsible for securing the application code and data stored within the instances. This includes applying security patches, configuring firewalls, and encrypting sensitive data at rest and in transit.
- A customer using Amazon RDS for their database management needs to implement proper access controls and encryption mechanisms to protect their data. They are also responsible for setting up database backups and ensuring data integrity.
- An organization deploying resources in an Amazon VPC must configure security groups and network ACLs to control inbound and outbound traffic flow to their EC2 instances and other resources.

Note:

The AWS Shared Responsibility Model applies differently to various types of AWS services, which are mentioned as follows:

- *For Infrastructure as a Service (IaaS) offering like Amazon EC2 and Amazon S3, customers have more responsibility for configuring and securing their applications and data.*
- *For Platform as a Service (PaaS) offerings like AWS Lambda or Amazon RDS, AWS manages more of the underlying infrastructure, but customers still have responsibility for securing their applications and data.*

- *For Software as a Service (SaaS) offerings like Amazon WorkMail or Amazon QuickSight, AWS takes on more of the security responsibility, but customers are still responsible for user access and data usage within those services.*

Recommended Security Best Practices

- Implement strong identity and access management (IAM) policies to control user access to AWS resources.
- Encrypt sensitive data both at rest and in transit using AWS Key Management Service (KMS) or other encryption mechanisms.
- Regularly update and patch operating systems, applications, and AWS services to mitigate security vulnerabilities.
- Enable logging and monitoring for AWS services to detect and respond to security incidents promptly.
- Implement network security controls such as security groups, network ACLs, and AWS WAF to protect against unauthorized access and DDoS attacks.
- Follow the principle of least privilege by granting only necessary permissions to users and resources.
- Conduct regular security audits, assessments, and penetration testing to identify and remediate security weaknesses.
- Establish incident response and disaster recovery plans to mitigate the impact of security breaches or service disruptions.

Ensuring Security Compliance under the AWS Shared Responsibility Model

The AWS Shared Responsibility Model delineates the security responsibilities between AWS and its customers, which outlines the shared commitment to maintaining a secure cloud environment. While AWS manages the security of the cloud infrastructure, including the physical facilities, networking, and hypervisor, customers are responsible for securing their data, applications, identities, and access management within the AWS environment. To fulfill their security obligations effectively, customers must implement a comprehensive security strategy aligned with the principles of the Shared Responsibility Model.

Understanding Security Responsibilities

First and foremost, customers must gain a clear understanding of their security responsibilities as outlined by the Shared Responsibility Model. This involves familiarizing themselves with the division of responsibilities between AWS and the customer, which ensures accountability for specific security tasks and controls. AWS provides detailed documentation and guidance on the Shared Responsibility Model, including whitepapers, best practice guides, and compliance resources to help customers comprehend their obligations, and establish robust security practices.

Implementing Security Best Practices

To meet their security obligations, customers should adopt industry-standard security best practices and follow AWS's security recommendations when configuring and managing their AWS resources. This entails implementing strong identity and access management (IAM) policies to control user access and permissions, employing encryption mechanisms to protect data both at rest and in transit and regularly updating and patching operating systems, applications, and AWS services to address security vulnerabilities.

Furthermore, customers should leverage AWS's comprehensive suite of security services and features like AWS Identity and Access Management (IAM), AWS Key Management Service (KMS), AWS CloudTrail, AWS Config, and AWS Security Hub to enhance security visibility, control, and compliance. By utilizing these services, customers can strengthen their security posture, detect and respond to security incidents, and demonstrate compliance with regulatory requirements and industry standards.

Continuous Security Monitoring and Compliance

Continuous security monitoring and compliance are essential components of maintaining a secure AWS environment. Customers should regularly assess their security posture and adherence to security standards and regulations through security audits, assessments, and penetration testing. By conducting thorough evaluations of their AWS environment, identifying security weaknesses and vulnerabilities, and remedying them promptly, customers can mitigate the risk of security breaches and data exposures.

Additionally, customers should stay informed about security updates, advisories, and new features released by AWS, and promptly apply relevant patches and updates to their AWS resources to address emerging security threats and vulnerabilities. AWS provides timely notifications and alerts through various channels including the AWS Management Console, AWS Personal Health Dashboard, and AWS Trusted Advisor, which enable customers to stay vigilant and proactive in safeguarding their AWS environment.

Engaging with AWS Professional Services and Partners

For customers seeking additional support and expertise in security implementation and compliance, AWS offers Professional Services engagements and certified consulting partners specializing in security assessments, architecture reviews, and guidance on security best practices. By engaging with AWS Professional Services or certified partners, customers can benefit from tailored security solutions, expert recommendations, and hands-on assistance in designing, implementing, and optimizing their security controls and processes.

Cultivating a Security-Conscious Culture

Lastly, customers should foster a security-conscious culture within their organization by promoting security awareness, training, and education among employees and stakeholders. By providing comprehensive security training programs, resources, and awareness campaigns, organizations can empower their workforce to recognize and mitigate security risks, adhere to security policies and procedures, and contribute to the overall security posture of the AWS environment.

Conclusion

In conclusion, ensuring security compliance under the AWS Shared Responsibility Model requires a proactive and multifaceted approach that encompasses understanding security responsibilities, implementing security best practices, continuous security monitoring and compliance, engagement with AWS Professional Services and partners, and cultivating a security-conscious culture. By adhering to these principles and practices, customers can effectively fulfill their security obligations and maintain a secure and resilient AWS environment.

In the next chapter, we will delve into the core services of AWS, including Compute, Storage, and more. You will not only learn about these essential components but also get hands-on experience with some key services offered by AWS. Get ready to dive deeper into the practical aspects of building and managing applications on the AWS platform.

Points to Remember

- **AWS Well-Architected Framework:** Offers best practices for optimizing cloud workloads across six pillars: operational excellence, security, reliability, performance efficiency, cost optimization and sustainability
- **Operational Excellence:** Focuses on automating operations, testing recovery procedures, and scaling resources efficiently to enhance agility and reduce downtime
- **Security:** Emphasizes robust identity management, comprehensive monitoring, and a defense-in-depth approach to protect data and systems from threats
- **Reliability:** Ensures that workloads recover automatically from failures, test recovery procedures regularly, and scale horizontally for increased availability
- **Performance Efficiency:** Encourages the use of advanced technologies, global deployments, and serverless architectures to optimize performance and resource utilization

- **Cost Optimization:** Promotes Cloud Financial Management, consumption-based models, and efficient resource usage to minimize costs and maximize value
- **Sustainability:** Promotes understanding and minimizing the environmental impact of cloud workloads through efficient resource usage, adoption of renewable energy, and continuous improvement of sustainability practices
- **Shared Responsibility Model:** Defines security responsibilities between AWS and customers and emphasizes on collaboration to ensure a secure cloud environment
- **Security Best Practices:** Include implementing strong authentication, encryption, and monitoring mechanisms to safeguard data and assets
- **Meeting Security Obligations:** Customers can ensure compliance with the Shared Responsibility Model by implementing recommended security measures and continuously monitoring and updating their environment.

Multiple Choice Questions

1. What is the primary goal of the AWS Well-Architected Framework?
    a. To provide free security services to AWS customers
    b. To ensure optimal design and security of workloads on AWS
    c. To allocate responsibility for security between AWS and its customers
    d. To enforce strict security measures on AWS infrastructure
2. Which of the following are key pillars of the AWS Well-Architected Framework? (Select all that apply.)
    a. Operational Excellence
    b. Cost Optimization
    c. Sustainability
    d. Performance Efficiency
3. Your company is planning to deploy a new application on AWS. Who is responsible for ensuring that the application follows security best practices?
    a. AWS
    b. The Customer
    c. Both AWS and the Customer
    d. Third-party Security Providers

4. What does the Shared Responsibility Model define?
    a. The shared ownership of AWS services between AWS and its customers
    b. The shared responsibility for financial costs between AWS and its customers
    c. The shared infrastructure resources between AWS and its customers
    d. The shared accountability for security between AWS and its customers
5. Which of the following are considered the customer's responsibility under the Shared Responsibility Model? (Select all that applies)
    a. Physical security of AWS data centers
    b. Patch management of EC2 instances
    c. Network and firewall configuration
    d. Data encryption in transit
6. Your company experienced a security breach on an AWS-hosted application. According to the Shared Responsibility Model, what steps should your company take to investigate and mitigate the breach?
    a. Notify AWS support and wait for their response.
    b. Analyze logs and data to identify the root cause of the breach.
    c. Increase security measures on all AWS resources.
    d. Shift all responsibilities to AWS for resolving the issue.
7. What is the role of AWS in the Shared Responsibility Model? (Select all that apply.)
    a. AWS is responsible for securing the physical infrastructure of AWS data centers.
    b. AWS is responsible for managing customer data and applications.
    c. AWS is responsible for implementing security measures in customer workloads.
    d. AWS is responsible for customer data privacy and compliance.
8. Which of the following are examples of security best practices recommended under the Shared Responsibility Model? (Select all that apply.)
    a. Regularly updating software patches
    b. Encrypting data at rest and in transit
    c. Configuring IAM policies and roles
    d. Monitoring network traffic for suspicious activity

9. Which AWS Well-Architected Framework pillar addresses reducing energy consumption and cost impact from running resource-intensive AI workloads such as training large models? (Select all that apply.)
    a. Performance Efficiency
    b. Cost Optimization
    c. Sustainability
    d. Reliability
10. Under the Shared Responsibility Model for GenAI services like Amazon Bedrock, which of the following are customer responsibilities? (Select TWO)
    a. Encrypting data used for model fine-tuning
    b. Securing physical data centers where the models are hosted
    c. Governing how prompts and outputs handle sensitive data
    d. Ensuring redundancy of the global AWS backbone
    e. Applying network-level DDoS protection for Bedrock APIs

Answers

1. b
2. a, b, c, d
3. c
4. d
5. b, c, d
6. b
7. a, c
8. a, b, c, d
9. b, c
10. a, c

References

- https://docs.aws.amazon.com/wellarchitected/latest/framework/cost-dp.html
- https://aws.amazon.com/solutions/case-studies/finra/
- https://docs.aws.amazon.com/whitepapers/latest/aws-risk-and-compliance/shared-responsibility-model.html

CHAPTER 5
AWS Core Services – Part I

Introduction

Now that we have laid a solid foundation by exploring fundamental aspects of AWS such as the Well-Architected Framework, Shared Responsibility Model, and the intricate Global Infrastructure, it is time to delve deeper into the core services offered by AWS. In this chapter, we will provide you with essential information tailored specifically for your exam preparation. While we will cover each service comprehensively enough to equip you with the knowledge needed to excel, remember that for those eager to explore further, AWS documentation is always available for more in-depth insights. Additionally, to enhance your understanding and practical skills, we will include hands-on sessions towards the end of the chapter, which will allow you to familiarize yourself with key services through interactive exercises. So, let us embark on this journey to master the core AWS services and ace your certification exam!

Structure

In this chapter, we will explore the various products in core services in AWS Cloud Environment, which are as follows:

- Compute Services
- Storage Services
- Database Services

Compute Services

Compute services form the backbone of AWS and provide the processing power needed to run everything from simple applications to advanced AI workloads. These services give businesses the flexibility to choose the right environment, whether it is virtual machines, containers, or serverless functions, to meet their unique needs. Let us explore these services provided by AWS in detail.

Amazon Elastic Compute Cloud (EC2)

Amazon Elastic Compute Cloud (EC2) is a foundational service within the AWS ecosystem that allows users to rent virtual servers, which are also known as instances, in the cloud. Imagine EC2 as a giant pool of computers that you can tap into whenever you need computing power. Here is how it works:

Key Features

- **Virtual Computing Environment:** EC2 enables users to launch instances, which are virtual computers running in the cloud. These instances can run various operating systems such as Windows, Linux, or MacOS, offering the same flexibility as traditional computers.
- **Instance Variety:** EC2 offers a wide range of instance types optimized for different use cases such as general-purpose computing, high-performance computing, memory-intensive applications, or graphics processing. This variety allows users to choose the instance type that best suits their specific workload requirements.
- **Complete Control:** Once launched, EC2 instances provide users with complete control over their computing environment. Users can install any software, configure operating system settings, and access instances remotely, tailoring them to their specific requirements.
- **Scalability:** EC2 provides users with the ability to scale their computing resources up or down based on demand. This scalability is essential for handling sudden spikes in traffic or scaling down during periods of low activity, while optimizing costs and performance.
- **Integration with AWS Services:** EC2 seamlessly integrates with other AWS services and enables users to build complex and powerful applications. For example, users can store data on Amazon S3, use a managed database service such as Amazon RDS, or set up auto-scaling based on CloudWatch metrics.

Benefits

- **Elasticity:** EC2 provides users with elasticity, which enables them to quickly scale compute resources up or down based on demand. This elasticity ensures optimal performance and cost-effectiveness for applications.

- **Cost-Effectiveness:** Users only pay for the compute capacity they use with EC2, with various pricing models available to optimize costs based on workload requirements. This cost-effectiveness allows users to minimize expenses while maximizing computing power.
- **Flexibility:** EC2 offers users a wide range of instance types optimized for different use cases, providing the flexibility to choose the right instance type for their specific needs. This flexibility ensures that users can tailor their computing environment to match their workload requirements precisely.
- **Customization:** EC2 instances are highly customizable, allowing users to configure them to meet their specific requirements. Users have full control over the operating system, software, and networking settings, enabling them to tailor each instance to their application's unique needs.
- **Reliability and Security:** EC2 offers a highly reliable environment with built-in redundancy and failover mechanisms to ensure applications remain available even in the event of hardware failures. Additionally, EC2 instances are protected by multiple layers of security such as Security Groups, Network ACLs, and encryption which ensure the confidentiality and integrity of data and applications.

Instance Types

In the benefits section, we briefly mentioned the variety of instance types available with EC2 for users to leverage. Now, let us delve into this aspect in more detail.

Amazon EC2 offers users a diverse selection of over 750 instance types tailored to meet various computing needs. These instances are optimized with different combinations of CPU, memory, storage, and networking capabilities that provide users with the flexibility to select the most suitable resources for their applications. Each instance type includes multiple sizes, which allows users to scale resources according to workload requirements.

The table here illustrates some of the EC2 instance families, and their intended use cases:

EC2 Instance Family	Purpose/Design
C	Compute-optimized instances tailored for compute-intensive tasks
D	Designed for heavy data usage; ideal for applications such as file servers and data warehouses
F	Equipped with FPGA hardware acceleration for applications requiring high-speed processing
G	Designed for graphics-intensive workloads that require high-performance graphics processing
H	Designed with up to 16 TB of HDD-based local storage, optimized for applications with high disk throughput requirements

EC2 Instance Family	Purpose/Design
I	Optimized for storage I/O-intensive workloads such as NoSQL databases and data warehouses
M	General-purpose instances suitable for a wide range of applications, such as app servers
P	Instances with dedicated GPU resources; ideal for applications requiring GPU acceleration
R	Memory-optimized instances suitable for memory-intensive workloads
T	Cost-effective instances, including options like T2-micro, suitable for low-cost computing needs
U	High-memory instances offering bare metal performance; ideal for in-memory databases like SAP HANA & Apache Spark
X	Built for heavy memory usage applications such as SAP HANA and Apache Spark
Z	Featuring fast CPU, high memory, and NVMe-based SSDs; suitable for demanding workloads requiring high overall performance

Table 5.1: *List of Key Instance Families in AWS EC2*

Beyond running traditional web and enterprise workloads, EC2 instances are now widely used for AI training and inference, with specialized hardware like AWS Trainium and Inferentia chips designed to accelerate deep learning models.

Amazon EC2 Naming Convention

The naming convention for Amazon EC2 instances typically follows a pattern that includes the instance type, size, and other specifications.

It usually appears as:

```
instance-type.instance-size.instance-options
```

Here is what each part of the naming convention represents:

- **Instance Type:** This indicates the general purpose or specialized use case for the instance, such as "t" for general-purpose instances or "c" for compute-optimized instances.
- **Instance Size:** This refers to the size or capacity of the instance, usually denoted by a letter or a combination of letters and numbers, such as "micro" or "large."
- **Instance Options:** This part of the naming convention may include additional specifications, such as the generation of the instance ("gen"), the presence of local storage ("local"), or the presence of a GPU ("gpu").

For example, an EC2 instance named "`t2.micro`" indicates a general-purpose instance ("t") with a small size ("micro"). Similarly, an instance named "`c5.large`" denotes a compute-optimized instance ("c5") with a medium size ("large").

This naming convention helps users quickly identify and select the appropriate instance type and size for their specific workload requirements.

Pricing Model for Amazon EC2

The pricing model for Amazon EC2 instances offers flexibility and options to suit various usage scenarios. Here are the key components of the EC2 pricing model:

- **On-Demand Instances:**
    - Pay for compute capacity by the hour or by the second, with no long-term commitments or upfront payments required
    - Suitable for applications with short-term, spiky, or unpredictable workloads
- **Reserved Instances (RIs):** Offer significant savings compared to on-demand pricing by allowing users to commit to a specific instance configuration for a 1-year or 3-year term:
    - **Standard RIs** provide a discount of up to 72% off on-demand prices, while **Convertible RIs offer flexibility** to change instance attributes.
    - **Scheduled RIs** are available to launch within specified time windows.

Reserved Instances Purchase Options

- **Standard Reserved Instances:** Offer a discount of up to 72% compared to on-demand instance pricing, with the flexibility to change the availability zone, instance size, and networking type
- **Convertible Reserved Instances:** Provide additional flexibility such as the ability to use different instance families, operating systems, or tenancies over the reserved instance term with a discount of up to 66% compared to on-demand instances

Reserved Instances Payment Options

- **All Upfront:** Pay for the entire reserved instance term with one upfront payment, while providing the largest discount compared to on-demand instance pricing.
- **Partial Upfront:** Make a low upfront payment and then be charged a discounted hourly rate for the instance for the duration of the reserved instance term.
- **No Upfront:** No upfront payment required, with a discounted hourly rate for the duration of the term.

Spot Instances

- Enable users to bid for unused EC2 capacity, potentially offering significant cost savings compared to on-demand pricing
- Provide up to 90% discount on prices, making them highly cost-effective for applications with flexible start and end times or those that can tolerate interruptions

Dedicated Hosts and Instances

- **Dedicated Hosts:** Provide physical servers dedicated exclusively to users' use, offering complete control over instance placement and predictable performance
- **Dedicated Instances:** Run on dedicated hardware but share the underlying server with other instances from the same AWS account

Savings Plans

- Offer flexible pricing options and provide savings of up to 72% on EC2 usage compared to on-demand prices
- Lower prices for a commitment to a consistent amount of usage, regardless of instance family, size, OS, tenancy, or AWS Region
    - **Compute Savings Plans:** Provide flexibility and help reduce costs by up to 66% automatically applied to EC2 instance usage, Fargate, or Lambda usage
    - **EC2 Instance Savings Plans:** Offer savings of up to 72% in exchange for a commitment to usage of individual instance families in a Region

Therefore, by understanding and leveraging these pricing options, users can optimize their EC2 usage to maximize cost savings while meeting performance and scalability needs.

Amazon Machine Image (AMI)

An Amazon Machine Image (AMI) is a special type of virtual appliance used to create a virtual machine within the Amazon Elastic Compute Cloud (EC2). It acts as a template for the root volume of an EC2 instance and contains the operating system, applications, libraries, data, and associated configuration settings.

AMIs are crucial in the context of EC2 because they enable users to launch instances quickly and easily with pre-configured environments tailored to their specific needs. Instead of starting from scratch to install and configure the operating system and software stack, users can simply select an appropriate AMI and launch an instance based on that image. This streamlines the deployment process, saves time, and ensures consistency across multiple instances.

Moreover, AMIs allow users to capture and replicate customized environments, while facilitating scalability and reproducibility. They also support backup and disaster recovery strategies by providing a snapshot of the instance's state at a particular point in time.

Amazon Machine Images (AMIs) come in various types, each serving different purposes and found in different locations, which are mentioned as follows:

- **Amazon-Managed AMIs:** These AMIs are provided and maintained by AWS. They are available in the AWS Management Console under the "AMI" section when launching a new EC2 instance. Examples include Amazon Linux, Ubuntu Server, and Windows Server.

- **Community AMIs:** Community AMIs are created and shared by AWS users within the AWS Marketplace. They can be found in the AWS Marketplace by searching for specific keywords or browsing through categories. Examples include AMIs with pre-installed software applications, specialized configurations or custom operating system distributions contributed by the community.
- **Custom AMIs**: Custom AMIs are created by users based on their specific requirements and configurations. They can be found in the "My AMIs" section of the AWS Management Console. Examples include AMIs customized with specific software configurations, security settings, or application dependencies tailored to the user's needs.

In conclusion, Amazon Elastic Compute Cloud (Amazon EC2) offers a versatile and scalable solution for hosting virtual server instances in the cloud. With a wide selection of instance types optimized for different use cases, flexible pricing options including on-demand instances, reserved instances, spot instances, and savings plans, EC2 provides cost-effective solutions for various workload requirements. The availability of Amazon Machine Images (AMIs) further enhances EC2's flexibility, allowing users to choose from a range of pre-configured operating systems and software configurations or create their own custom images tailored to their specific needs. With its reliability, scalability, and cost-effectiveness, EC2 remains a cornerstone service in the AWS ecosystem, and empowers businesses to build and deploy applications with ease in the cloud.

Exercise 5.1: Test Your Cloud Knowledge

1. What is the primary goal of Amazon EC2?
    a. To provide free security services to AWS customers
    b. To ensure optimal design and security of workloads on AWS
    c. To allocate responsibility for security between AWS and its customers
    d. To enforce strict security measures on AWS infrastructure
2. Which of the following instance types is optimized for heavy data usage, such as file servers and data warehouses?
    a. D - DATA
    b. R - RAM
    c. M - MAIN
    d. C - COMPUTE
3. Which pricing model offers significant savings compared to on-demand pricing by allowing users to commit to a specific instance configuration for a 1-year or 3-year term?
    a. Spot Instances
    b. On-Demand Instances

   c. Reserved Instances
   d. Dedicated Hosts

4. Which type of AMI allows users to create a virtual machine within the Amazon EC2?
   a. Community AMIs
   b. AWS Marketplace AMIs
   c. My AMIs
   d. All the above

5. Which option allows users to bid for unused EC2 capacity, and offers significant cost savings compared to on-demand pricing?
   a. On-Demand Instances
   b. Reserved Instances
   c. Spot Instances
   d. Dedicated Hosts

Answers

1. b
2. a
3. c
4. d
5. c

Amazon Elastic Container Service (ECS)

Amazon Elastic Container Service (ECS) is a part of AWS Compute and is designed for managing Docker containers effortlessly. It is like a container babysitter for your applications, while ensuring that they run smoothly on clusters of EC2 instances.

Key Features

- **No Cluster Hassle:** ECS eliminates the headache of setting up and managing your own cluster infrastructure. You do not have to worry about installing or scaling clusters; ECS handles it all for you.
- **Simple API Calls:** With ECS, launching and stopping container applications is as easy as making a phone call. Just use simple API commands to control your containers and check on your clusters' status in real-time.

- **Two Launch Types**: ECS offers two launch types: EC2 and Fargate. EC2 gives you more control over infrastructure, while Fargate automates everything, so you do not have to worry about cluster optimization.
- **Integration with AWS Services:** ECS seamlessly integrates with other AWS services like security groups, load balancers, and storage volumes. It is like having a full toolbox at your disposal for building and managing your containerized applications.
- **Elastic Container Registry (ECR):** ECS works together with ECR, a managed Docker registry service. It is where you store, manage, and deploy your Docker container images, which makes the deployment process smoother and more efficient.
- **Simple Pricing:** With ECS, you only pay for the AWS resources you use, such as EC2 instances and storage volumes. There are no upfront fees or commitments, so you can scale your applications without breaking the bank.
- **Efficient Container Management:** ECS streamlines the deployment process, allowing you to focus on building and scaling your applications without getting bogged down by infrastructure management.

In essence, Amazon ECS takes the complexity out of container management, while allowing you to deploy, scale, and manage your applications with ease.

Amazon Elastic Container Registry (ECR)

Amazon Elastic Container Registry (ECR) is a fully managed container image registry that makes it easy to store, manage, and deploy Docker container images. It eliminates the need to operate your own container repositories, providing a secure and scalable environment for container-based application workflows.

Key Features

- **Fully Managed:** AWS handles the infrastructure, so you do not have to manage your own container repositories or storage.
- **Secure Storage:** Images are encrypted at rest and in transit, with fine-grained access controls present through AWS IAM.
- **Seamless Integration:** AECR works natively with Amazon ECS, EKS, and AWS Fargate, which allows for smooth container deployments.
- **High Availability:** It is built on AWS infrastructure with replication across availability zones to ensure resilience.
- **Automated Scanning:** AECR provides image scanning to detect vulnerabilities, helping maintain security compliance.

Amazon ECR simplifies container management by providing a secure, reliable, and integrated image repository within AWS. With its managed nature, developers can focus on building and deploying applications rather than maintaining container infrastructure.

AWS Lambda

AWS Lambda revolutionizes the way developers build and deploy applications by offering a serverless platform that scales automatically and integrates seamlessly with other AWS services, while allowing for efficient event-driven execution of code.

Key Features

- **Serverless Computing:** AWS Lambda is the epitome of serverless computing. It allows you to run code without provisioning or managing servers. You just upload your code and Lambda takes care of the rest.
- **Event-Driven Architecture:** Lambda operates on an event-driven architecture. It responds to events triggered by other AWS services or custom events in your application. For example, it can automatically execute code in response to changes in data stored in Amazon S3 or updates to an Amazon DynamoDB table.
- **Pay-Per-Use Model:** Lambda follows a pay-per-use pricing model. You only pay for the compute time your code consumes and the number of requests it processes. There is no charge when your code is not running.
- **Automatic Scaling:** Lambda automatically scales your code by running as many instances as needed to handle the incoming requests. You do not have to worry about provisioning or managing infrastructure to accommodate varying workloads.
- **Support for Multiple Languages:** Lambda supports multiple programming languages, including Node.js, Python, Java, C#, Go, and Ruby. You can write your code in the language you're most comfortable with.
- **Stateless Execution:** Each Lambda function executes in its own isolated environment, which ensures stateless execution. This means you do not have to worry about managing sessions or maintaining state between function invocations.
- **Integrations with AWS Services:** Lambda seamlessly integrates with various AWS services, such as Amazon S3, DynamoDB, SNS, SQS, and more. This allows you to build highly scalable and event-driven architectures using a combination of serverless services.

Lambda is suitable for a wide range of use cases, including real-time file processing, data processing, IoT device management, web application backends, and more. Its flexibility and scalability make it ideal for building serverless applications.

AWS Fargate

AWS Fargate is a serverless compute engine for containers that lets you run applications without managing servers or clusters. It works with both Amazon ECS and Amazon EKS, which allows developers to focus solely on building applications while AWS handles the infrastructure.

Key Features

- **Serverless Containers:** Removes the need to provision or manage EC2 instances for running containers
- **On-Demand Scaling:** Automatically scales containerized workloads up or down based on demand
- **Integration with ECS and EKS:** Works seamlessly with both ECS and EKS, providing flexibility in container orchestration
- **Security by Design:** Isolates each workload with its own kernel runtime environment for better security
- **Cost Efficiency:** You only pay for the exact CPU and memory resources used during container execution.

AWS Fargate simplifies container deployment by removing server management and scaling concerns. It enables developers to run containerized applications efficiently, while reducing operational overhead.

AWS Elastic Beanstalk

AWS Elastic Beanstalk simplifies the process of deploying, managing, and scaling applications in the AWS cloud. With its managed platform, automatic scaling, built-in monitoring, and integration with other AWS services, Elastic Beanstalk empowers developers to focus on building great applications without worrying about the underlying infrastructure.

Key Features

- **Managed Platform:** AWS Elastic Beanstalk is a fully managed Platform as a Service (PaaS) offering from AWS. It abstracts away the underlying infrastructure complexities, while allowing developers to focus solely on deploying and managing their applications.
- **Easy Deployment:** With Elastic Beanstalk, deploying your application is as simple as uploading your code. It supports a variety of programming languages and frameworks like Java, .NET, Node.js, Python, Ruby, Go, Docker, and more.
- **Automatic Scaling:** Elastic Beanstalk automatically handles the scaling of your application based on traffic levels. It can dynamically adjust the number of EC2 instances running your application to ensure optimal performance and availability.
- **Built-in Monitoring and Management:** Elastic Beanstalk provides built-in monitoring and management capabilities, which allows you to easily monitor the health and performance of your application through the AWS Management Console or command-line interface.

- **Application Health Monitoring:** Elastic Beanstalk continuously monitors the health of your application and automatically replaces any instances that become unhealthy. This ensures that your application remains available and responsive to user requests.
- **Flexible Environment Configurations:** Elastic Beanstalk offers a range of environment configurations to suit different types of applications like web servers, worker environments, and more. You can customize parameters such as instance types, network settings, and auto-scaling policies to meet your specific requirements.
- **Integration with Other AWS Services:** Elastic Beanstalk seamlessly integrates with other AWS services, such as Amazon RDS for database management, Amazon S3 for storage, Amazon SQS for message queuing, and more. This allows you to build and deploy complex applications with ease.
- **Cost-Effective Pricing:** Elastic Beanstalk follows a pay-as-you-go pricing model, where you only pay for the AWS resources (such as EC2 instances, S3 storage, and so on) used by your application. There are no upfront fees or long-term commitments, which makes it cost-effective for both small and large-scale deployments.

Use Case: Imagine that you are a startup developing a new Node.js web application that needs to scale quickly to accommodate growing user demand. With AWS Elastic Beanstalk, you can easily deploy your application code and configuration, which allows Elastic Beanstalk to automatically handle provisioning, load balancing, and auto-scaling of the underlying infrastructure. As your application gains traction, Elastic Beanstalk seamlessly scales resources to match demand, while ensuring optimal performance and reliability without the need for manual intervention. With built-in monitoring and integration with other AWS services such as Amazon RDS for database management, Elastic Beanstalk provides a cost-effective and hassle-free solution for startups to deploy and manage scalable web applications in the cloud.

AWS Batch

AWS Batch is a fully managed service provided by Amazon Web Services (AWS) that enables developers, scientists, and engineers to efficiently run batch computing workloads in the cloud. It dynamically provisions the optimal quantity and type of compute resources (such as virtual CPUs and memory) based on the specific requirements of your jobs. By abstracting the underlying infrastructure management, AWS Batch simplifies the process of executing large-scale batch computing tasks, which allows users to focus on developing and running their applications without worrying about provisioning, scaling, or managing compute resources.

Key Features

- **Job Scheduling:** AWS Batch allows you to define and schedule batch computing jobs using simple job definitions. You can specify parameters such as Docker container images, resource requirements, and dependencies, thereby enabling flexible job configurations.

- **Resource Provisioning:** With AWS Batch, you can specify your desired compute environment, including the type and size of instances, storage configurations, and networking settings. The service automatically provisions and scales the compute resources based on the workload requirements, while optimizing resource utilization and cost efficiency.
- **Job Queues:** AWS Batch organizes batch computing jobs into logical queues, which allows you to prioritize and manage job execution based on factors such as job priority, resource availability, and dependencies between jobs. This helps ensure efficient resource utilization and job scheduling.
- **Docker Integration:** AWS Batch seamlessly integrates with Docker containers, enabling you to package and deploy your batch computing applications as containerized tasks. This facilitates consistent and reproducible execution environments, simplifying application development and deployment workflows.
- **Monitoring and Logging:** AWS Batch provides built-in monitoring and logging capabilities that allow you to track the progress of your batch jobs, monitor resource utilization, and diagnose any issues that may arise during job execution. You can leverage Amazon CloudWatch metrics and logs to gain insights into job performance and troubleshoot potential issues.

Use Case: Consider a genomics research project that involves analyzing large volumes of DNA sequencing data. With AWS Batch, researchers can define batch computing jobs to process and analyze DNA sequences, leveraging custom bioinformatics algorithms packaged as Docker containers. AWS Batch automatically provisions the necessary compute resources based on the job requirements, allowing researchers to efficiently scale their computational workloads as needed. By abstracting the underlying infrastructure management, AWS Batch enables researchers to focus on developing and optimizing their bioinformatics pipelines, while accelerating the pace of scientific discovery in genomics research.

AWS Lightsail

AWS Lightsail is a simplified and easy-to-use Virtual Private Server (VPS) service offered by Amazon Web Services (AWS). It provides developers, small businesses, and individuals with a straightforward way to launch and manage virtual private servers, databases, and storage solutions in the cloud. AWS Lightsail offers pre-configured server configurations and a user-friendly management console, which makes it an ideal choice for users who require a low-cost and straightforward solution for hosting websites, web applications, blogs, and development projects.

Key Features

- **Pre-Configured Instances:** AWS Lightsail offers a range of pre-configured virtual server instances optimized for various use cases, such as web hosting, application development, and database management. Users can choose from a selection of instance sizes, operating systems, and software stacks to suit their specific requirements.
- **Easy Management Console:** The AWS Lightsail management console provides a simplified interface for launching, managing, and monitoring virtual private servers, databases, and storage instances. Users can easily deploy and configure resources without the need for deep technical expertise, making it accessible to developers and non-technical users alike.
- **Scalability and Flexibility:** Lightsail allows users to easily scale their resources up or down based on changing workload demands. With flexible pricing plans and on-demand instance provisioning, users can quickly adjust their resource allocation to accommodate fluctuations in traffic and application usage.
- **Integrated Networking:** AWS Lightsail includes built-in networking features such as static IP addresses, DNS management, and firewall configurations, which allow users to easily set up and manage their network infrastructure. This simplifies the process of configuring network settings for virtual private servers and ensures secure and reliable connectivity.
- **Snapshot Backups:** AWS Lightsail offers snapshot-based backups for instances and databases, allowing users to create point-in-time backups of their data and configurations. This enables users to easily restore their instances to a previous state in the event of data loss or system failures, and provide additional data protection.

Use Case: Consider a small e-commerce startup that wants to launch a new online store to sell handmade crafts. The startup team has limited technical expertise and resources but needs a reliable and cost-effective hosting solution to deploy their e-commerce website. With AWS Lightsail, the startup can quickly spin up a virtual private server instance with pre-configured settings for web hosting. They can choose an appropriate instance size and operating system, deploy their website code, and configure domain settings using the Lightsail management console. The integrated networking features in Lightsail allow the startup to set up custom domain names, SSL certificates, and firewall rules to secure their website and ensure reliable connectivity. As the e-commerce business grows, the startup can easily scale their resources and adapt to changing traffic patterns, all within the user-friendly environment of AWS Lightsail.

AWS Outposts

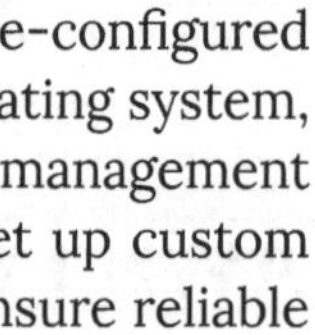

AWS Outposts is a fully managed service provided by Amazon Web Services (AWS) that extends AWS infrastructure and services to customers' on-premises data centers or co-location facilities. It allows customers to run AWS compute, storage, database, and other services locally, while providing a consistent hybrid cloud experience. With AWS Outposts, customers can seamlessly integrate on-premises environments with the AWS cloud and modernize their applications, improve performance, and meet data residency requirements while maintaining operational consistency across environments.

Key Features

- **Hybrid Cloud Consistency:** AWS Outposts provides a consistent infrastructure, services, and management experience across on-premises and cloud environments. This allows customers to leverage familiar AWS tools, APIs, and services to develop, deploy, and manage applications both on-premises and in the cloud, while ensuring operational consistency and simplifying hybrid cloud management.

- **Fully Managed Service:** AWS Outposts is a fully managed service, meaning AWS handles installation, configuration, monitoring, maintenance, and updates of the infrastructure and services deployed on Outposts. This allows customers to focus on their applications and workloads without worrying about managing underlying infrastructure components.

- **Broad Service Availability:** AWS Outposts supports a wide range of AWS services like Amazon EC2, Amazon EBS, Amazon RDS, Amazon ECS, Amazon EKS, Amazon S3, and more. Customers can choose from a catalog of AWS services to deploy on Outposts, which enables them to meet diverse application requirements and use cases.

- **Local Data Processing:** With AWS Outposts, customers can process data locally on-premises, minimizing latency and ensuring data sovereignty and compliance with regulatory requirements. This is particularly beneficial for applications that require low-latency access to on-premises data or have strict data residency requirements.

- **Seamless Integration with AWS:** AWS Outposts seamlessly integrates with AWS services running in the cloud, while allowing customers to extend their existing AWS workloads to on-premises environments and vice versa. This hybrid cloud architecture enables workload portability, scalability, and flexibility and empowers customers to innovate and adapt to changing business needs.

Use Case: Consider a financial institution that operates in a regulated industry with strict data residency requirements. The institution needs to process sensitive financial transactions locally to comply with data privacy regulations and reduce latency for real-time transactions. By deploying AWS Outposts in its on-premises data center, the institution can run AWS services such as Amazon EC2, Amazon RDS, and Amazon S3 locally, while enabling it to process transactions closer to customers' locations, and maintaining compliance with regulatory requirements. Additionally, the institution can seamlessly integrate its on-premises applications with AWS cloud services, which allows it to leverage the scalability, agility, and innovation of the cloud while meeting regulatory and performance needs.

Amazon Elastic Kubernetes Service (EKS)

Amazon Elastic Kubernetes Service (EKS) is a fully managed service that simplifies running Kubernetes clusters on AWS. It takes care of the heavy lifting, such as provisioning, scaling, and managing the control plane, so that organizations can focus on deploying and managing containerized applications.

Key Features

- **Managed Control Plane:** EKS automatically manages the Kubernetes control plane, including patching, upgrades, and high availability.
- **Seamless Integration:** Integrates natively with AWS services such as VPC, IAM, and CloudWatch, which makes it easier to build secure and observable workloads
- **Flexible Deployment:** Supports running Kubernetes workloads on Amazon EC2, AWS Fargate (for serverless containers), or even on-premises with EKS Anywhere
- **High Availability and Scalability:** Control plane nodes are spread across multiple Availability Zones, ensuring resilient and scalable clusters.
- **Upstream Compatibility:** EKS is certified Kubernetes conformant, so workloads and tools designed for open-source Kubernetes can run seamlessly.

Amazon EKS provides a reliable and secure way to run Kubernetes at scale without the operational overhead of managing clusters manually. It helps teams accelerate innovation by combining Kubernetes flexibility with AWS's scalability and integrations.

Exercise 5.2: Test Your Cloud Knowledge

1. Which AWS service provides a highly scalable container management service that supports Docker containers?
    a. AWS Batch
    b. AWS Lambda
    c. Amazon ECS
    d. AWS Elastic Beanstalk
2. Which AWS service allows users to deploy code without provisioning or managing servers, and automatically scales based on incoming requests?
    a. AWS Batch
    b. Amazon EC2
    c. AWS Lambda
    d. AWS Elastic Beanstalk

Answers

1. c
2. c

Storage Services

Storage is at the heart of every cloud workload and ensures that data is kept secure, durable, and readily available when needed. AWS offers a broad range of storage services designed to handle everything from frequently accessed business data to long-term archives. Let us explore key services in storage provided by AWS.

Amazon Simple Storage Service (S3)

Amazon Simple Storage Service is a scalable object storage service offered by AWS. It allows users to store and retrieve any amount of data from anywhere on the web.

Key points about Amazon S3

- **Scalability:** Amazon S3 is designed to scale storage resources both vertically and horizontally, which allows users to store virtually unlimited amounts of data.
- **Durability and Availability:** Amazon S3 boasts high durability, as data is stored across multiple devices and facilities within a region to ensure resilience against failures. It also offers high availability, with a Service-Level Agreement (SLA) guaranteeing 99.999999999% durability.
- **Object-Based Storage:** S3 is object-based, which means that it allows users to store objects or files of virtually any size, ranging from a few bytes to many terabytes. Each object is stored as a file along with its metadata and a unique identifier.
- **Security and Encryption:** Amazon S3 offers several features to ensure data security, including Server-Side Encryption (SSE), client-side encryption, Access Control Lists (ACLs), and bucket policies. Users can choose to encrypt data at rest and in transit for added protection.

- **Lifecycle Policies:** S3 allows users to define lifecycle policies to automatically transition objects between storage classes or delete them after a specified period. This helps optimize storage costs by moving infrequently accessed data to lower-cost storage tiers or deleting expired objects.
- **Versioning:** Versioning is a feature of S3 that allows users to keep multiple versions of an object in the same bucket. This provides protection against accidental deletion or overwrites, as users can restore previous versions of objects if needed.
- **Integration and Compatibility:** Amazon S3 integrates seamlessly with other AWS services such as Amazon EC2, Amazon RDS, and AWS Lambda, which makes it a versatile storage solution for various use cases. It also supports a wide range of third-party tools and applications.

Amazon S3 Storage Class: Amazon S3 offers different types of storage classes, each optimized for specific use cases and priced differently. Here are the main types of S3 storage classes based on pricing:

- **Standard:** Amazon S3 Standard is the default storage class and is designed for general-purpose storage of frequently accessed data. It offers high durability, availability, and low latency, which makes it suitable for a wide range of use cases. Standard storage is priced higher than other storage classes but offers the fastest access times.
- **Standard-IA (Infrequent Access):** S3 Standard-IA is designed for data that is accessed less frequently but requires rapid access when needed. It offers the same durability and availability as Standard storage but at a lower cost. Standard-IA is suitable for long-term storage of infrequently accessed data, such as backups and archives.
- **One Zone-IA:** S3 One Zone-IA is like Standard-IA but stores data in a single availability zone instead of across multiple zones. This makes it a more cost-effective option for storing data that does not require multi-AZ redundancy. However, it may not offer the same level of durability as Standard or Standard-IA storage.
- **Intelligent-Tiering:** S3 intelligent-tiering is designed for data with unknown or changing access patterns. It automatically moves objects between two access tiers: frequent access and infrequent access, which are based on usage patterns. Intelligent-tiering is priced slightly higher than standard storage, but it can optimize costs by automatically transitioning objects to the most cost-effective tier.
- **Glacier:** Amazon S3 Glacier is a low-cost storage class designed for long-term data archival and backup. It offers the lowest storage costs but with slower retrieval times, when compared to other storage classes. Glacier is suitable for data that is rarely accessed and can tolerate longer retrieval times, such as regulatory archives and compliance data.
    - **S3 Glacier Instant Retrieval:** S3 Glacier Instant Retrieval provides expedited access to data, allowing you to retrieve archived objects within milliseconds.

While offering faster retrieval times, S3 Glacier Instant Retrieval is priced higher compared to other S3 Glacier storage classes.

  - **S3 Glacier Flexible Retrieval:** S3 Glacier Flexible Retrieval offers flexible retrieval options, allowing you to choose between standard, bulk, or expedited retrieval speeds based on your specific needs. Compared to S3 Glacier Instant Retrieval, S3 Glacier Flexible Retrieval is priced lower, which makes it a cost-effective option for data that requires occasional access with flexible retrieval times.

- **Glacier Deep Archive:** S3 Glacier Deep Archive is the lowest-cost storage class offered by Amazon S3, designed for data that is accessed infrequently and can tolerate retrieval times of hours to days. It is ideal for long-term retention of data that is rarely accessed such as compliance records and digital preservation.

Thus, each of these storage classes offers different pricing options and access characteristics, which allow users to choose the most cost-effective option based on their specific storage requirements and access patterns.

Additional Facts to Know About Amazon S3

- **Data Persistence:** Amazon S3 provides persistent storage, which ensures data durability even after reboots, restarts, or power cycles.
- **Bucket Naming Rules:** Bucket names must be unique across all of AWS and should be between 3 to 63 characters in length (max 100 characters). They can only contain lowercase letters, numbers, and hyphens, and cannot be formatted as an IP address.
- **Object Components:** Objects in S3 consist of a key (name), value (data), version ID (for versioning), and metadata (information about the stored data).
- **Lifecycle Management:** Set rules to automatically transfer objects between storage classes at defined time intervals.
- **Versioning:** Automatically, maintain multiple versions of an object with versioning enabled.
- **Encryption:** Encryption can be enabled for both buckets and objects to enhance security.
- **Charges:** S3 pricing includes storage costs, request fees, storage management pricing, data transfer charges, and transfer acceleration fees.
- **Region Selection:** When creating a bucket, it is advisable to select the region closest to your users to minimize latency.
- **Additional Capabilities:** S3 offers features such as Transfer Acceleration for faster uploads, Requester Pays for charging requesters instead of bucket owners, tagging

objects for costing and billing purposes, triggering events with SNS, SQS, or Lambda, hosting static websites, and utilizing BitTorrent for retrieving publicly available objects.

- In addition to its storage classes and durability, Amazon S3 now supports **S3 Tables**, which lets you query structured data directly within S3 without needing to move it into a database. This bridges the gap between object storage and analytics as well as makes it easier to run AI/ML pipelines and business intelligence directly on data lakes.
- **Cross-Region Replication:** Amazon S3 allows you to replicate objects across different AWS regions to meet compliance requirements, minimize latency for distributed applications, or facilitate disaster recovery. This feature automatically copies objects from a source bucket in one region to a destination bucket in another region.

Exercise 5.3: Test Your Cloud Knowledge

1. Which is a key characteristic of Amazon S3 buckets?
    a. They can only store structured data.
    b. They are restricted to a single region.
    c. They do not support cross-region replication.
    d. They have a maximum size limit of 10 TB.
2. Which of the following is a valid naming rule for Amazon S3 bucket names?
    a. Names must be at least 10 characters long.
    b. Names can contain uppercase letters.
    c. Names can be up to 100 characters long.
    d. Names cannot contain hyphens.
3. Which feature of Amazon S3 allows you to automatically keep multiple versions of an object?
    a. Object Lock
    b. Object Lifecycle Policies
    c. Versioning
    d. Access Control Lists
4. Which is one of the additional capabilities offered by Amazon S3?
    a. Dynamic Web Hosting
    b. Server-Side Scripting
    c. Transfer Acceleration
    d. Virtual Machine Deployment

Answers

1. b
2. c
3. c
4. c

Amazon Elastic Block Store (EBS)

Amazon Elastic Block Store (EBS) is a block storage service provided by Amazon Web Services (AWS) that offers highly available and scalable storage volumes for use with Amazon EC2 instances. EBS volumes are designed to persist independently from the life of an EC2 instance, which makes them suitable for storing critical data that needs to survive instance termination.

One of the key features of Amazon EBS is its flexibility in terms of volume types, which allows users to tailor their storage performance and cost to specific workloads. There are several types of EBS volumes available:

- **General Purpose SSD (gp2):** This volume type offers a balance of price and performance for a wide variety of workloads, including boot volumes and small to medium-sized databases.
- **Provisioned IOPS SSD (io1):** This volume type is designed for applications that require high performance and low latency, such as databases and I/O-intensive workloads. Users can specify the desired level of IOPS (input/output operations per second) when creating io1 volumes.
- **Throughput Optimized HDD (st1):** This volume type is optimized for frequently accessed, throughput-intensive workloads, such as big data analytics and data warehouses. It provides low-cost, high-throughput storage for large, sequential I/O operations.
- **Cold HDD (sc1):** This volume type is optimized for infrequently accessed, throughput-intensive workloads with large block sizes, such as file servers and backup repositories. It offers the lowest storage cost per gigabyte among EBS volume types.
- **Magnetic (standard):** This is the original volume (also called previous generation volume) type offered by EBS and is suitable for workloads where cost is the primary consideration and performance requirements are modest. It provides baseline performance at the lowest cost per gigabyte.

In addition to volume types, Amazon EBS offers features such as snapshots, encryption, and Elastic Volumes. Snapshots allow users to create point-in-time backups of their volumes, which can be used for data protection, disaster recovery, and cloning volumes. Encryption-at-rest ensures that data stored on EBS volumes is encrypted using industry-standard encryption algorithms, which provides an additional layer of security for sensitive data. Elastic Volumes allow users to dynamically resize their EBS volumes without interrupting operations, while making them flexible to scale storage capacity up or down as needed.

Amazon Elastic File System (EFS)

Amazon EFS is a fully managed, scalable file storage service provided by AWS. It offers highly available, durable, and cost-effective storage for various applications.

Key Features

- **Scalability:** Automatically scales storage capacity up or down as files are added or removed. Amazon EFS supports petabyte-scale file systems with virtually unlimited storage capacity.
- **Availability and Durability:** Stores data across multiple availability zones within a region for high availability. Amazon EFS provides built-in redundancy to ensure data accessibility even during failures.
- **Access Protocols:** Supports NFSv4, which allows Linux-based EC2 instances to mount EFS file systems directly. Amazon EFS seamless integration with existing applications and workflows.
- **Performance:** Offers low-latency access to data and high throughput for read and write operations. Amazon EFS scales performance in response to varying workloads and data access patterns.
- **Security and Management:** Provides file system encryption to protect data at rest using AWS Key Management Service (KMS). Amazon EFS offers several monitoring and management tools for performance tracking, access control management, and alarm setup. It also allows for lifecycle management policies for automatic data movement to lower-cost storage classes.

Use Cases

- Content Repositories
- Big Data Analytics
- Media Processing

AWS Snowball

AWS Snowball is a petabyte-scale data transport solution that enables secure, efficient, and cost-effective transfer of large volumes of data into and out of the AWS cloud. It addresses challenges associated with transferring data over the internet by providing a rugged, tamper-resistant hardware device for offline data transfer.

Key Features

- **Physical Storage Device:** Snowball devices are rugged, tamper-resistant hardware appliances designed to securely transfer large amounts of data.
- **Available in Two Sizes:** Snowball and Snowball Edge are the two available sizes with storage capacities ranging from 50TB to 80TB (Snowball) and up to 80TB with onboard compute capabilities (Snowball Edge).
- **Data Transfer:** Facilitates high-speed data transfer by shipping the Snowball device to the customer's location for data upload. Supports various data transfer protocols, including NFS, SMB, and S3-compatible APIs.
- **Security and Encryption:** Implements strong encryption standards (256-bit encryption) to secure data during transit and storage. It also provides AWS Key Management Service (KMS) integration for managing encryption keys.
- **Integration with AWS**: Seamlessly integrates with AWS services such as S3, Glacier, and Snowball Edge compute instances for data processing. It enables easy import/export of data into/from AWS cloud storage services.
- **Ease of Use:** Amazon Snowball offers a simple, web-based console for ordering, tracking, and managing Snowball jobs. It also provides detailed job tracking features and monitors capabilities for real-time status updates.

Use Cases

- **Data Migration to AWS:** Transfer large datasets, backups, and archives to AWS cloud storage.
- **Disaster Recovery**: Create offline backups of critical data for disaster recovery purposes.

Amazon FSx

Amazon FSx is a fully managed file storage service that provides scalable and highly available file systems compatible with Windows and Lustre. It simplifies the deployment and management of file storage for a variety of use cases like business applications, analytics, and High-Performance Computing (HPC).

Key Features

- **Fully Managed Service:** Amazon FSx eliminates the overhead of managing file storage infrastructure by providing a fully managed service that handles setup, configuration, monitoring, and maintenance tasks. It automatically scales storage capacity and performance based on workload demands, while ensuring optimal performance without manual intervention.

- **Windows and Lustre File Systems:** Amazon FSx two types of file systems: Amazon FSx for Windows File Server and Amazon FSx for Lustre. These are explained as follows:
    - **FSx for Windows** File Server provides fully managed Windows file shares with support for Microsoft Active Directory integration, NTFS permissions, and features like shadow copies and encryption.
    - **FSx for Lustre** delivers high-performance, POSIX-compliant file systems optimized for compute-intensive workloads such as ML, simulation, and data analytics.
- **Integration with AWS Services:** Amazon FSx seamlessly integrates with other AWS services such as EC2, S3, and IAM, which allows applications to access FSx file systems securely and efficiently. Provides native integration with AWS Backup for automated backup and recovery of file system data.
- **High Availability and Durability:** Amazon FSx ensures high availability and durability through redundant storage and automatic failover mechanisms. It also offers built-in data redundancy options and Multi-Availability Zone (AZ) deployments to protect against component failures and maintain data integrity.
- **Performance Optimization:** Amazon FSx optimizes performance for various workloads by offering configurable throughput and IOPS options. FSx for Lustre leverages SSD storage and parallel file system architecture to deliver high throughput and low latency for data-intensive applications.

Use Cases

- **Shared File Storage:** Consolidate file shares for Windows-based applications, user home directories, and file-based workloads.
- **Windows Application Migration:** Lift and shift Windows applications to AWS cloud with native file storage support.
- **High-Performance Computing (HPC):** Accelerate data processing and simulation tasks with Lustre file systems optimized for HPC workloads.

AWS Backup

AWS Backup is a fully managed backup service that centralizes and automates data protection across AWS services and on-premises environments. It enables customers to create and manage backups of their data, ensuring business continuity, compliance, and data protection against accidental deletion, corruption, or loss.

Key Features

- **Centralized Backup Management:** AWS Backup provides a unified interface to manage backups across AWS services such as EBS, RDS, DynamoDB, and AWS Storage Gateway, as well as on-premises resources. It enables customers to define backup policies, set retention periods, and schedule backup jobs through a single console or API.
- **Automated Backup Orchestration:** AWS Backup automates backup scheduling, resource discovery, and policy enforcement to streamline backup operations and reduce manual intervention. Supports customizable backup plans with flexible scheduling options at daily, weekly, or custom intervals to meet specific business requirements.
- **Incremental Backup and Deduplication:** AWS Backup performs incremental backups by capturing only the changes made since the last backup, minimizing backup windows and storage costs. It also utilizes data deduplication techniques to eliminate redundant data across backups, while optimizing storage utilization and reducing storage costs.
- **Cross-Region and Cross-Account Backup:** AWS Backup allows customers to create cross-region and cross-account backups for improved data durability, compliance, and disaster recovery. It facilitates data replication and synchronization across AWS regions and accounts, while ensuring data availability and resilience against regional outages.
- **Lifecycle Management and Retention Policies:** AWS Backup supports customizable retention policies to manage backup data lifecycle, including retention periods, archival to cost-effective storage tiers, and automatic deletion of expired backups. It also enables customers to define lifecycle rules based on backup age, storage class, and compliance requirements to optimize storage costs and regulatory compliance.

Use Cases

- **Data Protection and Disaster Recovery:** Protect critical data and applications against data loss, corruption, and accidental deletion by creating regular backups with AWS Backup.
- **Compliance and Governance:** Ensure regulatory compliance and data governance by implementing backup and retention policies that align with industry standards and best practices.
- **Multi-Region and Multi-Account Backup:** Establish cross-region and cross-account backup strategies to enhance data resilience, compliance, and disaster recovery capabilities.

Exercise 5.4: Test your Cloud Knowledge

1. Which AWS service provides block-level storage volumes that can be attached to EC2 instances as durable and persistent storage?
   a. AWS Backup
   b. Amazon EBS
   c. Amazon Glacier
   d. Amazon EFS
2. Which AWS service offers managed file storage for archival and data lifecycle management, providing low-cost storage options with retrieval options ranging from instant to flexible?
   a. Amazon S3
   b. AWS Backup
   c. Amazon Glacier
   d. Amazon EFS

Answers

1. b
2. c

Database Services

Databases power the applications we use every day and store everything from customer records to financial transactions. AWS provides a rich portfolio of managed database services that eliminate the heavy lifting of setup, scaling, and maintenance, which allows businesses to focus on insights and innovation. In the following section, we will explore the major database offerings on AWS.

Amazon Relational Database Service (RDS)

Amazon Relational Database Service (RDS) is a managed database service (Online Transaction Processing, or OLPT) provided by AWS that simplifies the setup, operation, and scaling of relational databases in the cloud. With RDS, users can easily deploy, manage, and scale databases such as MySQL, PostgreSQL, Oracle, SQL Server, and MariaDB without needing to worry about the underlying infrastructure.

Key Features

- **Managed Service:** Amazon RDS takes care of routine database tasks such as provisioning, patching, backup, recovery, and scaling, which allows users to focus on their applications rather than managing the database infrastructure.
- **Multiple Database Engines:** RDS supports various popular relational database engines, including MySQL, PostgreSQL, Oracle, SQL Server, and MariaDB, which gives users the flexibility to choose the engine that best fits their application requirements.
- **Automated Backups and Point-in-Time Recovery:** RDS automatically performs backups of the database instance and transaction logs, which enables point-in-time recovery to any second within the retention period, typically up to 35 days.
- **High Availability and Fault Tolerance:** RDS provides built-in high availability by deploying database instances across multiple Availability Zones (AZs) within a region. In the event of a hardware failure or AZ outage, RDS automatically fails over to a standby replica to minimize downtime.
- **Scalability:** Users can easily scale their database instances vertically by resizing the instance class or horizontally by adding read replicas to offload read traffic and improve performance.
- **Security:** RDS offers robust security features, including network isolation using Amazon VPC, encryption at rest using AWS KMS, encryption in transit using SSL/TLS, and fine-grained access control through IAM roles and database user accounts.
- **Monitoring and Metrics:** RDS provides comprehensive monitoring and metrics through Amazon CloudWatch, which allow users to monitor database performance, set up alarms, and troubleshoot issues proactively.
- **Cost-Effective:** With RDS, users pay only for the resources they consume, with no upfront fees or long-term commitments. RDS offers various pricing options, including on-demand instances, reserved instances, and RDS free tier for new users to get started with minimal cost.

Use Cases

- **Web Applications:** RDS is well-suited for powering web applications, as it provides a scalable and reliable backend database infrastructure for applications deployed on EC2 instances or AWS Lambda.
- **Enterprise Applications:** RDS can be used to host databases that support mission-critical enterprise applications such as Customer Relationship Management (CRM), Enterprise Resource Planning (ERP), and Business Intelligence (BI) systems that require high availability, scalability, and security.

- **Analytics and Reporting**: RDS supports data warehousing and analytics workloads by providing integration with AWS services such as Amazon Redshift for data analytics and Amazon QuickSight for business intelligence and visualization.

These databases can now integrate more tightly with AI services through Amazon Bedrock, SageMaker, and generative AI assistants to enable customers to use their operational data in real-time AI applications.

Amazon Aurora

Amazon Aurora is a fully managed relational database engine developed by Amazon Web Services (AWS) that combines the performance and availability of high-end commercial databases with the simplicity and cost-effectiveness of open-source databases.

Key Features

- **Compatibility and Performance:** Amazon Aurora is compatible with MySQL and PostgreSQL and offers users the familiarity of popular database engines. It provides superior performance and scalability compared to traditional databases, thanks to its distributed, fault-tolerant architecture.
- **Storage and Replication**: Aurora uses a distributed, fault-tolerant storage system that automatically scales up to 128 TiB per database instance. Data is replicated six ways across three Availability Zones (AZs), which ensures durability and high availability.
- **Performance and Scalability:** Aurora delivers high performance for both read and write operations, often surpassing traditional databases' performance metrics. It supports up to 15 read replicas per database instance, while enabling horizontal scaling of read traffic.
- **Fault Tolerance and High Availability:** With automatic failover and data replication across multiple AZs, Aurora ensures high availability and minimal downtime in case of hardware failures or disruptions. Automatic failover to standby replicas ensures continuous availability of the database and protects against data loss.
- **Fully Managed Service:** Amazon Aurora is a fully managed service which handles routine database management tasks such as hardware provisioning, software patching, backups, and monitoring. This managed service model allows users to focus on application development and optimization without worrying about database infrastructure management.

Use Case

- **E-commerce Platforms:** Online retailers can leverage Aurora to handle large volumes of transactional data efficiently to ensure fast response times and seamless shopping experiences for customers.

- **Financial Services:** Banking and financial institutions rely on Aurora to power critical applications such as trading platforms, payment processing systems, and fraud detection algorithms, where low latency and high throughput are essential.
- **Gaming:** Gaming companies use Aurora to manage player profiles, game progress, and in-game transactions to provide a reliable and responsive gaming experience to millions of users worldwide.
- **Content Management Systems (CMS):** Media and publishing companies leverage Aurora to store and manage vast amounts of content like articles, videos, and images, while ensuring high availability and data integrity.
- **Healthcare:** Healthcare providers use Aurora to store Electronic Health Records (EHRs), patient data, and medical imaging files securely, while enabling real-time access to critical information for medical professionals and patients.

Comparing Amazon Aurora vs Amazon Relational Database Service

Aspect	Amazon Aurora	Amazon RDS
Architecture	Distributed	Traditional
Performance	High	Variable
Scalability	Elastic	Limited
Storage	Distributed	Block-Based
Replication	Multi-Master	Single-Master

Table 5.2: *Differences between Aurora and RDS*

Amazon DynamoDB

Amazon DynamoDB is a fully managed NoSQL database service provided by AWS and offers fast and predictable performance with seamless scalability. It is designed to handle large-scale, high-traffic applications with ease, while providing a flexible and highly available database solution for various use cases.

Key Features

- **Fully Managed:** DynamoDB is a fully managed service, which means that AWS takes care of administrative tasks such as hardware provisioning, setup, configuration, replication, backups, and patching, thereby allowing developers to focus on building applications.
- **Scalability:** DynamoDB offers seamless scalability with virtually unlimited throughput and storage capacity. It can automatically scale up or down based on demand, while ensuring consistent performance regardless of workload fluctuations.

- **Performance:** DynamoDB delivers single-digit millisecond latency for read and write operations, which makes it ideal for applications that require low-latency data access. It achieves this performance by using SSD storage and distributed data architecture.
- **Flexible Data Model:** DynamoDB supports both key-value and document data models, while providing flexibility in data representation. It allows users to store and retrieve structured, semi-structured, and unstructured data, which makes it suitable for a wide range of applications.
- **High Availability and Durability:** DynamoDB is designed for high availability and durability, with data replication across multiple availability zones within a region. It offers built-in fault tolerance and automatic data replication to ensure data durability and resilience to failures.
- **Security:** DynamoDB offers robust security features like encryption at rest and in transit, fine-grained access control using AWS Identity and Access Management (IAM), and integration with AWS Key Management Service (KMS) for encryption key management.
- **Global Tables:** DynamoDB Global Tables allow users to replicate data across multiple AWS regions, while enabling low-latency access to data from anywhere in the world. It ensures data locality and disaster recovery capabilities for globally distributed applications.
- **On-Demand and Provisioned Capacity Modes:** DynamoDB offers flexible pricing options with on-demand and provisioned capacity modes. On-demand capacity mode automatically scales to accommodate varying workloads, while provisioned capacity mode allows users to specify read and write capacity units based on anticipated workload requirements.

Use Cases

- **Web and Mobile Applications:** DynamoDB is well-suited for web and mobile applications requiring low-latency data access such as user profiles, session management, and real-time analytics.
- **Gaming:** DynamoDB can power various gaming use cases like player profiles, leaderboards, in-game transactions, and game state storage due to its fast and scalable data storage capabilities.
- **IoT Applications:** DynamoDB is ideal for IoT applications handling large volumes of sensor data, device telemetry, and event streams. It can store, process, and analyze IoT data in real-time, thus enabling actionable insights and automation.
- **Ad Tech:** DynamoDB is commonly used in ad tech platforms for storing and processing user behavior data, ad impressions, clickstream data, and campaign analytics, providing real-time targeting and personalization capabilities.

- **Content Management Systems:** DynamoDB can serve as a backend database for content management systems, handling content metadata, user preferences, access control lists, and media files with its scalable and performant storage capabilities.

Let us look at a Comparison between Relational Database vs NoSQL Database for better clarity:

Feature	Relational Database (RDS)	NoSQL Database (DynamoDB)
Data Model	Structured (tables, rows, columns)	Flexible (schema-less, key-value pairs)
Scalability	Vertical (adding resources to a single server)	Horizontal (adding more servers/ nodes)
Schema Flexibility	Requires predefined schema, rigid structure	Schema-less, adaptable to changing data
Query Language	SQL (Structured Query Language)	NoSQL (varies by database type)
ACID Transactions	Supports ACID transactions for data integrity	Eventual consistency, eventual consistency guarantees
Use Cases	Complex relationships, transactions	High scalability, flexible data models

Table 5.3: *Comparing Relational Database to NoSQL Database*

Amazon ElasticCache

Amazon ElastiCache is a fully managed in-memory caching service provided by AWS. It simplifies the deployment, operation, and scaling of distributed in-memory caches in the cloud. ElastiCache supports two popular open-source in-memory caching engines: **Redis** and **Memcached**. Through ElastiCache, you can offload the burden of setting up and maintaining caching infrastructure, which allows you to focus on building high-performance, scalable applications.

Key Features

- **Performance:** By storing frequently accessed data in-memory, ElastiCache accelerates the performance of applications, while reducing latency and improving overall responsiveness.
- **Scalability:** ElastiCache allows you to easily scale your caching infrastructure by adding or removing nodes to meet changing demands. It supports both vertical scaling (resizing individual nodes) and horizontal scaling (adding more nodes to the cache cluster).
- **High Availability:** ElastiCache enhances the reliability of applications by providing automatic failover and data replication features. In Redis, Multi-AZ with automatic failover ensures high availability, while Memcached relies on a replicated cache strategy.

- **Managed Service:** AWS handles the administrative tasks associated with managing and monitoring the caching environment, including software patching, hardware provisioning, and cluster maintenance, which frees you from operational overhead.
- **Compatibility:** ElastiCache is compatible with popular caching engines such as Redis and Memcached, which allows you to leverage familiar tools and libraries to integrate caching into your applications seamlessly.

Use Cases

- **Session Store Caching:** Storing user session data in-memory to improve session management and enhance user experience.
- **Database Caching:** Caching frequently accessed database queries or results to reduce database load and improve application performance.
- **Content Caching:** Caching static content such as images, HTML files, or API responses to accelerate content delivery and reduce latency.

Amazon DocumentDB

Amazon DocumentDB is a fully managed, highly available, and scalable document database service provided by AWS. It is compatible with MongoDB, which means that you can use existing MongoDB drivers, libraries, and tools with DocumentDB without needing to rewrite your applications. DocumentDB is designed to provide the performance, scalability, and availability required for modern, mission-critical applications.

Key Features

- **Compatibility:** Amazon DocumentDB is compatible with MongoDB, which allows you to seamlessly migrate existing MongoDB applications to Amazon DocumentDB without modifying your code. It supports MongoDB APIs, drivers, and tools, thereby making it easy to transition to a managed service environment.
- **Managed Service:** Amazon DocumentDB is a fully managed service, which means that AWS handles administrative tasks such as hardware provisioning, software patching, setup, configuration, monitoring, and backups. This allows you to focus on building and scaling your applications without worrying about database management overhead.
- **Scalability:** Amazon DocumentDB is designed for horizontal scalability, which allows you to scale your database cluster by adding or removing instances to meet changing workload demands. It automatically partitions data across multiple instances and provides read scalability through replica sets, while enabling high-performance read operations.
- **High Availability:** DocumentDB provides built-in high availability with automated failover and continuous backups to ensure data durability and fault tolerance. It

replicates data across multiple Availability Zones (AZs) within a region, while providing resilience against AZ-level failures.

- **Performance:** DocumentDB delivers low-latency, high-throughput performance for read-heavy workloads, making it suitable for applications that require fast response times and real-time analytics. It leverages SSD-based storage and a distributed, fault-tolerant architecture to optimize query performance and data access.
- **Security:** DocumentDB integrates with AWS Identity and Access Management (IAM) for authentication and authorization, which allow you to control access to your database resources. It supports encryption at rest and in transit, while ensuring data security and compliance with regulatory requirements.
- **Fully Managed Backups:** DocumentDB automatically takes continuous backups of your data and stores them in Amazon S3, while providing point-in-time recovery and enabling you to restore your database to any specific point in time within the retention period.

Use Cases

- **Content Management Systems (CMS):** Storing and managing structured and unstructured content such as articles, blogs, and media files in a flexible and scalable document database
- **Product Catalogs:** Building and maintaining product catalogs for e-commerce platforms, while enabling fast and efficient querying of product information and attributes
- **User Profiles and Personalization:** Storing and querying user profiles and preferences for personalized recommendations, content delivery, and targeted marketing campaigns

Amazon Neptune

Amazon Neptune is a fully managed graph database service provided by AWS. It is designed to store and query highly connected data sets, making it ideal for applications that require complex relationships and traversals, such as social networks, recommendation engines, fraud detection, and knowledge graphs.

Key Features

- **Fully Managed:** Amazon Neptune is a fully managed service, which means that AWS handles administrative tasks such as hardware provisioning, software patching, setup, configuration, monitoring, and backups. This allows you to focus on developing and optimizing your graph applications without worrying about database management overhead.

- **Graph Database Engine:** Neptune is built on a purpose-built, high-performance graph database engine that is optimized for storing and querying graph data. It supports property graph and RDF graph models, while providing flexibility for different types of graph applications.
- **Highly Available:** Neptune provides built-in high availability with automated failover and continuous backups to ensure data durability and fault tolerance. It replicates data across multiple Availability Zones (AZs) within a region, while providing resilience against AZ-level failures.
- **Scalability:** Neptune is designed for horizontal scalability and allows you to scale your graph database cluster by adding or removing instances to meet changing workload demands. It automatically partitions data across multiple instances and provides read scalability through replica sets, while enabling high-performance graph traversals.
- **Performance:** Neptune delivers low-latency, high-throughput performance for graph queries, which make it suitable for applications requiring real-time analytics and complex graph traversals. It leverages SSD-based storage and a distributed, fault-tolerant architecture to optimize query performance and data access.
- **Compatibility:** Neptune supports popular graph query languages such as Gremlin and SPARQL, as well as APIs and drivers for popular programming languages. This allows you to use existing tools, libraries, and frameworks with Neptune without needing to learn new query languages or APIs.
- **Security:** Neptune integrates with AWS Identity and Access Management (IAM) for authentication and authorization, which allow you to control access to your graph database resources. It supports encryption at rest and in transit, while ensuring data security and compliance with regulatory requirements.

Use cases

- **Social Networks:** Modelling and analysing social networks to identify communities, influencers, and patterns of interaction
- **Recommendation Engines:** Generating personalized recommendations for products, content, or connections based on user preferences and behaviour
- **Fraud Detection:** Identifying fraudulent activities such as money laundering or cyber-attacks, by analysing patterns and connections in large datasets

Conclusion

In conclusion, this chapter has provided an in-depth explaination of AWS compute services, storage services, and database services, while highlighting their key features and use cases. We have gained insights into the versatility and scalability offered by compute services such as EC2, Lambda, and ECS, while enabling them to efficiently manage their computing resources.

Storage services such as S3, EBS, and Glacier are known for their durability, scalability, and cost-effectiveness as they cater to diverse storage needs. Additionally, database services such as RDS and DynamoDB have been discussed for their managed solutions, which ensures high availability, reliability, and performance for various applications.

In the next chapter, we will delve into AWS products in migration and transfer, network and content delivery, and developer tools to further expand our understanding of AWS offerings and capabilities.

Points to Remember

AWS Compute Services

- **EC2 (Elastic Compute Cloud):** Provides resizable compute capacity in the cloud
- **Lambda:** Runs code in response to triggers without provisioning or managing servers
- **Elastic Beanstalk:** Deploys and manages applications in the AWS Cloud without worrying about infrastructure details
- **Batch:** Runs batch computing workloads on the AWS Cloud
- **ECS (Elastic Container Service):** Highly scalable container management service that supports Docker containers
- **Outposts:** Brings native AWS services, infrastructure, and operating models to virtually any data centre, co-location space, or on-premises facility
- **Lightsail:** Launches virtual private servers, storage, and databases in the cloud
- **Fargate:** A serverless compute engine that runs containers without the need to manage servers
- **EKS:** A fully managed service for running Kubernetes workloads securely and at scale
- **ECR:** A managed container registry for storing, securing, and deploying Docker images

AWS Storage Service

- **S3 (Simple Storage Service):** Scalable object storage for data storage and retrieval
- **EBS (Elastic Block Store):** Provides persistent block-level storage volumes for use with EC2 instances
- **EFS (Elastic File System):** Fully managed file storage for EC2 instances
- **Glacier:** Low-cost storage for data archiving and long-term backup
- **FSx (File System):** Fully managed file storage service built on native Windows and Lustre file systems
- **Backup:** Centralized backup service that makes it easier to manage and automate backups across AWS services

- **Snowball:** Transfers large amounts of data into and out of AWS using physical storage appliances
- **Elastic Disaster Recovery:** A fully managed service that helps quickly recover applications and data to AWS, while minimizing downtime and data loss during disruptions

AWS Database Services

- **RDS (Relational Database Service):** Managed relational databases in the cloud
- **DynamoDB:** Fully managed NoSQL database service
- **Aurora:** Fully managed relational database compatible with MySQL and PostgreSQL
- **ElastiCache:** In-memory caching service for improving application performance
- **DocumentDB:** Fully managed document database service compatible with MongoDB
- **Neptune:** Fully managed graph database service that makes it easy to build and run applications that work with highly connected datasets

Multiple Choice Questions

1. Which AWS database service is purpose-built for applications requiring fast performance at any scale? (Select all that apply)
    a. Amazon RDS
    b. Amazon Aurora
    c. Amazon DynamoDB
    d. Amazon DocumentDB
2. Which feature of Amazon S3 enables running analytics queries directly on data stored in S3 without moving it to a database? (Select all that apply)
    a. S3 Glacier Deep Dive
    b. S3 Lifecycle policies
    c. S3 versioning
    d. S3 Tables
3. In which scenario would you choose Amazon Neptune over other AWS database services? (Select all that apply)
    a. Building highly scalable, graph-based applications
    b. Storing and querying structured, semi-structured, or unstructured data
    c. Deploying traditional relational databases with MySQL or PostgreSQL compatibility
    d. Managing time-series data with built-in analytics capabilities

4. Which AWS database service is ideal for applications requiring millisecond latency and seamless scalability for real-time workloads?
    a. Amazon RDS
    b. Amazon Aurora
    c. Amazon DynamoDB
    d. Amazon Neptune
5. In which use case would you consider using Amazon DocumentDB over other AWS database services? (Select all that apply)
    a. Migrating existing MongoDB workloads to a fully managed service
    b. Building serverless applications with DynamoDB compatibility
    c. Analyzing large volumes of time-series data with built-in analytics
    d. Managing relational databases with high availability and compatibility with MySQL or PostgreSQL
6. Which AWS database service offers compatibility with SQL (Structured Query Language) and is suitable for migrating existing MySQL, PostgreSQL, Oracle, or SQL Server databases to the cloud? (Select all that apply)
    a. Amazon RDS
    b. Amazon Aurora
    c. Amazon DynamoDB
    d. Amazon Neptune
7. Which AWS database service is purpose-built for applications requiring fast, predictable performance with compatibility for the PostgreSQL database engine? (Select all that apply)
    a. Amazon RDS
    b. Amazon Aurora
    c. Amazon DynamoDB
    d. Amazon DocumentDB
8. In which scenario would you choose Amazon Timestream over other AWS database services? (Select all that apply)
    a. Storing and analyzing time-series data from IoT sensors or applications
    b. Managing highly relational datasets with complex interconnections
    c. Building graph-based applications with optimized traversal queries
    d. Hosting traditional SQL databases with built-in security and compliance features

9. Which AWS database service is fully managed and provides compatibility with MongoDB, allowing you to run MongoDB workloads at scale? (Select all that apply)
   a. Amazon RDS
   b. Amazon Aurora
   c. Amazon DynamoDB
   d. Amazon DocumentDB
10. Your team is building a customer-facing web application that needs to handle millions of users globally. To ensure low latency and automatic scaling, they want a managed NoSQL database that can scale without manual intervention. Which AWS service is the best fit?
   a. Amazon RDS
   b. Amazon Aurora
   c. Amazon DynamoDB
   d. Amazon DocumentDB
11. Which of the following AWS storage services are suitable for long-term archival of infrequently accessed data? (Select all that apply)
   a. Amazon S3 Glacier
   b. Amazon EBS
   c. Amazon FSx
   d. AWS Backup
12. In which scenarios would you typically use Amazon EFS? (Select all that apply)
   a. Storing frequently accessed data that requires low latency
   b. Hosting static websites with high availability
   c. Sharing files across multiple EC2 instances
   d. Storing application backups in a durable and scalable manner
13. What are the key features of AWS Snowball? (Select all that apply)
   a. High-speed data transfer device for large data sets
   b. Securely transport data between your data center and AWS
   c. Provides low-latency access to frequently accessed data
   d. Automatically synchronizes data between on-premises and AWS storage

14. Which AWS storage service provides durable, scalable object storage suitable for a wide range of use cases, including data lakes, backup and restore, disaster recovery, and analytics?
    a. Amazon EBS
    b. Amazon S3
    c. Amazon Glacier
    d. AWS Storage Gateway
15. In which scenario would you use Amazon FSx for Windows File Server? (Select all that apply)
    a. Hosting a web application that requires high availability
    b. Running a Windows-based enterprise application that needs shared file storage
    c. Archiving infrequently accessed data for compliance purposes
    d. Backing up data from on-premises Windows servers to the cloud
16. Which AWS service allows you to run containerized applications on a managed cluster of Amazon EC2 instances?
    a. Amazon EC2
    b. Amazon ECS
    c. Amazon EKS
    d. AWS Lambda
17. What is the purpose of Amazon Machine Images (AMIs)?
    a. To store and manage Docker containers
    b. To provide a template for creating virtual machine instances
    c. To manage relational databases in the cloud
    d. To provision dedicated hosts for your applications
18. What is the key benefit of AWS Lambda?
    a. Provides managed Kubernetes clusters
    b. Allows you to run Docker containers
    c. Scales automatically based on demand
    d. Provides virtual private servers
19. Which AWS service allows you to run batch computing workloads?
    a. Amazon EC2
    b. Amazon ECS

c. AWS Batch

d. AWS Elastic Beanstalk

20. What is the primary purpose of AWS Outposts?

a. To extend AWS services to on-premises locations

b. To manage containerized applications

c. To provide a serverless computing environment

d. To manage relational databases in the cloud

Answers

1. b, c
2. d
3. a
4. c
5. a, d
6. a
7. d
8. a
9. d
10. d
11. a
12. c, d
13. a, b
14. b
15. b
16. b
17. b
18. c
19. c
20. a

References

- https://docs.aws.amazon.com/index.html - Documents for each service are present in this link.

CHAPTER 6
AWS Core Services - Part II

Introduction

In this chapter, we will delve into AWS core services and focus on migration and transfer, network and content delivery, and developer tools. Building on our previous exploration of compute services, storage services, and database services, we will now expand our understanding of essential AWS offerings across these critical areas.

Migration and transfer services facilitate the seamless transition of data and applications to the AWS cloud. From AWS Database Migration Service (DMS) to AWS Transfer Family, these services ensure minimal disruption and downtime, while enabling organizations to harness the full potential of the cloud. Additionally, we will explore Network & Content Delivery services like Amazon Virtual Private Cloud (VPC), AWS Direct Connect, and Amazon CloudFront, which provide secure, scalable networking solutions. Finally, we will delve into Developer Tools like AWS CodePipeline, AWS CodeCommit, and AWS Cloud9, empowering developers with integrated solutions for streamlined application development and deployment workflows. Through this exploration, readers will gain valuable insights into leveraging these core AWS services effectively to drive innovation and success in the cloud.

Structure

In this chapter, will learn about the following topics:

- Migration and Transfer
- Network and Content Delivery
- Developer Tools

Migration and Transfer Services

AWS Migration and Transfer Services help organizations move applications, databases, and data from on-premises or other clouds into AWS quickly and securely. These services reduce downtime, simplify complex migrations, and provide tools to plan, track, and optimize the entire migration journey. Let us explore the services from AWS.

AWS Database Migration Service (DMS)

AWS Database Migration Service (DMS) is a fully managed service that enables you to migrate your databases to AWS quickly and securely. With DMS, you can migrate your databases to AWS with minimal downtime, which enables you to take advantage of the scalability, reliability, and security of the AWS Cloud.

Key Features

- **Database Compatibility:** DMS supports a wide range of databases, including MySQL, PostgreSQL, Oracle, SQL Server, MongoDB, and more. This allows you to migrate your databases regardless of the source or target database platform.
- **Continuous Data Replication:** DMS enables continuous data replication from your source database to your target database, while ensuring minimal downtime during the migration process. This ensures that your data is always up-to-date on the target database.
- **Schema Conversion:** DMS can automatically convert the schema of your source database to match the target database and eliminates the need for manual schema conversion. This simplifies the migration process and reduces the risk of errors.

- **High Availability and Reliability:** DMS is designed to be highly available and reliable, with built-in features such as automatic failover and continuous monitoring. This ensures that your data migration process is smooth and uninterrupted.
- **Security and Compliance:** DMS encrypts data during transit and at rest, ensuring that your data is secure during the migration process. Additionally, DMS is compliant with various industry standards and regulations, which makes it suitable for use in regulated industries.

Use Cases

- **Database Consolidation:** DMS can be used to consolidate multiple databases into a single database platform, which reduces operational overhead and improving efficiency.
- **Database Migration to the Cloud:** DMS enables you to migrate your on-premises databases to the AWS Cloud, which allows you to take advantage of the scalability, reliability, and cost-effectiveness of cloud computing.
- **Database Replication:** DMS can be used for database replication, which enables you to create high-availability configurations, disaster recovery solutions, and read replicas for your databases.

AWS Migration Hub

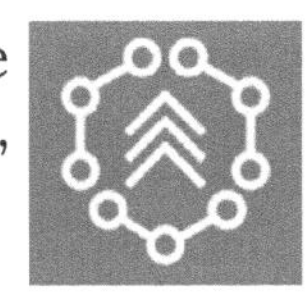

AWS Migration Hub is a service that provides a centralized hub for tracking the progress of application migrations to the AWS cloud. It enables you to plan, track, and monitor migrations across multiple AWS and partner migration tools.

Key Features

- **Centralized Migration Tracking:** Migration Hub offers a single console where you can track the progress of application migrations across multiple AWS services and tools. It provides a unified view of migration status, progress, and resource utilization, while allowing you to monitor migrations more effectively.
- **Integration with Migration Tools:** Migration Hub integrates with various AWS and partner migration tools like AWS Server Migration Service (SMS), AWS Database Migration Service (DMS), AWS DataSync, AWS Snow Family, and third-party migration tools. This integration enables you to use your preferred migration tools while still leveraging the capabilities of Migration Hub for centralized tracking and management.
- **Migration Status and Progress:** Migration Hub provides real-time status updates and progress tracking for each migration task like insights into resource discovery, assessment, replication, testing, and cutover phases. It offers detailed metrics and reports to help you understand the overall status of your migration projects and identify any issues or bottlenecks.

- **Grouping and Tagging:** Migration Hub allows you to group related resources and migration tasks into application groups, which makes it easier to manage and track migrations for specific applications or business units. You can also tag resources with custom metadata to organize and categorize them based on your migration requirements.
- **Collaboration and Visibility:** Migration Hub supports collaboration among team members involved in migration projects by providing shared access to migration data and insights. It offers Role-Based Access Control (RBAC) to control user permissions and access levels, ensuring that only authorized users can view or modify migration data.

Use Cases

- **Enterprise-Wide Migration Management:** Migration Hub is suitable for enterprises with complex IT environments and multiple migration projects. It enables centralized management and tracking of all migration activities across different teams, departments, and AWS accounts.
- **Multi-Cloud Migrations:** Migration Hub can be used to track migrations to AWS from on-premises environments, other cloud providers, or hybrid cloud configurations. It offers visibility into the entire migration process, regardless of the source or destination environment.
- **Migration Performance Optimization:** Migration Hub allows organizations to identify performance bottlenecks, optimize migration workflows, and improve migration efficiency. It provides data-driven insights into migration progress, resource utilization, and cost implications, while enabling continuous improvement and optimization of migration strategies.

AWS Application Discover Service

AWS Application Discovery Service is a tool designed to help organizations plan their migration to the cloud by discovering and collecting information about their on-premises applications and infrastructure.

It offers the following features:

- **Agentless Discovery:** There is no need to install software agents on servers or devices.
- **Infrastructure Visualization:** It provides visualizations of your infrastructure and shows interconnections.
- **Dependency Mapping:** It identifies dependencies between applications, servers, databases, and so on.
- **Inventory Collection:** It gathers detailed inventory and metadata information about on-premises assets.
- **Integration:** It seamlessly integrates with other AWS migration tools.

AWS Application Migration Service (AWS MGN)

AWS Application Migration Service (AWS MGN) is the **primary service for migrating servers and applications to AWS**. It automates the lift-and-shift (rehost) process, which enables you to move workloads from physical servers, virtual machines, or other cloud environments into AWS with minimal downtime. Instead of rebuilding or redesigning applications, AWS MGN replicates your existing servers in real-time and then launches them as Amazon EC2 instances once you are ready to cut over. This approach significantly reduces the complexity, time, and cost of migration.

Key Features

- **Continuous Replication:** MGN continuously replicates source servers into AWS and ensures that data is always up to date during migration.
- **Minimal Downtime:** By keeping the target environment synchronized, final cutover requires only a short downtime window.
- **Automated Conversion:** The service automatically converts source infrastructure into cloud-ready Amazon EC2 instances, which removes the need for manual reconfiguration.
- **Scalability:** Supports large-scale migrations of thousands of servers simultaneously
- **Testing Before Cutover:** You can launch non-disruptive test instances in AWS to validate functionality before completing the migration.
- **Cost Optimization:** After cutover, AWS MGN provides recommendations to right-size and optimize EC2 instances and storage for cost efficiency.
- **Security and Compliance:** Data replication is encrypted in transit and the service supports common compliance standards.

Use Case

Enterprises use AWS MGN when they need to quickly migrate legacy applications and workloads into AWS without rewriting code or making architectural changes.

AWS Migration Evaluator

AWS Migration Evaluator (formerly known as **TSO Logic**) is a service that helps organizations **analyze and plan their move to AWS**. Instead of jumping directly into migration, it provides detailed insights into your current IT environment—servers, applications, and workloads—and builds a **business case for cloud adoption**.

Think of it as a "pre-migration assessment tool" that estimates costs, identifies opportunities for savings, and shows you what your infrastructure might look like once it is running on AWS.

Key Features

- **Comprehensive Discovery:** Collects information about on-premises servers, virtual machines, and workloads to create a clear picture of your IT estate
- **Cost Modeling:** Generates detailed cost estimates of running the same workloads in AWS, including right-sized EC2 instances, storage options, and licensing considerations
- **Business Case Development:** Builds a data-driven business case that compares current costs to projected AWS costs, which helps the leadership justify the migration
- **Right-Sizing Recommendations:** Identifies over-provisioned resources and suggests optimized AWS configurations to avoid unnecessary spending
- **Customizable Scenarios:** Allows you to adjust assumptions such as reserved instances, savings plans, or regional deployments to see different cost outcomes
- **Licensing Analysis:** Evaluates existing software licensing (Windows, SQL Server, and so on) and shows how Bring Your Own License (BYOL) options could reduce expenses

Use Case

Organizations use Migration Evaluator before starting a migration project to gain **financial clarity and executive alignment**. It is especially useful when decision-makers need concrete, data-backed justification for cloud adoption.

AWS Schema Conversion Tool (AWS SCT)

AWS Schema Conversion Tool (SCT) helps you **migrate databases from one engine to another** by automatically converting database schema, code, and objects. For example, you can move from commercial engines like Oracle or SQL Server to open-source engines such as Amazon Aurora PostgreSQL or MySQL. SCT analyzes your source database, identifies incompatible objects, and suggests workarounds when automated conversion isn't possible. It also supports migrating application code that relies on database APIs, functions, and procedures, thereby making it easier to modernize workloads during migration.

Exercise 6.1: Test Your Cloud Knowledge

1. What does AWS Application Discovery Service primarily provide?
    a. Agent-based discovery
    b. Visualization of cloud infrastructure
    c. Real-time data synchronization
    d. Load balancing configuration

2. Which AWS service helps automatically convert database schemas and code objects when migrating from one database engine (such as Oracle or SQL Server) to another (such as Amazon Aurora PostgreSQL)?
    a. AWS Database Migration Service (DMS)
    b. AWS Schema Conversion Tool (SCT)
    c. AWS Application Migration Service (MGN)
    d. AWS Migration Evaluator
3. Which AWS service helps organizations plan their migration to the cloud by discovering and collecting information about their on-premises applications and infrastructure?
    a. AWS DataSync
    b. AWS Transfer Family
    c. AWS Application Discovery Service
    d. AWS Migration Hub

Answers

1. b
2. b
3. c

Network and Content Delivery

AWS network and content delivery services provide the backbone for securely connecting applications, users, and data across the globe while ensuring low latency, high availability, and seamless performance. From private connectivity to global content distribution, these services form the foundation of modern cloud architectures. Let us explore the AWS services which enable network and content delivery.

Amazon Virtual Private Cloud (VPC)

Amazon Virtual Private Cloud (VPC) is a service that allows you to launch AWS resources in a logically isolated virtual network. With VPC, you have complete control over your virtual networking environment such as selecting your IP address range, creating subnets, and configuring route tables and network gateways. VPC provides a secure and scalable environment for deploying your applications and services within the AWS cloud.

Key Features

- **Isolated Networking**: VPC allows you to create multiple isolated virtual networks within the AWS cloud, which enable you to securely launch resources like EC2 instances, RDS databases, and Lambda functions within your own virtual network.
- **Custom IP Addressing**: You can define your own IP address range (CIDR block) for your VPC, allowing you to choose IP addresses that match your organization's internal network addressing scheme.
- **Subnet Creation:** Within your VPC, you can create multiple subnets, each with its own CIDR block, availability zone placement, and route table configuration. Subnets provide segmentation within your VPC and enable you to control traffic flow between different parts of your network.
- **Internet Gateway:** VPC allows you to attach an Internet Gateway (IGW) to your virtual network, enabling communication between instances in your VPC and the public internet. This allows your resources to access external services and for external users to access resources hosted in your VPC.
- **Security Groups and Network ACLs:** VPC provides security features such as security groups and network Access Control Lists (ACLs) to control inbound and outbound traffic to your instances. Security groups act as a virtual firewall for your instances, while network ACLs provide subnet-level filtering.
- **VPN and Direct Connect:** VPC supports VPN connections and AWS Direct Connect, allowing you to establish secure connections between your on-premises data centre or corporate network and your VPC. This allows the creation of hybrid cloud architectures and establishes secure communication between your on-premises resources and AWS cloud resources.

Amazon Route 53

Amazon Route 53 is a scalable and highly available Domain Name System (DNS) web service provided by AWS. It effectively routes end users to applications by translating human-readable domain names into IP addresses.

Key Features

- **Domain Registration:** Route 53 allows you to register domain names and manage their DNS records using a simple and intuitive interface. You can purchase new domain names directly from Route 53 or transfer existing domains from other registrars.
- **DNS Management:** With Route 53, you can create and manage DNS records for your domain, including A records for IPv4 addresses, AAAA records for IPv6 addresses,

CNAME records for aliasing one domain name to another, MX records for email routing, and more.

- **Global DNS Resolution:** Route 53 provides global anycast routing, ensuring low-latency DNS resolution for end users worldwide. It uses a global network of DNS servers strategically located around the world to route DNS queries to the nearest available server.

- **Health Checks and Failover:** Route 53 can monitor the health of your application endpoints using health checks. If an endpoint fails a health check, Route 53 can automatically route traffic away from the unhealthy endpoint to healthy ones, improving the availability and reliability of your application.

- **Traffic Management:** Route 53 offers traffic management features such as weighted routing, latency-based routing, and geolocation routing. These features allow you to distribute incoming traffic across multiple endpoints based on different criteria such as geographic location or endpoint health.

- **Integration with AWS Services:** Route 53 seamlessly integrates with other AWS services, such as Elastic Load Balancing (ELB), Amazon CloudFront, and AWS Global Accelerator. You can use Route 53 to route traffic to these services, providing a scalable and reliable architecture for your applications.

AWS Direct Connect

AWS Direct Connect is a dedicated network connection service that enables enterprises to establish private connectivity between their on-premises data centers and AWS cloud infrastructure. By bypassing the public internet, Direct Connect offers enhanced security, reliability, and consistent network performance for mission-critical workloads.

Key Features

- **Dedicated Connection:** Direct Connect provides a dedicated network connection, allowing enterprises to establish private connectivity directly to AWS.

- **Private Virtual Interfaces (VIFs):** Customers can provision multiple private VIFs to separate and prioritize traffic flows, which ensures efficient network management.

- **Predictable Performance:** By bypassing the public internet, Direct Connect offers predictable network performance with low latency and consistent bandwidth, which is ideal for latency-sensitive applications.

- **Flexible Bandwidth Options:** Direct Connect offers flexible bandwidth options ranging from 50 Mbps to 100 Gbps, which allows enterprises to scale their connectivity based on their requirements.

- **Direct Connect Gateway:** The Direct Connect gateway feature enables customers to extend their connectivity to multiple Virtual Private Clouds (VPCs) across different AWS Regions, while simplifying network management in a multi-region environment.
- **Global Reach:** With Direct Connect, enterprises can establish connections in multiple AWS Regions worldwide, while providing global reach and enabling hybrid cloud deployments across geographically distributed data centres.
- **Secure Connectivity:** Direct Connect connections are private and dedicated, ensuring secure data transmission between on-premises environments and AWS cloud resources. Additionally, customers can encrypt data in transit using AWS VPN or AWS Direct Connect dedicated connections.
- **Enterprise-Grade SLAs:** AWS Direct Connect offers enterprise-grade Service Level Agreements (SLAs) for availability and performance, providing assurance of reliable connectivity for critical workloads.

Elastic Load Balancer (ELB)

Elastic Load Balancer (ELB) is an AWS service that automatically distributes incoming application traffic across multiple targets such as Amazon EC2 instances, containers, and IP addresses, to ensure high availability, fault tolerance, and scalability of applications.

Key Features

- **Automatic Traffic Distribution:** ELB automatically distributes incoming traffic across multiple targets within a single or multiple Availability Zones to ensure optimal resource utilization and application availability.
- **High Availability:** ELB operates across multiple Availability Zones to provide fault tolerance and high availability for applications, automatically routing traffic away from unhealthy targets and rerouting traffic to healthy targets.
- **Intelligent Health Checks:** ELB continuously monitors the health of registered targets by performing health checks and automatically detecting and routing traffic away from unhealthy targets to maintain application availability.
- **SSL/TLS Termination:** ELB supports SSL/TLS termination, which allows it to offload SSL/TLS encryption and decryption tasks from backend servers, while improving performance and reducing the computational overhead on target instances.
- **Layer 4 and Layer 7 Load Balancing:** ELB supports both Layer 4 (TCP) and Layer 7 (HTTP/HTTPS) load balancing, while enabling it to route traffic based on application-specific information such as HTTP headers, paths, and cookies.
- **Path-Based Routing:** With path-based routing, ELB can route traffic to different backend services based on the URL paths specified in HTTP requests, thus allowing for flexible application routing and deployment strategies.

- **Cross-Zone Load Balancing:** ELB evenly distributes traffic across all healthy targets in all registered availability zones, while providing a more balanced distribution of traffic and reducing latency for end users.

AWS Transit Gateway

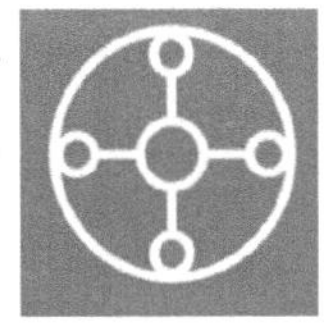

AWS Transit Gateway is a fully managed service that simplifies the connectivity between Amazon Virtual Private Clouds (VPCs), on-premises networks, and other AWS services. It acts as a hub that centralizes network traffic routing, which enables organizations to scale and manage their network infrastructure more efficiently.

Key Features

- **Centralized Hub:** AWS Transit Gateway serves as a central hub for connecting multiple VPCs, on-premises data centers, and remote networks, while simplifying network architecture and reducing the complexity of managing point-to-point connections.
- **Hub-and-Spoke Architecture:** With a hub-and-spoke architecture, AWS Transit Gateway allows organizations to connect thousands of VPCs and on-premises networks using a single gateway, while facilitating efficient communication and traffic routing between network resources.
- **Inter-Region Peering:** AWS Transit Gateway supports inter-region peering, enabling organizations to establish private connectivity between VPCs located in different AWS Regions, while improving redundancy, fault tolerance, and disaster recovery capabilities.
- **Dynamic Routing:** AWS Transit Gateway supports dynamic routing protocols such as Border Gateway Protocol (BGP), while allowing for automated route propagation and efficient traffic forwarding between connected networks, as well as ensuring optimal network performance and scalability.
- **VPN and Direct Connect Integration:** AWS Transit Gateway seamlessly integrates with AWS VPN and AWS Direct Connect services, which allows organizations to establish secure, private connections between on-premises data centers and AWS resources via encrypted VPN tunnels or dedicated network links.

Amazon CloudFront

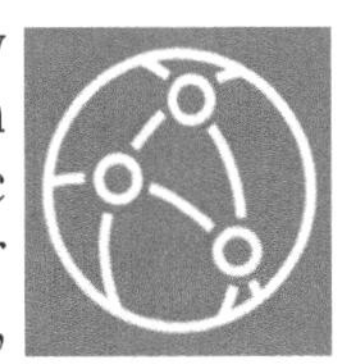

Amazon CloudFront is a Content Delivery Network (CDN) service provided by AWS that accelerates the delivery of web content to users across the globe with low latency and high transfer speeds. It works by caching static and dynamic content at distributed globally edge locations closer to end-users. Whenever a user requests content, CloudFront delivers it from the nearest edge location, while reducing latency and improving the overall user experience.

Key Features

- **Global Content Delivery:** With a network of edge locations spanning major cities worldwide, CloudFront ensures fast and reliable content delivery to users, regardless of their geographical location.
- **Low Latency:** By caching content at edge locations, CloudFront reduces the distance between users and servers, resulting in lower latency and faster load times for websites and applications.
- **High Transfer Speeds:** CloudFront optimizes content delivery by automatically selecting the fastest route and using high-speed, dedicated network connections between edge locations and origin servers.
- **Security:** CloudFront offers robust security features, including DDoS protection, SSL/TLS encryption, and integration with AWS Web Application Firewall (WAF) to protect against common web exploits and attacks.
- **Scalability:** CloudFront scales automatically to handle large volumes of traffic, while ensuring consistent performance even during traffic spikes or surges in demand.
- **Customization:** Users can customize and control various aspects of content delivery, such as caching behaviour, content compression, and HTTP headers, to optimize performance and meet specific requirements.

AWS Global Accelerator

AWS Global Accelerator is a networking service provided by AWS that improves the availability and performance of applications for global users by directing traffic to optimal endpoints over the AWS global network. It operates by using a fixed entry point, called a static IP address, and the AWS global network to route user requests to the nearest AWS edge locations.

Key Features

- **Global Reach:** AWS Global Accelerator leverages the vast AWS global network to ensure low-latency and high-performance delivery of traffic to users across the world, regardless of their geographic location.
- **Anycast IP Addresses:** Global Accelerator uses Anycast IP addresses to route traffic to the nearest edge location, while reducing latency and improving application performance for end-users.
- **Health Checking:** Global Accelerator continuously monitors the health of endpoints (such as EC2 instances, Application Load Balancers, or Elastic IP addresses) and automatically directs traffic away from unhealthy endpoints to maintain application availability.

- **Traffic Distributions:** Users can customize traffic distributions based on their specific requirements, such as dividing traffic between multiple endpoints based on weights or defining endpoint groups for different application environments (for example, production, staging).
- **Accelerated DNS Resolution:** AWS Global Accelerator provides accelerated DNS resolution to reduce the time it takes to resolve DNS queries, while improving the overall responsiveness of applications.

AWS Site-to-Site VPN

AWS Site-to-Site VPN is a networking service that allows secure communication between on-premises networks and AWS cloud resources over the internet using encrypted tunnels. It enables organizations to extend their existing on-premises infrastructure to the AWS Cloud securely.

Key Features

- **Encrypted Communication:** Site-to-Site VPN establishes encrypted IPsec tunnels between customer gateway devices in the on-premises network and virtual private gateways in the AWS Cloud, while ensuring the confidentiality and integrity of data in transit.
- **Secure Connectivity:** It provides a secure and private connection between on-premises networks and AWS VPCs, which allows organizations to securely access AWS resources such as EC2 instances, RDS databases, and S3 storage from their corporate network.
- **High Availability:** Site-to-Site VPN supports redundancy and failover mechanisms, which allows organizations to configure multiple VPN tunnels for high availability and reliability. In case of tunnel or gateway failures, the traffic is automatically rerouted to alternative paths.
- **Scalability:** It scales to support large-scale deployments, accommodating multiple VPN connections and high traffic volumes between on-premises data centers and AWS regions.
- **Compatibility:** Site-to-Site VPN is compatible with a wide range of customer gateway devices, including hardware-based VPN appliances, software-based VPN solutions, and virtual appliances, while ensuring flexibility in deployment options.
- **Cost-Effective:** Compared to dedicated leased lines or MPLS connections, Site-to-Site VPN offers a cost-effective solution for establishing secure connections between on-premises networks and the AWS Cloud as organizations pay only for the data transferred over the VPN tunnels.

AWS PrivateLink

AWS PrivateLink enables you to securely connect your Virtual Private Cloud (VPC) to supported AWS services, partner services, or your own applications, without exposing traffic to the public internet. Instead of routing data through public endpoints, AWS PrivateLink creates an Elastic Network Interface (ENI) in your VPC that serves as a private access point.

Key Features

- **Private Connectivity:** Keeps all traffic on the AWS private network, while improving security and reducing exposure to internet-based threats
- **Simplified Access:** Eliminates the need for complex firewall rules or NAT gateways to reach AWS services privately
- **Service Publishing:** You can create your own services in one VPC and securely share them with other AWS accounts or VPCs via PrivateLink.
- **High Availability:** Built on AWS's highly available and scalable infrastructure and ensures reliable connectivity
- **Compliance-Friendly:** Helps organizations meet compliance requirements by preventing sensitive data from traversing the public internet

Use Case

A financial institution may use PrivateLink to connect its internal VPC directly to Amazon S3 or Kinesis without exposing any data over the internet, while ensuring both **low latency and enhanced security**.

Exercise 6.2: Test Your Cloud Knowledge

1. Which AWS service provides private connectivity between VPCs, AWS services, and on-premises applications without traversing the public internet?
   a. AWS Direct Connect
   b. Amazon CloudFront
   c. AWS PrivateLink
   d. AWS Transit Gateway
2. What is the primary purpose of AWS Direct Connect?
   a. Load balancing incoming traffic across multiple EC2 instances
   b. Establishing private connectivity between an on-premises network and AWS
   c. Distributing content to users globally with low latency
   d. Transferring data between different AWS regions

3. Which AWS service is used to distribute content to users globally with low latency by caching data at edge locations?
    a. AWS Direct Connect
    b. AWS Global Accelerator
    c. Amazon Route 53
    d. Amazon CloudFront
4. Which AWS service provides managed VPN connections between an on-premises network and an AWS VPC?
    a. AWS Direct Connect
    b. AWS Transit Gateway
    c. AWS Site-to-Site VPN
    d. Amazon VPC Peering

Answers

1. c
2. b
3. d
4. c

Developer Tools

AWS Developer Tools streamline the software development lifecycle by helping teams build, test, and deploy applications faster with automation and integrated workflows. These services empower developers to collaborate efficiently and deliver high-quality code at scale. Let us explore the AWS services that enable developer productivity.

AWS Code Pipeline

AWS CodePipeline is a continuous integration and continuous delivery (CI/CD) service that automates the build, test, and deployment phases of your release process. It allows you to model, visualize, and automate the steps required to release your software. With AWS CodePipeline, you can create pipelines that connect various AWS services and third-party tools, which enable you to deliver updates quickly and reliably to your applications.

Key Features

- **Pipeline Model:** AWS CodePipeline allows you to define a series of stages and actions that represent your release process. Each stage can contain one or more actions such as building code, running tests, and deploying applications.
- **Integration with AWS Services:** AWS CodePipeline seamlessly integrates with other AWS services such as AWS CodeBuild for building code, AWS CodeDeploy for deploying applications, and AWS CodeCommit for storing and versioning code repositories.
- **Third-Party Integrations:** In addition to AWS services, AWS CodePipeline supports integration with third-party tools and services through custom actions and webhooks. This flexibility allows you to incorporate your existing tools and processes into your CI/CD pipelines.
- **Automated Deployments:** AWS CodePipeline automates the deployment process by triggering pipeline executions based on events, such as code commits, pull requests, or scheduled builds. This automation reduces manual intervention and ensures consistent and repeatable deployments.
- **Visual Pipeline Editor:** AWS CodePipeline provides a visual editor that allows you to create and edit pipelines using a drag-and-drop interface. This makes it easy to design and customize your release process without writing code.
- **Artifact Management:** Throughout the pipeline execution, AWS CodePipeline manages the flow of artifacts (for example, source code, build artifacts) between stages and actions. This ensures that each stage receives the necessary inputs and outputs to perform its tasks.
- **Monitoring and Notifications:** AWS CodePipeline offers built-in monitoring capabilities, including real-time pipeline execution status and detailed execution logs. Additionally, you can configure notifications to alert stakeholders of pipeline events and failures.

AWS CodeBuild

AWS CodeBuild is a fully managed continuous integration service that compiles source code, runs tests, and produces software packages that are ready for deployment. It automates the build, test, and packaging phases of the software development lifecycle, which enables developers to focus on writing code without worrying about infrastructure management.

Key Features

- **Build Environments:** AWS CodeBuild provides pre-configured build environments for popular programming languages, frameworks, and build tools, including Java, Python, Node.js, Docker, and more. It supports custom build environments, allowing developers to define their own build configurations using Docker images.
- **Managed Build Infrastructure:** AWS CodeBuild manages the build infrastructure, including compute resources, build environments, and scaling capacity, while eliminating the need for developers to provision and manage build servers. It automatically scales compute resources based on the size and complexity of the build workload.
- **Flexible Build Configurations:** AWS CodeBuild supports build specifications written in YAML or JSON format, which allows developers to define build phases, commands, environment variables, and artifacts. Build configurations can be version-controlled alongside the source code, while enabling reproducible builds and traceability.
- **Parallel and Distributed Builds:** AWS CodeBuild supports parallel and distributed builds, allowing multiple build projects to run concurrently and accelerate build times. It provides options for caching dependencies and artifacts between builds, thus improving performance and reducing build times for subsequent runs.
- **Custom Build Environments:** AWS CodeBuild allows developers to create custom build environments using Docker images, while enabling support for specific dependencies, libraries, and build tools. Custom build environments can be shared across teams and projects, which ensures consistency and reproducibility in the build process.

AWS Command Line Interface (CLI)

The AWS Command Line Interface (CLI) is a unified tool that enables users to interact with various AWS services from the command line. It provides a convenient way to manage AWS resources and automate tasks and thus makes it a valuable tool for developers, system administrators, and DevOps engineers. The AWS CLI is built on top of the AWS SDKs, which allows users to access the same functionality programmatically through scripts and automation workflows. With the AWS CLI, users can perform a wide range of tasks, including managing EC2 instances, S3 buckets, IAM users and roles, CloudFormation stacks, and much more, all from the command line. It supports tab completion, command history, and shell scripting, providing a flexible and efficient environment for managing AWS resources.

Key Features

- **Unified Tool:** Provides a single interface to interact with multiple AWS services
- **Command Line Interface:** Allows users to execute commands directly from the terminal or command prompt

- **Automation:** Enables automation of AWS tasks through scripts and automation workflows
- **Wide Range of Tasks:** Supports a wide range of tasks, including resource management, data manipulation, and service configuration
- **Extensibility:** Offers extensive support for shell scripting and integration with other command-line tools
- **SDK Integration:** Built on top of the AWS SDKs; allows users to access AWS functionality programmatically
- **Tab Completion and Command History:** Supports tab completion for commands and maintains a command history for efficient navigation.

AWS X-Ray

AWS X-Ray is a service that allows developers to analyse and debug distributed applications, such as those built using microservices architecture. It provides insights into how services are performing and interacting with each other, while helping developers to identify performance bottlenecks, errors, and issues within their applications. With X-Ray, developers can trace requests as they flow through different components of their application, visualize the entire request path, and identify areas for optimization and improvement.

The key features of AWS X-Ray include distributed tracing, service map visualization, performance monitoring, and anom aly detection.

AWS Kiro (agentic AI IDE, launched mid-2025)

AWS introduced **Kiro** as a next-generation, AI-powered IDE designed to help developers move from concept to production with clarity and control. Unlike traditional "vibe coding" tools, Kiro uses **spec-driven development**; it transforms prompts into structured **user stories with explicit acceptance criteria**, generates technical designs and task plans, and keeps everything in sync. Built-in **hooks**, which are automated triggers on file changes, help enforce quality and consistency. Kiro includes advanced features like **Model Context Protocol (MCP) support**, **agentic chat, steering rules**, and **automated code checks** to catch errors early. Currently available in preview, Kiro has attracted strong user interest, prompting temporary usage limits and a waitlist. It is an ideal example of how AI is reshaping software delivery practices.

Conclusion

As we conclude our exploration of AWS Core Services encompassing migration and transfer, network and content delivery, and developer tools, we have gained invaluable insights into the foundational components of the AWS ecosystem. From seamless data migration to robust networking solutions and efficient development workflows, these services form the backbone of cloud computing, which empower organizations to innovate and thrive in the digital landscape.

Looking ahead, our journey continues into the realm of AWS security, management, and governance, and aapplication integration tools. These critical areas further bolster the AWS infrastructure, ensuring robust security, efficient resource management, and seamless integration of applications and services. By diving deeper into these domains, readers will unlock the keys to building resilient, scalable, and secure cloud environments. Stay tuned as we explore these essential pillars of AWS, while equipping you with the knowledge and tools to navigate the complexities of cloud computing with confidence and proficiency.

Points to Remember

Migration and Transfer Services

- **AWS Database Migration Service (DMS):** Helps migrate databases to AWS quickly and securely
- **AWS Transfer Family:** Provides fully managed SFTP, FTPS, and FTP services
- **AWS Migration Hub:** Tracks the progress of application migrations
- **AWS Application Discovery Service**: Helps plan application migration projects
- **AWS Application Migration Service (MGN):** Used when you want to quickly move whole servers and apps to AWS without rebuilding them
- **AWS Migration Evaluator:** Used to figure out how much money you will save (or spend) by moving your systems to AWS before you start migrating
- **AWS Schema Conversion Tool (SCT):** Used when you want to shift a database from one type (like Oracle) to another (like Aurora PostgreSQL) and need the code and structure converted automatically

Network and Content Delivery

- **Amazon VPC (Virtual Private Cloud):** Isolates cloud resources and provides network customization
- **Amazon Route 53:** Scalable DNS (Domain Name System) web service
- **AWS Direct Connect:** Establishes a dedicated network connection from on-premises to AWS
- **Elastic Load Balancer:** Automatically distributes incoming application traffic across multiple targets
- **AWS Transit Gateway:** Centrally manages and scales connectivity across thousands of Amazon VPCs
- **Amazon CloudFront:** Fast content delivery network (CDN) service

- **AWS Global Accelerator:** Improves the availability and performance of your applications with local or global users
- **AWS Site-to-Site VPN:** Connects your on-premises networks to AWS securely
- **AWS PrivateLink:** *Used when you want to connect securely to AWS services from your* VPC *without sending traffic over the public internet*

Developer Tools

- **AWS CodePipeline:** Automates the continuous integration and continuous delivery (CI/CD) pipeline
- **AWS CodeBuild:** Builds and tests code in the cloud
- **AWS Command Line Interface (CLI):** Unified tool to manage AWS services from the command line
- **AWS X-Ray:** Analyzes and debugs distributed applications such as those built using microservices architecture

Multiple Choice Questions

1. Which AWS service helps track the progress of application migrations?
    a. AWS DataSync
    b. AWS Database Migration Service (DMS)
    c. AWS Migration Hub
    d. AWS Application Discovery Service

2. A company wants to move hundreds of on-premises servers to AWS with **minimal downtime** and without rebuilding their applications. Which AWS service should they use?
    a. AWS Application Migration Service (MGN)
    b. AWS Database Migration Service (DMS)
    c. AWS Transfer Family
    d. AWS Migration Hub

3. Which AWS service helps establish a dedicated network connection from on-premises to AWS?
    a. Amazon VPC
    b. AWS Direct Connect
    c. Elastic Load Balancer
    d. AWS Transit Gateway

4. Which AWS service distributes incoming application traffic across multiple targets?
   a. Amazon VPC
   b. Elastic Load Balancer
   c. AWS Transit Gateway
   d. Amazon Route 53
5. Which AWS service provides a fast Content Delivery Network (CDN) service?
   a. AWS Transfer Family
   b. AWS Global Accelerator
   c. Amazon CloudFront
   d. AWS Site-to-Site VPN
6. Which AWS tool allows you to manage AWS resources from your terminal or command prompt using scripts and commands?
   a. AWS Management Console
   b. AWS SDKs
   c. AWS CLI (Command Line Interface)
   d. AWS CloudShell
7. A developer team wants a managed service to automatically run **unit tests and package applications** every time they push code to GitHub. Which AWS service best fits this use case?
   a. AWS CodeCommit
   b. AWS CodeBuild
   c. AWS Lambda
   d. AWS CloudFormation
8. Which AWS service automates the software release process by orchestrating build, test, and deployment workflows?
   a. AWS CodePipeline
   b. AWS CodeDeploy
   c. AWS CodeCommit
   d. AWS CodeArtifact

9. A company is troubleshooting a **serverless application built with AWS Lambda**. They want to trace requests end-to-end and pinpoint where latency issues occur. Which AWS service should they use?
    a. AWS CloudWatch
    b. AWS X-Ray
    c. AWS Config
    d. Amazon Inspector
10. Which new AWS service introduces a **spec-driven AI-powered IDE** that guides developers from natural-language requirements to production-ready code?
    a. Amazon Q Developer
    b. AWS CodeWhisperer
    c. AWS Kiro
    d. AWS Cloud9
11. A company is planning to migrate its on-premises database to AWS. Which AWS service can help with this migration process?
    a. AWS DataSync
    b. AWS Database Migration Service (DMS)
    c. AWS Transfer Family
    d. AWS Snowball
12. A developer needs to deploy a new web application to AWS and automatically scale the infrastructure based on incoming traffic. Which AWS service should the developer use?
    a. AWS Direct Connect
    b. AWS Elastic Load Balancer
    c. AWS CodeDeploy
    d. AWS CloudFront
13. A company wants to ensure low-latency access to its web application for users around the globe. Which AWS service can help achieve this requirement?
    a. AWS Direct Connect
    b. Amazon Route 53
    c. AWS Global Accelerator
    d. AWS Site-to-Site VPN

14. A development team wants to automate their entire release process, including building code, running tests, and deploying applications to AWS whenever new code is committed. Which AWS service should they use?
    a. AWS CodeBuild
    b. AWS CodePipeline
    c. AWS Cloud9
    d. AWS X-Ray
15. An organization needs to securely connect its on-premises data centre to AWS without using the public internet. Which AWS service provides this capability?
    a. AWS Direct Connect
    b. Amazon Route 53
    c. AWS Global Accelerator
    d. AWS Site-to-Site VPN
16. A healthcare company needs to connect its VPC securely to an AWS service for processing sensitive patient data. Compliance rules state that traffic **must not traverse the public internet**. Which AWS service should the company use?
    a. Amazon Route 53
    b. AWS Direct Connect
    c. AWS PrivateLink
    d. AWS Site-to-Site VPN
17. A company wants to distribute its media content globally with low latency and high transfer speeds. Which AWS service can fulfil this requirement?
    a. AWS Direct Connect
    b. Amazon Route 53
    c. AWS Global Accelerator
    d. AWS CloudFront
18. A company is migrating from an on-premises Oracle database to Amazon Aurora PostgreSQL. They want to keep the source database running during the migration and ensure the target stays updated with ongoing changes until cutover. Which AWS service should they use?
    a. AWS Schema Conversion Tool (SCT)
    b. AWS Database Migration Service (DMS)
    c. AWS Application Migration Service (MGN)
    d. AWS DataSync

19. A company is planning to migrate large volumes of data to AWS and requires a secure and efficient data transfer solution. Which AWS service is suitable for this use case?
    a. AWS DataSync
    b. AWS Database Migration Service (DMS)
    c. AWS Transfer Family
    d. AWS Snowball
20. A global team of developers needs secure access to AWS and on-premises resources from their laptops while working remotely. Which AWS service should they use?
    a. AWS Site-to-Site VPN
    b. AWS Client VPN
    c. AWS Direct Connect
    d. Amazon VPC Peering

Answers

1. c
2. a
3. b
4. b
5. c
6. c
7. b
8. a
9. b
10. c
11. b
12. b
13. c
14. b
15. d
16. c
17. d
18. b
19. d
20. b

Chapter 7
AWS Core Services - Part III

Introduction

In the previous chapter, we explored the core AWS services that form the foundation of any cloud environment, including compute, storage, networking, databases, migration tools, and developer tools. These services act as the building blocks for deploying and managing applications on AWS, helping organizations run workloads efficiently and scale as needed.

In this chapter, we shift focus to AWS security, management and governance, and application integration tools. We will examine how AWS secures the cloud through the shared responsibility model, along with the services that help customers protect their data and applications. We will also look at tools that enable organizations to monitor, automate, and govern their cloud environments, as well as services that support communication and integration between distributed application components. Together, these capabilities help build secure, well-managed, and scalable cloud architectures on AWS.

Structure

In this chapter, we will explore the following topics:

- Understanding Infrastructure Security
- Understanding Data Security

- Security, Identity and Compliance services of AWS
- Management and Governance Services of AWS
- Application Integration Services of AWS

Understanding Infrastructure Security

Before we jump into specific security services like our previous chapters, let us understand why we are focusing on infrastructure security first. Think of it as building a strong foundation for your house before adding fancy decorations. We will cover basic elements like Virtual Private Clouds (VPCs), security groups, and Network Access Control Lists (NACLs). These are like the locks and keys that keep your online space safe. Without them, your digital "*house*" could be vulnerable to bad actors. So, let us start with the basics to build a solid security foundation for your AWS "*home*."

- **Virtual Private Cloud (VPC)**
    - VPC enables you to create isolated sections of the AWS cloud, while providing network-level security.
    - It allows you to define private subnets, control inbound and outbound traffic with security groups and Network Access Control Lists (NACLs), and establish VPN connections for secure communication.
    - **Example:** By configuring VPC with private and public subnets, you can segregate sensitive data from public-facing applications, enhancing security.
- **Security Groups**
    - Security groups act as virtual firewalls for your Amazon EC2 instances, while controlling inbound and outbound traffic based on specified rules.
    - You can define rules to allow only necessary traffic, such as SSH for administration or HTTP/HTTPS for web traffic, while blocking all other access.
    - **Example:** Configuring a security group to allow inbound SSH access only from specific IP addresses limits exposure to potential threats.
- **Network Access Control Lists (NACLs)**
    - NACLs are stateless firewalls that control traffic at the subnet level, while allowing you to set rules for both inbound and outbound traffic.
    - They provide an additional layer of security by filtering traffic before it reaches the instances.
    - **Example:** By configuring NACLs to deny inbound traffic from specific IP ranges or protocols, you can block potential attackers from accessing your network.

- **Internet Gateway**
    - An internet gateway facilitates communication between instances in your VPC and the internet.
    - It acts as a gateway for traffic destined for public IP addresses, while enabling instances to connect to the internet while preventing unsolicited inbound traffic.
    - **Example:** By attaching an internet gateway to your VPC, you enable instances in the VPC to access external services such as Amazon S3 or Amazon RDS securely.

These components work together to establish a secure and isolated environment within the AWS cloud, safeguarding your infrastructure from unauthorized access and potential threats. By implementing robust security measures at the infrastructure level, organizations can create a solid foundation for hosting their applications and data in the cloud.

Aspect	Security Groups	NACLs
Type of Control	Instance level	Subnet level
Stateful/Stateless	Stateful	Stateless
Evaluation Order	Applied before NACLs	Applied after Security Groups
Rules	Allow traffic	Allow and deny traffic
Number of Rules	Limited (up to 50)	More rules (up to 200)
Flexibility	Less flexible	More flexible
Logging	Yes	No

Table 7.1: *Comparing Security Groups and NACLs*

Understanding Data Security

Data security encompasses various components to ensure data integrity, confidentiality, and availability. These components include encryption, access controls, data backups, and monitoring.

- **Encryption:** AWS services like S3 offer encryption-at-rest features, automatically encrypting data stored in the bucket using Server-Side Encryption (SSE). This ensures that data remains encrypted while stored in S3, while protecting it from unauthorized access even if someone gains physical access to the underlying storage hardware.
- **Access Controls:** IAM allows for fine-grained access control over AWS resources, which enables administrators to define who can access specific resources and what actions they can perform. For example, IAM policies can restrict access to S3 buckets based on user roles or permissions.

- **Data Backups:** AWS Backup simplifies the process of creating and managing backups across various AWS services, including S3, EBS, and RDS. With AWS Backup, users can define backup schedules, retention policies, and lifecycle management rules to ensure data integrity and availability.
- **Monitoring:** AWS services such as CloudTrail and CloudWatch provide real-time monitoring and logging capabilities. CloudTrail records API activity and changes made to AWS resources, while CloudWatch monitors system performance metrics and triggers alerts based on predefined thresholds. These tools enable users to detect and respond to security incidents promptly.

By leveraging these built-in encryption mechanisms and services such as IAM, AWS Backup, CloudTrail, and CloudWatch, users can enhance data security and compliance with regulatory requirements.

Now that the importance of a system's infrastructure and data security is clear, let us explore the AWS services that help users maintain the highest levels of security in the AWS Cloud environment.

Security, Identity, and Compliance

Security, Identity, and Compliance services in AWS provide the tools to protect your data, manage access, and ensure adherence to regulatory requirements. These services help you build a secure cloud foundation by combining identity management, encryption, monitoring, and governance into one cohesive framework.

AWS Identity and Access Management (IAM)

AWS Identity and Access Management (IAM) is a centralized service that helps you manage access to AWS resources securely. It enables you to control who can access your resources and what actions they can perform.

IAM consists of several key components, including:

- **Users:** IAM allows you to create individual users within your AWS account, each with their own set of credentials (such as a username and password). Users represent the individuals or entities that interact with your AWS resources.

Example: John Smith, an IT administrator, creates an IAM user named "**Jane_Doe**" for a new developer joining the team. He assigns permissions to Jane that allow her to access specific AWS resources required for her job, such as EC2 instances for development and S3 buckets for storing code.

- **Groups:** Groups are collections of IAM users. You can assign permissions to groups to easily manage access for multiple users who require the same level of permissions. Instead of assigning permissions to each user individually, you can assign them to groups and then add users to those groups.

  Example: In a large organization, there are multiple teams, including Development, Operations, and Marketing. The IT administrator creates IAM groups named "**DevTeam**," "**OpsTeam**," and "**MarketingTeam**" and assigns relevant permissions to each group. When new employees join these teams, the administrator simply adds them to the appropriate IAM group, automatically granting them the necessary permissions.

- **Roles:** IAM roles are like users, but they are intended for use by AWS services or applications rather than individual users. Roles define a set of permissions and can be assumed by AWS services, applications, or other entities. Roles are often used to grant permissions to resources within an AWS account or to enable cross-account access.

  Example: A web application hosted on EC2 instances needs to access resources in an S3 bucket. Instead of embedding long-term credentials directly into the application's code, the developer creates an IAM role named "**WebAppRole**" with permissions to access the S3 bucket. The application running on the EC2 instances assumes this role to obtain temporary security credentials, while enhancing security and reducing the risk of credential exposure.

- **Policies:** IAM policies are JSON documents that define permissions. They specify the actions that are allowed or denied on which AWS resources. Policies can be attached to users, groups, roles, or AWS resources directly. IAM policies are the primary mechanism for controlling access to AWS resources.

To understand policies better, let us look at how organizations can utilize policies for in their operations.

Scenario: An organization wants to enforce strict security measures to prevent unauthorized access to sensitive data stored in its S3 buckets. They need to ensure that only authorized users and applications have access to specific S3 buckets, and that access is granted based on the principle of least privilege.

Solution: The organization creates IAM policies to define permissions and attach them to IAM users, groups, or roles as needed. Here is how they might implement this:

1. **IAM Policy for S3 Access:**

   a. The organization creates a custom IAM policy named "**S3AccessPolicy**" that allows read and write access to specific S3 buckets.

b. This policy includes a list of actions allowed (for example, `s3:GetObject`, `s3:PutObject`) and specifies the ARN (Amazon Resource Name) of the S3 buckets to which the policy applies.

c. The policy also includes conditions to restrict access based on IP address, time of day, or other factors, if necessary.

2. **Attaching Policies:**
   a. The organization attaches the "`S3AccessPolicy`" to IAM users, groups, or roles that require access to the specified S3 buckets.
   b. For example, they attach the policy to the "`DevTeam`" IAM group to grant S3 access to developers, or to an IAM role assumed by an EC2 instance running an application that needs to read/write data to the S3 buckets.

3. **Testing and Validation:**
   a. The organization tests the permissions by simulating different access scenarios using IAM policy simulator or by performing real-world tests.
   b. They verify that users, groups, or applications have the appropriate level of access to the S3 buckets without granting unnecessary permissions.

By using IAM policies, the organization can effectively control access to their S3 buckets, enforce security best practices, and ensure compliance with regulatory requirements. Policies provide granular control over permissions, which allows organizations to tailor access permissions to their specific security needs.

Feature	IAM Users	IAM Groups	IAM Roles
Description	Individual entities representing users	Collections of users with similar permissions	Entities with temporary credentials for applications or services
Use Case	Used for individual human users	Used to group users with similar access needs	Used to grant permissions to AWS services, applications, or users
Authentication	Can log in with their own credentials	Can log in with their own credentials	Not intended for interactive logins, used by applications or services
Permissions	Can have policies attached directly	Can have policies attached directly	Can have policies attached directly
	Can belong to multiple groups	Can belong to multiple groups	Can be associated with multiple policies
	Permissions are granted individually or via group membership	Users inherit permissions from the group they belong to	Assume a role to temporarily assume permissions

Feature	IAM Users	IAM Groups	IAM Roles
Management	Managed individually	Managed as a collection	Managed as a collection
	Users can be added to and removed from groups	Users can be added to and removed from groups	Roles can be created, modified, and deleted

Table 7.2: *Comparing Key Aspects of IAM Users, Groups and Roles*

IAM offers several features and capabilities to help you manage access to your AWS resources effectively:

- **Granular Permissions:** IAM allows you to define fine-grained permissions using policies. You can specify permissions at the API level, resource level, or even down to the level of individual actions within a service.
- **Multi-Factor Authentication (MFA):** IAM supports MFA, which adds an extra layer of security to user authentication. With MFA enabled, users must provide a second form of authentication (such as a one-time password from a hardware token or mobile app) in addition to their username and password.
- **Identity Federation:** IAM supports identity federation, which allows you to grant temporary access to AWS resources for users authenticated through external identity providers (such as Active Directory, LDAP, or SAML-based identity providers).
- **Access Control Lists (ACLs):** IAM provides Access Control Lists (ACLs) that allow you to control access to individual S3 buckets and objects. You can use ACLs to grant read or write access to specific users or groups.
- **IAM Access Analyzer:** IAM Access Analyzer helps you analyze resource policies to identify unintended access and resource sharing across AWS accounts. It helps you identify and remediate security risks by providing findings for your resources.
- **IAM Identity Centre: IAM Identity Center (formerly AWS Single Sign-On)** is a cloud-based service that simplifies access management across AWS accounts and business applications. It enables you to centrally create or connect user identities, assign fine-grained permissions, and provide single sign-on access to multiple AWS accounts, the AWS Management Console, and third-party SaaS applications. By integrating with external identity providers (such as Microsoft Active Directory or Okta), IAM Identity Center supports a seamless login experience while enforcing security best practices such as multi-factor authentication and least-privilege access. This service helps organizations reduce administrative overhead, strengthen security, and provide users with consistent and secure access to the resources they need.

Overall, IAM is a fundamental service in AWS that enables you to manage access to your resources securely by controlling who can access your resources and what actions they can perform.

Amazon Key Management Service (KMS)

Amazon Key Management Service (KMS) is a fully managed service that makes it easy for you to create and control the encryption keys used to encrypt your data. With KMS, you can manage the lifecycle of encryption keys, control access to them, and audit their usage without having to build or maintain your own key management infrastructure.

Key Features

- **Centralized Key Management:** KMS provides a central location to create, store, and manage cryptographic keys used for encryption across various AWS services and applications.
- **Secure and Scalable:** KMS is designed to be highly secure and scalable, which ensures that your encryption keys are protected and available when needed, even as your workload grows.
- **Integration with AWS Services:** KMS seamlessly integrates with other AWS services, which allows you to easily encrypt and decrypt data stored in services such as S3, EBS, RDS, and Redshift.
- **Granular Access Control:** KMS allows you to define fine-grained access policies to control who can create, manage, and use encryption keys, which help you enforce security best practices and compliance requirements.
- **Built-in Auditing and Compliance:** KMS provides detailed audit logs and integrates with AWS CloudTrail for monitoring and tracking key usage, which help you meet regulatory and compliance requirements.

Developers can use Amazon KMS to encrypt sensitive data at rest and in transit, while ensuring the confidentiality and integrity of their data. KMS can be particularly useful in scenarios where data security and compliance are critical, such as protecting customer data, financial information, and intellectual property.

Amazon Cognito

Amazon Cognito is a fully managed identity and access management service that allows you to add user sign-up, sign-in, and access control to your web and mobile apps quickly and easily. It provides authentication, authorization, and user management features to help you securely manage user identities and access to your applications.

Key Features

- **User Authentication:** Cognito supports user authentication through various methods, including username/password, social identity providers such as Facebook and Google, and enterprise identity providers such as SAML and OIDC.

- **User Pools:** With Cognito User Pools, you can create a customizable user directory to store user profiles, manage sign-up and sign-in processes, and enable Multi-Factor Authentication (MFA) for added security.
- **Federated Identities:** Cognito Federated Identities allows you to authenticate users through third-party identity providers (such as Amazon, Facebook, or Google) and obtain temporary, limited-privilege AWS credentials to access AWS resources securely.
- **Secure Access Control:** Cognito lets you define fine-grained access controls and permissions for your users, groups, and resources, which allows you to enforce least privilege access and protect sensitive data.

Developers can use Amazon Cognito to implement user authentication and authorization features in their web and mobile applications without the need to manage infrastructure for user management and access control. It is particularly useful for scenarios where you need to authenticate users, manage user identities and profiles, and control access to resources securely across different platforms and devices.

Amazon GuardDuty

Amazon GuardDuty is a threat detection service that continuously monitors for malicious activity and unauthorized behavior in your AWS environment. It analyzes various data sources such as VPC Flow Logs, CloudTrail logs, and DNS logs to identify potential security threats and anomalies.

Key Features

- **Threat Detection:** GuardDuty uses machine learning algorithms and threat intelligence feeds to detect common attack patterns such as unusual API calls, compromised instances, and unauthorized access attempts.
- **Intelligent Insights:** It provides detailed findings and actionable insights about detected threats such as severity levels, affected resources, and recommended remediation steps to help you prioritize and respond to security incidents effectively.
- **Centralized Management:** GuardDuty offers a centralized dashboard where you can view and manage security findings from across your AWS accounts and regions, which makes it easier to monitor your entire infrastructure for security threats.
- **Automated Remediation:** GuardDuty can automatically trigger response actions such as disabling compromised instances or blocking suspicious IP addresses through AWS Lambda functions or CloudWatch Events to mitigate security risks in real-time.

Developers and security teams can use Amazon GuardDuty to enhance the security posture of their AWS environments by proactively detecting and responding to security threats and vulnerabilities. It provides continuous monitoring and threat intelligence capabilities, which helps organizations to improve their overall security posture and compliance with industry standards and regulations.

Amazon Inspector

Amazon Inspector is a security assessment service that helps identify potential security vulnerabilities in your AWS environment. With Amazon Inspector, you can easily assess the security of your AWS resources and identify any security issues or misconfigurations.

Key Features

- **Comprehensive Security Assessments:** Amazon Inspector performs thorough security assessments of your AWS resources including EC2 instances, container images, and AWS Lambda functions, as well as code repositories.
- **Customizable Assessment Templates:** You can create custom assessment templates to focus on specific security concerns or compliance requirements.
- **Continuous Monitoring:** Amazon Inspector continuously monitors your AWS environment for security issues and alerts you to any potential threats.
- **Integration with AWS Config:** Amazon Inspector integrates with AWS Config, which allows you to view and manage the configuration of your AWS resources.

As a developer, you can use Amazon Inspector to:

- Identify security vulnerabilities in your AWS environment and take steps to remediate them.
- Ensure compliance with security standards and regulations, such as PCI DSS, HIPAA, and GDPR.

Amazon Macie

Amazon Macie is a security service that uses machine learning to automatically discover, classify, and protect sensitive data in your AWS environment. With Amazon Macie, you can easily identify and secure sensitive data such as personal information, financial data, and intellectual property.

Key Features

- **Automatic Data Discovery and Classification:** Amazon Macie uses ML to automatically discover and classify sensitive data in your AWS environment, including data stored in S3 buckets, databases, and other data stores.
- **Customizable Data Classification:** You can create custom data classification models to identify specific types of sensitive data that are relevant to your organization.
- **Data Protection:** Amazon Macie provides several data protection options, such as encryption, access controls, and data masking, to help secure sensitive data.

- **Integration with AWS Lake Formation:** Amazon Macie integrates with AWS Lake Formation, which allows you to easily analyze and query data from multiple sources.

As a developer, you can use Amazon Macie to:

- Identify and protect sensitive data in your AWS environment, while ensuring compliance with data privacy regulations such as GDPR, HIPAA, and CCPA.
- Automate data classification and protection, which reduces the need for manual processes and increasing the accuracy of data classification.

AWS Certificate Manager (ACM)

AWS Certificate Manager (ACM) is a service that allows you to easily provision, manage, and deploy SSL/TLS certificates for your AWS resources. With ACM, you can ensure secure communication between your customers and your web applications, APIs, and other services.

Key Features

- **Easy Certificate Management:** ACM simplifies the process of obtaining, renewing, and managing SSL/TLS certificates for your AWS resources.
- **Integration with AWS Services:** ACM integrates with many AWS services, including Elastic Load Balancer, Amazon Route 53, and Amazon CloudFront, which makes it easy to deploy certificates across your AWS environment.
- **Customizable Certificate Management:** You can create custom certificate templates to meet your specific security needs and also import your own certificates into ACM.
- **Automatic Certificate Renewal:** ACM automatically renews certificates before they expire, which ensures that your applications and services remain secure and available.

As a developer, you can use ACM to:

- Easily provision and manage SSL/TLS certificates for your AWS resources to ensure secure communication with your customers.
- Simplify the certificate management process and reduce the need for manual processes and minimizing the risk of certificate-related outages.

AWS CloudHSM

AWS CloudHSM (Hardware Security Module) offers secure cryptographic key storage and cryptographic operations to safeguard sensitive data and meet compliance requirements in the cloud. It provides dedicated Hardware Security Modules (HSMs) within the AWS cloud infrastructure, which enables customers to generate, store, and manage encryption keys securely.

Key Features

- **Hardware Security Module (HSM) Integration:** AWS CloudHSM seamlessly integrates with your existing applications and cryptographic libraries, which allows you to offload sensitive cryptographic operations to dedicated HSMs.
- **Secure Key Storage:** CloudHSM provides FIPS 140-2 Level 3 validated HSMs, while ensuring the highest level of security for storing cryptographic keys. Keys never leave the HSM unencrypted, thus enhancing data protection.
- **Customizable Access Controls:** Administrators have granular control over access permissions and policies for cryptographic keys, while allowing them to define who can access keys and under what circumstances. This enhances security and compliance.
- **High Availability and Durability:** CloudHSM clusters are deployed across multiple Availability Zones (AZs) within a region, while providing high availability and durability for cryptographic key operations and ensuring business continuity.
- **Scalability and Performance:** With the ability to scale HSM capacity up or down based on demand, CloudHSM offers consistent and predictable performance for cryptographic operations, while meeting the needs of both small-scale and enterprise-level applications.

Developers can leverage AWS CloudHSM to enhance the security of their applications by offloading cryptographic operations such as key generation, encryption, decryption, and signing to dedicated hardware security modules.

AWS Firewall Manager

AWS Firewall Manager is a centralized security management service provided by AWS that allows administrators to configure and manage firewall rules across multiple AWS accounts and resources. It simplifies the process of enforcing and managing security policies for AWS resources, while ensuring consistent protection and compliance across an organization's cloud infrastructure.

Key Features

- **Centralized Security Management:** AWS Firewall Manager enables administrators to define and enforce security policies centrally across multiple AWS accounts and resources, while providing a unified approach to security management.
- **Automated Rule Enforcement:** Administrators can create security rules and policies using AWS WAF (Web Application Firewall) or AWS Shield Advanced, and automatically enforce these rules across all resources within their AWS environment.
- **Compliance and Governance:** Firewall Manager helps organizations maintain compliance with regulatory requirements and industry standards by providing visibility into security policy enforcement and compliance status across their AWS infrastructure.

- **Customizable Security Rules:** Administrators can create custom security rules tailored to their organization's specific security requirements such as blocking certain types of traffic or allowing access only from specified IP ranges and apply these rules consistently across their AWS environment.

Developers and administrators can use AWS Firewall Manager to streamline security management and ensure consistent enforcement of security policies across their AWS infrastructure.

AWS Secrets Manager

AWS Secrets Manager is a service provided by AWS that helps you securely store, manage, and retrieve sensitive information such as API keys, passwords, and database credentials. It enables you to centralize the management of your application secrets, while ensuring that they are encrypted and protected both at rest and in transit.

Key Features

- **Secure Storage:** AWS Secrets Manager encrypts your secrets using AWS Key Management Service (KMS) keys, while ensuring they are securely stored and protected from unauthorized access. Secrets are encrypted both at rest and in transit, providing end-to-end security.
- **Centralized Management:** Secrets Manager allows you to centralize the management of your application secrets, which makes it easier to rotate, manage access controls, and audit usage. You can store secrets for multiple applications and services in a single, centralized location.
- **Secret Rotation:** Secrets Manager automates the process of rotating your secrets, such as database passwords and API keys, on a schedule or in response to specific events. This helps improve security by regularly updating sensitive credentials without requiring manual intervention.
- **Integration with AWS Services:** Secrets Manager seamlessly integrates with other AWS services such as Amazon RDS, Amazon Redshift, and Amazon DocumentDB, which allows you to securely retrieve and inject secrets directly into your applications and infrastructure.
- **Auditing and Monitoring:** Secrets Manager provides audit logs and monitoring capabilities, which allows you to track access to your secrets, monitor rotation activity, and detect any unauthorized access attempts in real-time.

Developers can use AWS Secrets Manager to enhance the security of their applications by securely storing and managing sensitive information such as database credentials, API keys, and encryption keys.

AWS Security Hub

AWS Security Hub is a comprehensive security service provided by AWS that helps you centrally manage and automate security compliance checks across your AWS environment. It provides a unified view of your security posture, aggregating findings from various AWS services and third-party security tools, and enables you to prioritize and remediate security issues effectively.

Key Features

- **Centralized Security Dashboard**: Security Hub offers a centralized dashboard that provides a unified view of your security posture across your AWS accounts and regions. It aggregates security findings from various AWS services such as Amazon GuardDuty, Amazon Inspector, and AWS Firewall Manager, as well as integrated third-party security tools.
- **Continuous Security Monitoring**: Security Hub continuously monitors your AWS environment for security issues, compliance violations, and potential vulnerabilities. It automatically ingests security findings from AWS services and external providers, which enables you to identify and respond to security threats in real-time.
- **Security Standards and Compliance**: Security Hub provides built-in security standards and compliance checks based on industry best practices and regulatory requirements such as CIS AWS Foundations Benchmark, PCI DSS, and AWS Foundational Security Best Practices.
- **Automated Remediation**: Security Hub allows you to automate the remediation of security findings using AWS Lambda functions or other AWS services. You can define custom response and remediation actions to address security issues quickly and efficiently, which reduces the time to resolution.

Developers and security teams can use AWS Security Hub to gain visibility into their AWS security posture, identify and prioritize security issues, and automate the remediation of security findings.

AWS Shield

AWS Shield is a managed Distributed Denial of Service (DDoS) protection service that safeguards web applications running on AWS against DDoS attacks.

Key Features

- **Automatic Protection:** Shield provides automatic detection and mitigation of DDoS attacks, while protecting your applications without any intervention.
- **Always-On:** It offers continuous protection, ensuring your applications remain available and responsive during DDoS attacks.

- **Global Coverage:** Shield protects against attacks targeting applications hosted on AWS globally, across multiple AWS Regions.
- **Layer 3, 4, and 7 Protection:** It defends against network and application layer DDoS attacks, mitigating threats at different levels of the OSI model.
- **Cost-Effective:** Shield is included at no additional cost for all AWS customers, with optional paid plans offering advanced features for higher protection levels.

Developers can integrate AWS Shield into their applications effortlessly to automatically protect against DDoS attacks, while ensuring continuous availability without manual intervention.

AWS WAF

AWS WAF (Web Application Firewall) is a scalable web application firewall service that helps protect your web applications from common web exploits that could affect application availability, compromise security, or consume excessive resources.

Key Features

- **Managed Web Application Firewall:** AWS WAF provides a managed solution to protect web applications from common attack patterns such as SQL injection, cross-site scripting, and more.
- **Customizable Rules:** It allows you to create custom rules to filter web traffic based on IP addresses, HTTP headers, URI strings, or request attributes, which provides granular control over web application traffic.
- **Managed Rulesets:** AWS WAF offers managed rulesets developed by AWS security experts and industry leaders, which can be easily deployed to provide immediate protection against common threats without the need for custom rule creation.
- **Real-Time Monitoring and Metrics:** It provides real-time visibility into web traffic and security events through Amazon CloudWatch metrics and AWS WAF logs, which allows you to monitor and analyze traffic patterns and security threats effectively.

Developers can use AWS WAF to enhance the security of their web applications by implementing customizable rules to filter and block malicious traffic.

Amazon Detective

Amazon Detective is a fully managed service by AWS that helps to analyze, investigate, and identify the root cause of security findings or suspicious activities across your AWS resources.

Key Features

- **Automated Data Analysis:** Amazon Detective automatically collects log data from your AWS resources such as VPC Flow Logs, CloudTrail logs, and GuardDuty findings, and uses ML algorithms to analyze and correlate this data to identify potential security issues.
- **Graphical Investigation Interface:** It provides a graphical user interface that visualizes security findings and related resource behaviors, making it easier for security teams to investigate and understand complex security incidents.
- **Security Insights:** Amazon Detective generates security insights and recommendations based on its analysis of your AWS environment, which helps you prioritize and focus on the most critical security issues.
- **Behavioral Analysis:** It performs behavioral analysis to detect unusual activity patterns and anomalies across your AWS resources, which allows you to identify potential security threats and unauthorized access attempts.

Developers and security teams can use Amazon Detective to improve the security of their AWS environment by gaining insights into security incidents, identifying potential threats, and responding to security issues more effectively.

Amazon Audit Manager

Amazon Audit Manager is an AWS service designed to help you simplify the process of assessing and managing compliance with industry standards and regulations. It automates evidence collection and streamlines the audit process, which makes it easier to demonstrate compliance to auditors and stakeholders.

Key Features

- **Automated Assessments:** Audit Manager automates the collection of evidence from AWS services and resources, while streamlining the assessment process and reducing manual effort.
- **Prebuilt Frameworks:** It provides prebuilt frameworks for common regulatory standards such as GDPR, HIPAA, and SOC 2 to allow you to assess compliance against these standards efficiently.
- **Custom Assessments:** Audit Manager allows you to create custom assessments tailored to your organization's specific requirements, while providing flexibility to assess compliance with internal policies and industry-specific regulations.
- **Centralized Evidence Repository:** It offers a centralized repository for storing evidence collected during assessments, which makes it easy to track and manage compliance data over time.

- **Integration with AWS Services:** Audit Manager integrates with other AWS services such as AWS Config and AWS Security Hub, which enables you to leverage existing data sources and automate evidence collection from your AWS environment.

Developers and compliance teams can use Amazon Audit Manager to streamline the compliance assessment process, reduce manual effort, and maintain a centralized repository of compliance evidence.

Other AWS Security Services

AWS Artifact is a central resource that provides on-demand access to AWS compliance reports and security documentation. Organizations can download audit artifacts such as Service Organization Control (SOC) reports, ISO certifications, and Payment Card Industry (PCI) reports to demonstrate compliance with regulatory standards. By offering self-service access to these documents, AWS Artifact helps businesses streamline their compliance processes, reduce audit preparation time, and gain confidence in AWS's adherence to global security frameworks.

AWS Directory Service enables you to run Microsoft Active Directory (AD) as a managed service in the AWS Cloud. With options like AWS Managed Microsoft AD and AD Connector, organizations can extend their existing on-premises directories or create cloud-native directories to manage users and groups. This integration makes it easier to provide single sign-on for applications, enforce group policies, and authenticate users seamlessly across AWS resources, thereby improving security while reducing administrative overhead.

AWS Resource Access Manager (RAM) is a service that allows you to securely share AWS resources across accounts within your organization. Instead of duplicating resources, you can centrally create services such as Amazon VPC subnets, Route 53 Resolver rules, or AWS License Manager configurations and share them with other accounts. This promotes better governance, cost efficiency, and consistency, while ensuring that multiple teams or business units can collaborate using the same infrastructure resources without unnecessary duplication.

Exercise 7.1: Test your cloud knowledge

1. Which AWS service provides managed DDoS (Distributed Denial of Service) protection for your web applications running on AWS?
    a. AWS WAF (Web Application Firewall)
    b. AWS Shield
    c. AWS Inspector
    d. Amazon GuardDuty

2. Which AWS service allows you to centrally manage and automate security compliance checks across your AWS environment?
    a. AWS Config
    b. AWS Security Hub
    c. AWS IAM
    d. AWS Firewall Manager
3. In AWS IAM, what is the primary purpose of an IAM role?
    a. Assigning permissions to users
    b. Defining policies for S3 buckets
    c. Delegating access to AWS resources without sharing credentials
    d. Enforcing multi-factor authentication
4. Which AWS service provides managed web application firewall capabilities to protect against common web exploits?
    a. Amazon Inspector
    b. AWS WAF (Web Application Firewall)
    c. AWS Shield
    d. AWS Firewall Manager
5. Which AWS service is used for managing access and permissions to AWS resources?
    a. AWS Inspector
    b. Amazon GuardDuty
    c. AWS IAM (Identity and Access Management)
    d. AWS Config

Answers

1. b
2. c
3. b
4. b
5. c

Management and Governance

Management and governance services in AWS give organizations the ability to monitor, automate, and control their cloud environments effectively. These services ensure visibility, compliance, and cost optimization, while helping teams operate securely and efficiently at scale.

Amazon CloudWatch

Amazon CloudWatch is a monitoring and observability service provided by AWS that collects and tracks metrics, logs, and events from AWS resources and applications. It enables developers, system administrators, and DevOps teams to gain insights into the performance, operational health, and behavior of their applications and infrastructure in real-time.

Key Features

- **Metrics Monitoring:** CloudWatch allows users to collect and monitor various metrics such as CPU utilization, network traffic, latency, and error rates from AWS services and custom applications. These metrics can be visualized on dashboards and used to set alarms for triggering notifications based on predefined thresholds.
- **Logs Monitoring:** CloudWatch Logs enables users to collect, monitor, and analyze log data generated by AWS resources and applications in real-time. It provides centralized log storage, search capabilities, and integration with AWS services for automated log analysis and troubleshooting.
- **Events Monitoring:** CloudWatch Events provides a stream of system events that describe changes in AWS resources, such as instance state changes, API calls, and scheduled events. Users can create event rules to trigger automated actions in response to specific events, enabling event-driven architectures and automated workflows.
- **Dashboards:** CloudWatch Dashboards allow users to create custom dashboards to visualize metrics and alarms from multiple AWS services and applications in a single view. Dashboards can be customized with widgets such as line charts, stacked graphs, and text widgets to provide real-time insights into system performance and health.
- **Alarms and Notifications:** CloudWatch Alarms enable users to set alarms on metrics and trigger notifications (via Amazon SNS) when the metric breaches predefined thresholds. Alarms can be configured to trigger actions such as sending notifications, while invoking AWS Lambda functions, or stopping/restarting EC2 instances.

Use Cases for Developers

- **Performance Monitoring:** Developers can use CloudWatch to monitor the performance of their applications and infrastructure in real-time, tracking metrics such as response times, error rates, and resource utilization to identify performance bottlenecks and optimize application performance.

- **Log Analysis:** CloudWatch Logs can be used by developers to collect and analyze log data generated by their applications, which enables them to troubleshoot issues, debug code, and gain insights into application behavior and user activity.
- **Automated Scaling:** CloudWatch Alarms can be used by developers to monitor application metrics such as CPU utilization or request latency and automatically scale resources up or down in response to changes in demand. This enables developers to maintain optimal performance and cost efficiency for their applications.

Other features of CloudWatch

- **Integration with AWS Services:** CloudWatch integrates seamlessly with other AWS services such as EC2, Lambda, S3, and RDS, which allows developers to collect and monitor metrics, logs, and events from a wide range of AWS resources and services.
- **Cost Management:** Developers should be aware of the cost implications of using CloudWatch, particularly for high-frequency monitoring and retention of log data. Understanding CloudWatch pricing models and optimizing monitoring configurations can help manage costs effectively.
- **Security and Compliance:** CloudWatch provides features for encrypting data at rest and in transit, while controlling access to monitoring data using IAM policies and enabling compliance with industry standards and regulations such as GDPR and HIPAA.
- **Global Availability:** CloudWatch is available in multiple AWS regions worldwide, which allows developers to monitor applications and infrastructure deployed globally and ensure consistent monitoring and observability across different geographic locations.

Amazon CloudFormation

Amazon CloudFormation is a service provided by AWS that enables developers to create and manage AWS infrastructure as code using templates. It allows you to define your infrastructure in a declarative format using JSON or YAML templates, which can then be provisioned and managed in a repeatable and automated manner.

Key Features

- **Infrastructure as Code (IaC):** CloudFormation enables you to define your AWS infrastructure in a template format, while allowing you to version-control, share, and provision infrastructure changes in a consistent and repeatable way.
- **Template-Based Provisioning:** You can create templates that describe the resources and their configurations needed for your applications. CloudFormation then

provisions and configures these resources automatically, while ensuring consistency and eliminating manual intervention.

- **Stack Management:** CloudFormation organizes resources into stacks, allowing you to manage and update related resources as a single unit. You can create, update, delete, and roll back stacks easily, simplifying the management of complex environments.
- **Change Sets:** Before making changes to your infrastructure, CloudFormation allows you to preview the changes using change sets. This enables you to review and approve proposed changes before they are applied, reducing the risk of unintended modifications.
- **Integration with AWS Services:** CloudFormation integrates with various AWS services, which enables you to provision a wide range of resources such as EC2 instances, S3 buckets, Lambda functions, and more, as part of your infrastructure templates.

Use Cases for Developers

- **Infrastructure Automation:** Developers can use CloudFormation to automate the provisioning and management of infrastructure resources needed for their applications to reduce manual effort and maintain consistency across environments.
- **Continuous Deployment:** CloudFormation templates can be integrated with CI/CD pipelines to automate the deployment of infrastructure changes alongside application code changes, while enabling continuous integration and deployment practices.

Amazon EC2 Auto Scaling

Amazon EC2 Auto Scaling is a service provided by AWS that automatically adjusts the number of EC2 instances in a fleet based on user-defined policies. It maintains application availability and performance by dynamically scaling EC2 capacity in response to changing demand.

Key Features

- **Automatic Scaling:** EC2 Auto Scaling automatically adds or removes EC2 instances based on metrics such as CPU utilization, network traffic, or custom application metrics. This ensures that the application always has the right amount of compute capacity to handle varying workloads.
- **Integration with AWS Services:** EC2 Auto Scaling seamlessly integrates with other AWS services such as Elastic Load Balancing (ELB) and Amazon CloudWatch, which allows you to create scalable and resilient architectures that respond dynamically to changes in demand.
- **Health Monitoring and Recovery:** EC2 Auto Scaling monitors the health of EC2 instances and replaces unhealthy instances automatically. It performs health checks on instances and terminates or replaces instances that fail health checks, thus ensuring high availability and reliability of applications.

Amazon CloudTrail

AWS CloudTrail is a service provided by AWS that enables governance, compliance, operational auditing, and risk auditing of your AWS account. It records API calls and actions taken by users, roles, or AWS services within your account and delivers detailed logs for analysis, monitoring, and security investigations.

Key Features

- **Audit Trail:** CloudTrail captures a comprehensive record of API calls and actions made within your AWS account like the identity of the caller, the time of the call, the request parameters, and the response elements.
- **Centralized Logging:** CloudTrail provides centralized logging of AWS API activity across multiple regions and accounts, which allows you to track changes and monitor account activity from a single location.
- **Security and Compliance:** CloudTrail helps organizations meet security and compliance requirements by providing an audit trail of user and resource activity, facilitating security analysis, incident response, and forensic investigations.
- **Visibility and Governance:** CloudTrail enables organizations to gain visibility into user actions, resource changes, and operational activities across their AWS infrastructure, which enhances governance, risk management, and compliance capabilities.

Use Case: Thus, by enabling CloudTrail logging, organizations can track user and resource activity within their AWS accounts, detect unauthorized access attempts, and ensure compliance with security policies and regulatory requirements.

AWS Config

AWS Config is a service provided by AWS that enables you to assess, audit, and evaluate the configuration of your AWS resources. It continuously monitors and records changes to resource configurations, which allows you to maintain compliance, troubleshoot operational issues, and improve security posture.

Key Features

- **Configuration History:** AWS Config maintains a detailed history of configuration changes to AWS resources, including resource attributes, relationships, and metadata. This enables you to track changes over time and understand the state of your infrastructure at any point in time.
- **Compliance Checks:** AWS Config allows you to define and enforce compliance rules and policies for your AWS resources. It performs continuous evaluations against these rules and generates compliance reports, which helps you to identify non-compliant resources and take corrective actions to maintain compliance.

- **Resource Inventory:** AWS Config provides a comprehensive inventory of your AWS resources, including details such as resource types, configurations, and relationships. This enables you to gain visibility into your infrastructure and understand resource dependencies and usage patterns.
- **Change Notifications:** AWS Config sends notifications when configuration changes occur to AWS resources, while allowing you to respond promptly to changes and take appropriate actions. Notifications can be delivered via Amazon SNS, enabling you to integrate with other AWS services and external systems.

Use Case: AWS Config can be used to track changes to security group configurations, identify instances with public IP addresses, and enforce encryption settings for S3 buckets.

AWS License Manager

AWS License Manager is a service provided by AWS that helps you manage your software licenses across your AWS infrastructure. It enables you to track, enforce, and optimize license usage to ensure compliance with software licensing agreements and minimize costs.

Key Features

- **License Tracking:** AWS License Manager allows you to track the usage of software licenses across your AWS accounts and resources, while providing visibility into license entitlements, allocations, and usage metrics.
- **License Entitlements:** You can define license entitlements for software products using AWS License Manager, thus specifying details such as license type, quantity, and terms of use. This enables you to enforce license compliance and prevent over-usage of licenses.
- **Automated Discovery:** AWS License Manager offers automated discovery of software installed on EC2 instances, which enables you to identify and inventory software deployments and their associated licenses.
- **License Consumption:** It provides real-time visibility into license consumption and usage patterns, which allows you to optimize license allocations, consolidate licenses, and avoid unnecessary license purchases.
- **Integration with AWS Services:** AWS License Manager integrates with other AWS services such as AWS Organizations, AWS Resource Groups, and AWS CloudFormation, which enable you to manage licenses at scale, enforce license policies, and automate license provisioning and management tasks.

Use Case: AWS License Manager can be used to monitor license usage for Microsoft SQL Server, Oracle Database, or other software products running on EC2 instances, and automatically allocate licenses based on usage metrics and license entitlements.

AWS Health Dashboard

The AWS Health Dashboard is a service provided by AWS that offers real-time status information about AWS services and regions. It provides visibility into the operational status of AWS resources and helps customers stay informed about service interruptions, performance issues, and scheduled maintenance events.

Key Features

- **Service Health Status:** The AWS Health Dashboard displays the current operational status of AWS services, including information about service disruptions, performance degradation, and availability issues. It categorizes incidents based on severity levels (such as informational, warning, and outage) to help users prioritize and respond to issues effectively.
- **Region-Specific View:** Users can view the health status of AWS services in specific regions or across all regions globally. This allows customers to assess the impact of service disruptions on their workloads and applications deployed in different AWS regions.
- **Personalized Notifications:** AWS Health Dashboard provides personalized notifications and alerts about service events and status changes. Users can subscribe to receive notifications via email, SMS, or Amazon SNS (Simple Notification Service), which enables proactive monitoring and timely communication about service incidents.
- **Scheduled Maintenance:** The dashboard includes information about scheduled maintenance events and upcoming changes to AWS services. It provides details about maintenance windows, affected resources, and recommended actions for customers to prepare for planned downtime or service interruptions.
- **Integration with AWS Organizations:** AWS Health Dashboard integrates with AWS Organizations, allowing users to view the health status of all linked accounts and Organizational Units (OUs) from a centralized dashboard. This enables organizations to monitor the health of their entire AWS environment and manage service incidents across multiple accounts and resources.

Use Case: A common use case for the AWS Health Dashboard is operational monitoring and incident response. Organizations can use the dashboard to monitor the health status of AWS services and regions, detect service disruptions or performance issues affecting their applications, and respond to incidents promptly.

AWS Service Catalog

AWS Service Catalog is a service provided by Amazon Web Services (AWS) that enables organizations to create and manage catalogs of approved IT services for use by their users, applications, and teams. It allows administrators to centrally manage and distribute approved resources and applications, enabling self-service provisioning while maintaining governance and compliance.

Key Features

- **Centralized Catalog Management:** Manage catalogs of approved IT services in a centralized location.
- **Governance and Compliance Controls:** Enforce policies, permissions, and compliance requirements for resource provisioning.
- **Versioning and Lifecycle Management:** Support versioning and lifecycle management for products and resources.
- **Customization and Extensibility:** Customize catalogs and products to specific use cases and requirements.

Use Case: A common use case for AWS Service Catalog is IT service management and governance. Organizations can use Service Catalog to create and manage catalogs of approved resources such as virtual machine images, software licenses, and infrastructure templates.

AWS Systems Manager

AWS Systems Manager is a management service provided by AWS that helps you automate and manage your AWS infrastructure and applications. It provides a unified user interface for managing operational tasks across your AWS resources, which allows you to automate administrative tasks, monitor system health, and maintain compliance.

Key Features

- **Automation:** Automate common administrative tasks and workflows using AWS Systems Manager Automation, which reduces manual effort and increasing operational efficiency.
- **Run Command:** Execute commands remotely on EC2 instances and other AWS resources at scale, which enables you to perform tasks such as software installations, patch management, and configuration updates.
- **State Manager:** Define and enforce desired configurations for your infrastructure using State Manager, while ensuring consistency and compliance across your environment.
- **Parameter Store:** Securely store and manage configuration data, secrets, and sensitive information using Parameter Store, and access them programmatically from your applications and automation workflows.
- **Patch Manager:** Automate patching of operating systems and applications on EC2 instances, while ensuring that your systems are up-to-date with the latest security patches and updates.
- **Session Manager:** Provides secure shell or CLI access to EC2 instances and on-premises servers without opening inbound ports or managing SSH keys, which enables safe remote administration with full activity logging and IAM-based access control.

Use Case: A common use case for AWS Systems Manager is managing and maintaining the operational health of your AWS infrastructure and applications. Organizations can use Systems Manager to automate administrative tasks such as software installations, patch management, and configuration updates across their EC2 instances and other AWS resources.

AWS Trusted Advisor

AWS Trusted Advisor is a service provided by AWS that helps you optimize your AWS infrastructure, improve performance, and reduce costs by providing real-time guidance and recommendations based on best practices and AWS usage patterns.

Key Features

- **Cost Optimization:** Analyze your AWS usage and spending patterns to identify cost optimization opportunities such as unused resources, idle instances, and over-provisioned capacity.
- **Performance Improvement:** Provide recommendations to improve the performance, availability, and security of your AWS infrastructure such as optimizing load balancer configurations, implementing caching strategies, and enhancing security settings.
- **Security Best Practices:** Evaluate your AWS environment against security best practices and compliance standards, while highlighting security vulnerabilities, misconfigurations, and potential security risks.
- **Fault Tolerance:** Assess the fault tolerance and resilience of your AWS architecture to identify single points of failure, resource bottlenecks, and potential reliability issues.
- **Service Limits Monitoring:** Monitor your AWS service limits and usage quotas, which alerts you when you approach or exceed service limits to prevent service disruptions and performance degradation.

Use Case: A common use case for AWS Trusted Advisor is cost optimization and resource management. Organizations can use Trusted Advisor to analyze their AWS usage and spending, identify opportunities to reduce costs, and optimize resource utilization.

AWS Organizations

AWS Organizations is a service provided by AWS that helps you centrally manage and govern multiple AWS accounts within your organization. It enables you to consolidate billing, control access to AWS services and resources, and automate the management of accounts and policies at scale.

Key Features

- **Consolidated Billing:** Aggregate and consolidate billing for multiple AWS accounts under a single payer account, while simplifying cost management and providing a unified view of spending across the organization.
- **Account Organization:** Create and manage a hierarchy of AWS accounts within your organization, allowing you to group accounts by business unit, department, or environment (for example, development, testing, production, and so on).
- **Policy-Based Management:** Define and enforce policies and controls for AWS resources and services across your organization using Service Control Policies (SCPs), while ensuring compliance with security and governance requirements.
- **Consolidated Access Management:** Centrally manage access to AWS services and resources across multiple accounts using AWS Identity and Access Management (IAM) roles, which allows you to grant permissions based on roles and policies defined at the organization level.
- **Account Automation:** Automate the creation and management of AWS accounts and resources using AWS Organizations APIs and AWS CloudFormation, which enable you to provision accounts, apply policies, and enforce standards consistently.

Use Case: A common use case for AWS Organizations is managing multi-account environments and enforcing governance and compliance policies. Organizations can use AWS Organizations to create and manage a hierarchy of AWS accounts, define centralized policies for security and compliance, and automate the provisioning and management of accounts and resources.

Brief Description on Some Other Management Services

The following is a list of other AWS management services:

- **AWS Management Console:** The AWS Management Console provides a user-friendly web interface for accessing and managing AWS services and resources.

  Use Case: Managing EC2 instances, S3 buckets, and other AWS resources without the need for command-line access.

- **AWS Well-Architected Tool:** The AWS Well-Architected Tool offers a framework for reviewing and enhancing the architecture of AWS workloads.

  Use Case: Evaluating an existing AWS workload against best practices to identify areas for improvement in terms of security, reliability, and cost optimization.

- **AWS Control Tower:** AWS Control Tower helps set up and govern a secure, multi-account AWS environment based on AWS best practices.

Use Case: Establishing a centralized governance model for managing multiple AWS accounts and ensuring compliance with organizational standards and policies.

- **AWS Compute Optimizer** is a recommendation service that analyzes your AWS resource usage (such as EC2 instances, EBS volumes, and Lambda functions) and suggests optimal configurations to improve performance and reduce costs. By leveraging machine learning models trained on millions of workloads, Compute Optimizer helps you right-size resources and avoid both over-provisioning and under-provisioning.
- **AWS Service Quotas** enables you to view and manage the limits (quotas) of AWS services in your account such as the number of EC2 instances or VPCs you can create. It provides dashboards, notifications, and automated request options to increase quotas, which helps you proactively plan capacity and avoid disruptions caused by hitting service limits.

Exercise 7.2 Test Your Cloud Skills

1. What is the primary purpose of AWS CloudTrail?
   a. Deploying and managing applications
   b. Monitoring and recording AWS API activity
   c. Configuring network security rules
   d. Analyzing website traffic patterns
2. Which AWS service enables you to define and manage your AWS infrastructure as code using templates?
   a. AWS CloudTrail
   b. AWS CloudFormation
   c. AWS Systems Manager
   d. AWS Lambda

Answers

1. b
2. b

Application Integration

Application Integration services in AWS enable different applications, services, and components to communicate seamlessly within a distributed environment. These services provide messaging, event-driven processing, and workflow orchestration, which allows you to build scalable, decoupled, and resilient cloud applications.

Amazon Simple Queue Service (SQS)

Amazon SQS is a fully managed message queuing service that enables you to decouple and scale microservices, distributed systems, and serverless applications.

Use Case: A common use case for SQS is handling asynchronous message processing in distributed systems. For example, you can use SQS to decouple components of an e-commerce application such as order processing and inventory management, while ensuring reliable message delivery and scaling.

Amazon Simple Notification Service (SNS)

Amazon SNS is a fully managed pub/sub messaging service that enables you to send notifications to distributed systems, mobile devices, and other endpoints.

Use Case: An example use case for SNS is sending notifications to mobile devices in real-time. For instance, a ride-sharing application can use SNS to notify drivers and passengers about ride requests, updates, and promotions, while ensuring timely communication and engagement.

AWS Step Functions

AWS Step Functions is a fully managed workflow orchestration service that enables you to coordinate and automate multi-step tasks and workflows.

Use Case: A common use case for Step Functions is automating business processes and workflows with multiple steps and decision points. For example, an e-commerce platform can use Step Functions to orchestrate the order fulfillment process, while coordinating tasks such as inventory check, payment processing, shipping, and handling exceptions and retries.

Amazon EventBridge

Amazon EventBridge is a serverless event bus service that enables you to connect and route events between AWS services, SaaS applications, and your own custom applications.

Use Case: An example use case for EventBridge is building event-driven architectures for real-time data processing and analytics. For instance, a streaming analytics platform can use EventBridge to ingest and process events from multiple sources such as IoT devices, web applications, and third-party services, while triggering real-time analytics and insights generation.

Amazon API Gateway

Amazon API Gateway is a fully managed service that enables you to create, publish, maintain, monitor, and secure APIs at any scale.

Use Case: A common use case for API Gateway is building and exposing RESTful APIs for web and mobile applications. For example, a mobile application can use API Gateway to access backend services such as user authentication, data retrieval, and business logic, while providing seamless integration with the backend infrastructure.

Conclusion

In this chapter, we delved into a variety of essential AWS services spanning security, management tools, and application integration. From safeguarding data and managing infrastructure to seamlessly integrating applications, AWS offers a comprehensive suite of services to meet diverse needs. As we transition to the next chapter, we will explore additional AWS services such as Analytics, Machine Learning, IoT, and Gen AI, while unlocking even more possibilities for innovation and growth. For readers, engaging with end-of-chapter questions will not only reinforce understanding but also provide practical insights into leveraging AWS effectively. Stay tuned for an exciting journey into the world of AWS solutions, where possibilities are limitless.

Points to Remember

Security Services

- **AWS Identity and Access Management (IAM):** Manages user access and permissions to AWS resources securely
- **AWS Key Management Service (KMS):** Creates and controls cryptographic keys used to encrypt data
- **AWS CloudHSM:** Securely generates, stores, and manages cryptographic keys in hardware security modules
- **AWS WAF:** Protects web applications from common web exploits and attacks
- **Amazon Cognito:** Provides authentication, authorization, and user management for web and mobile apps
- **Amazon GuardDuty:** Continuously monitors and detects threats in AWS accounts and workloads

- **Amazon Inspector:** Analyzes the security and compliance of AWS resources and applications
- **Amazon Macie:** Discovers, classifies, and protects sensitive data stored in AWS
- **AWS Certificate Manager (ACM):** Provisions, manages, and deploys SSL/TLS certificates for AWS resources
- **AWS Firewall Manager:** Centrally configures and manages AWS WAF rules and AWS Shield Advanced protections
- **AWS Secrets Manager:** Securely stores, manages, and rotates credentials, API keys, and other secrets
- **AWS Security Hub:** Centrally manages and automates security and compliance checks across AWS accounts
- **AWS Shield:** Protects against DDoS attacks and safeguard web applications running on AWS
- **Amazon Detective:** Investigates and analyzes security incidents and suspicious activities in AWS

Management and Governance Services

- **Amazon CloudWatch:** Monitors and collects metrics, logs, and events from AWS resources and applications
- **AWS CloudFormation:** Creates and manages AWS infrastructure as code using templates
- **Amazon EC2 Auto Scaling:** Automatically adjusts the number of EC2 instances to maintain application availability and performance
- **AWS Health Dashboard:** Provides real-time status and notifications about AWS services and resources
- **AWS Service Catalog:** Creates and manages catalogs of approved IT services for use by users and teams
- **AWS Trusted Advisor:** Optimizes AWS infrastructure, improve performance, and reduce costs based on best practices
- **AWS Organizations:** Centrally manages and governs multiple AWS accounts within an organization

Application Integration Tools

- **Amazon SQS:** Decouples and scales microservices and distributed systems with fully managed message queuing
- **Amazon SNS:** Sends notifications to distributed systems, mobile devices, and other endpoints

- **AWS AppSync:** Builds scalable GraphQL APIs to securely access and manipulate data from multiple sources
- **AWS Step Functions:** Orchestrates and automates multi-step tasks and workflows using visual workflows

Multiple Choice Questions

1. Which AWS service provides authentication, authorization, and user management for web and mobile apps?
    a. AWS Identity and Access Management (IAM)
    b. Amazon Cognito
    c. AWS Key Management Service (KMS)
    d. Amazon Macie
2. In a scenario where an organization needs continuous monitoring and detection of threats in their AWS accounts and workloads, which service would be most appropriate?
    a. Amazon GuardDuty
    b. AWS Certificate Manager (ACM)
    c. AWS Security Hub
    d. AWS WAF
3. Which AWS service would be best suited for protecting web applications from common web exploits and attacks?
    a. AWS Shield
    b. AWS Firewall Manager
    c. Amazon Inspector
    d. AWS Secrets Manager
4. Which AWS service allows users to securely store, manage, and rotate credentials, API keys, and other secrets?
    a. AWS Key Management Service (KMS)
    b. Amazon Macie
    c. AWS Secrets Manager
    d. AWS Firewall Manager

5. Which of the following AWS services are used for managing cryptographic keys and encryption? (Select all that applies)
    a. AWS Key Management Service (KMS)
    b. Amazon Macie
    c. AWS CloudHSM
    d. AWS Shield
6. In a scenario where an organization wants to protect against DDoS attacks and safeguard web applications running on AWS, which service should they use?
    a. AWS Shield
    b. AWS Firewall Manager
    c. AWS WAF
    d. Amazon Inspector
7. Which AWS service provides a central dashboard to manage and automate security and compliance checks across AWS accounts?
    a. AWS GuardDuty
    b. AWS Security Hub
    c. AWS Config
    d. Amazon Detective
8. In a scenario where an organization needs to monitor and log AWS API activity for auditing and compliance purposes, which service should they use?
    a. AWS CloudTrail
    b. Amazon Inspector
    c. AWS GuardDuty
    d. AWS Security Hub
9. Which of the following AWS services can be used to protect web applications from common web exploits and attacks? (Select all that applies)
    a. AWS Shield
    b. AWS Firewall Manager
    c. AWS WAF
    d. AWS Macie

10. Which AWS service enables organizations to centrally configure and manage AWS WAF rules and AWS Shield Advanced protections?
    a. AWS WAF
    b. AWS Firewall Manager
    c. Amazon Macie
    d. AWS Secrets Manager

Answers

1. b
2. a
3. a
4. c
5. a, c
6. a
7. b
8. a
9. a, c
10. b

Reference

https://docs.aws.amazon.com/index.html - Documents for each services can be accessed via this link.

Chapter 8
Other AWS Services

Introduction

In the previous chapter, we explored how AWS helps organizations secure, manage, and govern their cloud environments, while enabling seamless integration between application components. Building on that foundation, this chapter turns its attention to how AWS enables innovation through services in analytics, machine learning, Internet of Things (IoT), and other specialized functional domains.

As organizations generate and consume increasing volumes of data, AWS provides tools to analyze information, extract insights, and make data-driven decisions at scale. At the same time, services in machine learning, frontend development, and IoT allow businesses to build intelligent applications, deliver engaging user experiences, and connect physical devices to the cloud. Alongside these, AWS continues to expand into specialized areas such as media, blockchain, and emerging technologies, giving customers the flexibility to experiment and innovate. In this chapter, we will explore these service categories, their use cases, and how they fit into modern cloud architectures.

Structure

In this chapter we will explore the following topics:

- Overview of AWS Analytics Services and Use Cases

- Overview of AWS ML Services and Use Cases
- Overview of AWS IoT Services and Use Cases
- Overview of Additional AWS Services for Specific Use Cases

Amazon Redshift

Amazon Redshift is a fully managed, petabyte-scale data warehouse service in the cloud. It allows you to efficiently analyze large datasets using standard SQL and existing business intelligence tools.

Key Features

- **Columnar Storage:** Data is stored in columns rather than rows, which enables faster query performance by reading only the columns needed for a query.
- **Parallel Processing:** Redshift distributes query execution across multiple nodes for high performance and scalability.
- **Integration:** Redshift integrates with various AWS services such as Amazon S3, AWS Glue, and Amazon QuickSight.
- **Automatic Scaling:** Redshift automatically adds or removes nodes based on workload demands to ensure consistent performance.
- **Security:** Redshift provides advanced security features such as encryption at rest and in transit, IAM integration, and VPC support.

Use Cases

- **Data Warehousing:** Organizations use Amazon Redshift to store and analyze large volumes of structured data for business intelligence, reporting, and analytics.
- **Log Analysis:** Companies leverage Amazon Redshift to analyze logs from web servers, applications, and IoT devices to gain insights into user behavior, system performance, and security threats.

AWS Glue

AWS Glue is a fully managed Extract, Transform, and Load (ETL) service that makes it easy to prepare and load data for analytics. It automates much of the heavy lifting involved in data preparation, which allows you to focus on analysis rather than infrastructure.

Key Features

- **Data Catalog:** AWS Glue provides a centralized metadata repository where you can discover, search, and manage metadata for your datasets.

- **ETL Jobs:** AWS Glue allows you to define, schedule, and run ETL jobs to transform and prepare data for analytics.
- **Serverless:** AWS Glue runs on serverless infrastructure, automatically scaling up or down based on the workload, without the need for provisioning or managing servers.
- **Integration:** AWS Glue seamlessly integrates with various AWS services such as Amazon S3, Amazon RDS, Amazon Redshift, and Amazon Athena.
- **Data Quality:** AWS Glue offers built-in data quality checks and transformations to ensure data accuracy and consistency.

Use Cases

- **Data Integration:** Use AWS Glue to integrate data from multiple sources, including databases, data warehouses, and streaming sources into a unified data lake or data warehouse.
- **Data Preparation:** Employ AWS Glue to clean, transform, and enrich raw data to make it suitable for analysis, reporting, and ML.

Amazon EMR

Amazon EMR (Elastic MapReduce) is a cloud-based big data platform that simplifies the processing and analysis of large datasets using popular open-source frameworks such as Apache Hadoop, Apache Spark, Apache Hive, Apache HBase, and Presto. It enables you to run big data applications quickly and cost-effectively, while processing petabytes of data at scale.

Key Features

- **Scalability:** Amazon EMR allows you to easily scale your cluster up or down to handle varying workloads, while ensuring optimal performance and resource utilization.
- **Flexibility:** Amazon EMR supports a wide range of big data processing frameworks, which gives you the flexibility to choose the right tool for your specific use case.
- **Security:** Amazon EMR provides built-in security features such as encryption at rest and in transit, IAM integration, and VPC support to ensure the confidentiality and integrity of your data.
- **Cost Optimization:** Amazon EMR offers pay-as-you-go pricing with no upfront costs, allowing you to only pay for the resources you use and scale your cluster based on demand.
- **Integration:** Amazon EMR seamlessly integrates with other AWS services such as Amazon S3, Amazon Redshift, Amazon DynamoDB, and AWS Glue for data storage, analytics, and ETL.

Use Cases

- **Data Processing:** Amazon EMR is ideal for processing large volumes of data, performing tasks such as log analysis, ETL, data transformation, and batch processing.
- **Data Analytics:** Use Amazon EMR to run interactive SQL queries, perform data analytics, and generate insights from your big data datasets using tools such as Apache Hive, Apache Spark, and Presto.
- **Machine Learning (ML):** Amazon EMR can be used as a platform for building and deploying ML models at scale, while leveraging frameworks such as Apache Spark MLlib and TensorFlow.

Amazon Kinesis

Amazon Kinesis is a platform for real-time data streaming and analytics. It enables you to ingest, process, and analyze streaming data in real-time, while allowing you to quickly extract actionable insights and respond to events as they happen.

Key Features

- **Data Ingestion:** Amazon Kinesis allows you to ingest large volumes of streaming data from various sources such as IoT devices, clickstreams, log files, and social media feeds.
- **Real-time Processing:** It provides the ability to process streaming data in real-time using services such as Amazon Kinesis Data Streams, Amazon Kinesis Data Firehose, and Amazon Kinesis Data Analytics.
- **Scalability:** Amazon Kinesis is designed to scale seamlessly to handle any amount of streaming data, which allows you to accommodate fluctuating workloads and bursty traffic patterns.
- **Integration:** It integrates with other AWS services such as Amazon S3, Amazon Redshift, Amazon Elasticsearch Service, and AWS Lambda for storage, analytics, and processing of streaming data.
- **Durability and Reliability:** Amazon Kinesis ensures data durability and reliability by replicating data across multiple availability zones within a region and providing built-in fault tolerance.

Use Cases

- **Real-Time Analytics:** Amazon Kinesis is used for real-time analytics applications such as monitoring website clickstreams, analyzing sensor data from IoT devices, and detecting anomalies in log files.

- **Stream Processing:** It enables stream processing applications such as data transformation, aggregation, and filtering in real-time, which allows you to derive insights and take immediate actions on streaming data.
- **Data Integration:** Amazon Kinesis facilitates the integration of streaming data with other AWS services and third-party tools, which enables you to build end-to-end streaming data pipelines for various use cases.

Within Amazon Kinesis there are three other services that are explained as follows:

Amazon Kinesis Video Streams

Amazon Kinesis Video Streams is a fully managed AWS service for ingesting, storing, processing, and analyzing video streams at scale. It enables you to securely stream video from millions of devices to AWS for real-time and batch processing.

Use Cases

- **Video Surveillance:** Capture and process video streams from surveillance cameras deployed in smart cities, buildings, and public spaces for real-time monitoring and analysis.
- **Video Analytics:** Analyze live and recorded video streams to extract insights, detect objects, recognize faces, and identify patterns for applications such as security, safety, and retail analytics.

Amazon Kinesis Data Streams

Amazon Kinesis Data Streams is a massively scalable and durable real-time data streaming service. It allows you to continuously ingest and process large volumes of streaming data from various sources with low latency.

Use Cases

- **Real-time Analytics:** Analyze website clickstreams, sensor data, and social media feeds in real-time to gain insights into user behavior, monitor application performance, and detect anomalies.
- **Log and Event Processing:** Ingest and process application logs, system logs, and event data in real-time for monitoring, troubleshooting, and security analysis.

Amazon Kinesis Data Firehose

Amazon Kinesis Data Firehose is a fully managed service for ingesting, transforming, and loading streaming data into data lakes, data warehouses, and analytics services.

Use Cases

- **Data Lake Ingestion:** Ingest streaming data into Amazon S3 data lakes for centralized storage, analysis, and reporting.
- **Real-time Analytics:** Deliver streaming data to Amazon Redshift, Amazon Elasticsearch Service, or Splunk for real-time analysis and visualization of data insights.

Amazon OpenSearch Service

Amazon OpenSearch Service (formerly Amazon Elasticsearch Service) is a fully managed service that simplifies the deployment, operation, and scaling of Elasticsearch clusters in the AWS Cloud. It enables you to search, analyze, and visualize large volumes of data in real-time, while facilitating use cases such as log analytics, full-text search, and application monitoring.

Key Features

- **Fully Managed:** Amazon OpenSearch Service handles cluster provisioning, patching, monitoring, and backups, which allows you to focus on data analysis and application development.
- **Scalability:** Easily scale your cluster up or down to handle varying workloads and storage requirements, while ensuring optimal performance and cost efficiency.
- **Security:** Secure your data and cluster with built-in encryption, access controls, and VPC support to ensure data privacy and compliance with industry regulations.
- **High Availability:** Amazon OpenSearch Service automatically replicates data across multiple Availability Zones within a region to provide high availability and fault tolerance.

Use Cases

- **Log Analytics:** Ingest and analyze log data from applications, servers, and network devices to gain insights into system performance, detect anomalies, and troubleshoot issues.
- **Full-text Search:** Build powerful search capabilities into your applications to enable users to quickly find relevant information from large datasets such as product catalogs, documents, and web content.

Amazon QuickSight

Amazon QuickSight is a fully managed Business Intelligence (BI) service that enables you to easily create interactive dashboards and visualizations from your data. It allows you to derive insights and make data-driven decisions quickly and efficiently.

Key Features

- **Interactive Dashboards:** Create interactive and customizable dashboards with drag-and-drop functionality to visualize data and explore insights.
- **ML-powered Insights:** Utilize machine learning-powered features such as Auto-Narratives and ML Insights to automatically generate insights and narratives from your data.
- **Pay-per-Session Pricing:** Benefit from flexible pricing with pay-per-session pricing model, which allows you to pay only for the number of user sessions used each month.
- **Integration:** Seamlessly integrate with various data sources including Amazon Redshift, Amazon RDS, Amazon Aurora, Amazon S3, and third-party sources to access and analyze data.
- **Mobile Access:** Access and interact with dashboards and visualizations on the go using the Amazon QuickSight mobile app available for iOS and Android devices.

Use Cases

Business Reporting: Create interactive reports and dashboards to monitor Key Performance Indicators (KPIs), track business metrics, and communicate insights across your organization.

Amazon Athena

Amazon Athena is a serverless, interactive query service that makes it simple to analyze data directly in Amazon S3 using standard SQL. Unlike traditional databases, you do not need to set up infrastructure or load data into a system. With Athena, you point it to your data in S3, define a schema, and start querying within seconds. You only pay for the queries you run, which makes it highly cost-efficient for both ad-hoc and recurring analytics.

Key Features

- **Serverless Architecture:** No servers to provision or manage; queries scale automatically
- **SQL Support:** Uses familiar ANSI SQL syntax, which lowers the learning curve
- **Direct S3 Integration:** Query data in various formats (CSV, JSON, ORC, Avro, Parquet) without moving it
- **Federated Queries:** Extend queries beyond S3 to multiple data sources, including relational, NoSQL, and other AWS services
- **Integration with AWS Ecosystem:** Works seamlessly with AWS Glue Data Catalog, QuickSight for visualization, and Lake Formation for security and governance
- **Pay-Per-Query Model:** Charged only for the amount of data scanned, with potential savings through data partitioning and compressed columnar format

Use Case

A retail company stores millions of transaction logs and customer interaction records in Amazon S3. Instead of building and maintaining a data warehouse, they use Athena to query this data directly. Analysts can run SQL queries to identify sales trends, monitor product performance, and detect unusual patterns in customer activity—all without additional infrastructure. By combining Athena with QuickSight dashboards, the company delivers real-time business insights to decision-makers quickly and cost-effectively.

Machine Learning

Now let us understand the various applications of services offered by **Amazon Web Services** in Machine Learning. These services are used to build, train, and deploy machine learning models for real-world use cases such as recommendation systems, fraud detection, image and speech recognition, and predictive analytics, without requiring deep expertise in machine learning infrastructure.

Amazon SageMaker

Amazon SageMaker is a fully managed service that enables developers and data scientists to build, train, and deploy ML models quickly and easily. It provides a comprehensive set of tools and capabilities for every step of the machine learning workflow, from data labelling and preparation to model training and deployment.

Key Features

- **Managed Jupyter Notebooks:** Amazon SageMaker provides fully managed Jupyter notebooks that allow data scientists to explore and visualize data, prototype models, and collaborate with team members in a familiar environment.
- **Pre-built Algorithms:** SageMaker offers a library of pre-built machine learning algorithms and model frameworks that can be easily integrated into your workflows, which reduces the time and effort required for model development.
- **Automatic Model Tuning:** SageMaker automates the process of hyperparameter optimization, which allows you to easily tune your models for optimal performance without manual trial and error.
- **Scalable Training and Inference:** With SageMaker, you can scale training and inference horizontally across multiple instances to process large datasets and serve predictions to millions of users in real-time.
- **Model Deployment:** SageMaker simplifies the deployment of machine learning models with built-in hosting and deployment services, which enables you to deploy models as scalable and cost-effective RESTful APIs with just a few clicks.

Use Cases

- **Predictive Maintenance:** Use Amazon SageMaker to build and deploy predictive maintenance models that analyze equipment sensor data to predict failures and prevent downtime.
- **Personalized Recommendations:** Leverage Amazon SageMaker to develop recommendation systems that analyze user behavior and preferences to deliver personalized product recommendations in real-time.

Amazon Comprehend

Amazon Comprehend is a Natural Language Processing (NLP) service that enables you to analyze and extract insights from unstructured text data. It uses ML models to identify key entities, sentiments, and themes in text documents.

Use Cases

- **Sentiment Analysis:** Analyze customer feedback, reviews, and social media posts to understand sentiment trends, identify customer opinions, and monitor brand reputation.
- **Document Classification:** Automatically categorize documents, emails, and support tickets into predefined categories based on their content to facilitate document management and organization.

Amazon Lex

Amazon Lex is a service for building conversational interfaces (chatbots) using Natural Language Understanding (NLU) capabilities. It allows you to create interactive voice and text-based conversational experiences for applications.

Use Cases

- **Customer Support Chatbots:** Build chatbots that can answer frequently asked questions, provide product information, and assist customers with common inquiries, while reducing the workload on support teams.
- **Virtual Assistants:** Create virtual assistants for scheduling appointments, booking reservations, and performing tasks on behalf of users to enhance productivity and user experience.

Amazon Transcribe

Amazon Transcribe is an Automatic Speech Recognition (ASR) service that converts speech into text in real-time. It enables you to transcribe audio recordings, phone calls, and video content into accurate and readable text.

Use Cases

- **Transcription Services:** Transcribe recorded meetings, interviews, and conference calls into text transcripts for documentation, searchability, and analysis purposes.
- **Closed Captioning:** Generate closed captions for videos and live streams to make content accessible to hearing-impaired viewers and improve user engagement and retention.

Amazon Rekognition

Amazon Rekognition is a deep learning-based image and video analysis service. It allows you to analyze and extract meaningful information from images and videos such as objects, faces, and activities.

Use Cases

- **Facial Recognition:** Identify and verify individuals in images and videos for authentication, security, and surveillance applications.
- **Content Moderation:** Detects and filters inappropriate or unsafe content in images and videos to ensure compliance with content guidelines and protect users from harmful content.

Amazon Polly

Amazon Polly is a Text-to-Speech (TTS) service that allows you to convert text into lifelike speech in multiple languages and voices. It enables you to create audio content for various applications, including voice assistants, narration, and accessibility features.

Use Cases

- **Voice-enabled Applications:** Add voice capabilities to applications, devices, and services to provide spoken responses, notifications, and instructions to users.
- **E-learning and Accessibility:** Convert educational content, textbooks, and documents into audio format to make them accessible to visually impaired users and learners with reading difficulties.

Amazon Textract

Amazon Textract is a machine learning service that automatically extracts text and data from scanned documents, forms, and images. It enables you to analyze and process structured and unstructured data from documents in real-time.

Use Cases

- **Document Digitization:** Extract information from invoices, receipts, contracts, and forms to automate data entry, document processing, and content indexing.
- **Data Extraction:** Analyze and extract data fields such as names, addresses, and dates, from unstructured documents for analysis, validation, and integration with business systems.

Amazon Translate

Amazon Translate is a neural machine translation service that enables you to translate text between languages with high accuracy and fluency. It supports a wide range of language pairs and domains, which allows you to localize content for global audiences.

Use Cases

- **Multilingual Content Localization:** Translate website content, product descriptions, and user-generated content into multiple languages to reach international audiences and expand market reach.
- **Language Support:** Provide real-time translation capabilities in applications, chatbots, and customer support systems to facilitate communication between users who speak different languages.

Amazon Kendra

Amazon Kendra is an intelligent search service that uses machine learning algorithms to provide accurate and relevant search results across diverse data sources and formats. It enables users to quickly find information and insights within large enterprise repositories.

Use Cases

- **Enterprise Search:** Provide employees, customers, and partners with a unified search experience across internal documents, knowledge bases, FAQs, and support articles.
- **Customer Support:** Empower customer support teams to quickly access and retrieve relevant information to resolve inquiries, troubleshoot issues, and provide personalized assistance.

Amazon Bedrock

Amazon Bedrock is a managed service that makes foundation models from leading AI startup (Anthropic) and Amazon's own Titan and Nova models available through APIs. By using Amazon Bedrock, you can quickly incorporate state-of-the-art AI into your applications.

Key Features

- **High-Efficiency Neural Networks:** Amazon Titan models are pre-trained on vast amounts of data, which makes them powerful, general-purpose models. For example, Amazon Titan models are 1000x more powerful than the average smartphone and can perform inference at a fraction of the power.
- **Easy to Use:** Amazon Bedrock makes foundation models from leading AI startups and Amazon's own Titan models available through APIs. You just need to call an API to get started.
- **Fine-Grained Control:** You can control the level of detail in the output. For example, if you want the output in tabular format, you can specify this using the API.
- **Security:** Amazon Bedrock is designed with multiple layers of security, including data encryption at rest and in transit, to keep your data safe.

How Amazon Bedrock Works: Amazon Bedrock provides APIs that allow you to call the service and get the output in the form of a JSON or S3 object. For example, to get the weather forecast for a city, you can call the **`get_forecast`** API using the Amazon Bedrock client.

Use Cases

- **Fraud Detection:** By analyzing large amounts of data, Amazon Bedrock can detect fraudulent transactions and prevent financial losses for businesses.
- **Medical Diagnosis:** By analyzing patient data, Amazon Bedrock can help doctors make more accurate diagnoses and recommend the best treatment plans for patients.
- **Product Recommendations:** By analyzing user data, Amazon Bedrock can provide personalized product recommendations to users such as which products to buy or which books to read.

Amazon Q

Amazon Q is a generative AI-powered assistant introduced by AWS to help developers, business users, and analysts get answers and perform tasks faster using natural language. Instead of manually writing queries, searching through documentation, or navigating dashboards, users can simply "ask" Amazon Q in plain English and get precise, context-aware responses.

Amazon Q is available in multiple tailored experiences such as:

- **Amazon Q for Developers:** Integrated into IDEs (like Visual Studio Code) and AWS Console, which helps developers write, test, and troubleshoot code more efficiently. It can suggest code snippets, explain errors, and guide best practices using AWS documentation and your own project context.

- **Amazon Q for Business:** An enterprise-focused assistant that connects to internal data sources (for example, wikis, ticketing systems, knowledge bases) to answer employee questions, summarize documents, and automate workflows—all while respecting company security and access controls.
- **Amazon Q in QuickSight (QuickSight Q):** A natural language query feature in Amazon QuickSight. Instead of writing SQL queries or building reports manually, analysts can type questions such as "*What were our top-selling products last quarter in Europe?*" and instantly generate visual dashboards with charts and tables.

Use Cases

- **Developer Productivity:** A software team building a Lambda-based backend integrates Amazon Q into their IDE. Developers can ask, "*How do I connect DynamoDB with this Lambda function?*" and get sample code plus explanations instantly, which reduces the time spent searching documentation.
- **Business Decision-Making:** A customer support manager uses Amazon Q for Business connected to Zendesk and Confluence. They can ask, "*What are the top 5 recurring customer complaints this month?*" and Q automatically pulls insights from tickets and knowledge base articles, thus saving hours of manual reporting.
- **Data-Driven Insights:** A sales analyst opens QuickSight Q and types, "*Show me the year-over-year revenue growth for North America*". Q instantly generates a chart, highlights trends, and provides narrative insights. This removes the dependency on technical teams and speeds up decision-making across the organization.

End User Computing

Let us explore the services offered by AWS in the End User Computing segment. These End User Computing services offer flexible and secure solutions for accessing desktop applications and resources from anywhere, while enabling organizations to support remote workforces and enhance productivity.

Amazon AppStream 2.0

Amazon AppStream 2.0 is a fully managed application streaming service that enables users to stream desktop applications securely from the cloud to any device. It allows you to centrally manage and deliver applications to users without the need for complex software installations or downloads.

Use Case: A software development company wants to provide access to resource-intensive design tools to its remote design team. They use Amazon AppStream 2.0 to stream the applications to the designers' devices, allowing them to work efficiently on complex design projects from anywhere with an internet connection.

Amazon WorkSpaces

Amazon WorkSpaces is a managed Desktop-as-a-Service (DaaS) solution that provides virtual desktop environments in the cloud. It allows users to access their desktops and applications from anywhere using any supported device, whileproviding a consistent and secure desktop experience.

Use Case: A financial services company needs to provide its employees with secure access to corporate desktops and applications while working remotely. They deploy Amazon WorkSpaces to provide virtual desktops to employees, while ensuring data security and compliance with regulatory requirements and also enabling flexible remote work options.

Amazon WorkSpaces Web

Amazon WorkSpaces Web is a web-based client for accessing Amazon WorkSpaces virtual desktops directly from a web browser. It provides a lightweight and convenient way for users to access their WorkSpaces without the need for a dedicated client application.

Use Case: An employee needs to access their Amazon WorkSpaces desktop from a public computer in a library. Instead of installing a desktop client, they use Amazon WorkSpaces Web to securely connect to their virtual desktop, and access their files as well as applications from the web browser.

Frontend Web and Mobile

Frontend Web and Mobile services offer developers the tools and resources they need to build and deploy modern, scalable, and feature-rich applications for web and mobile platforms.

AWS Amplify

AWS Amplify is a set of tools and services for building scalable and secure cloud-powered applications for web and mobile platforms. It provides features such as authentication, data storage, analytics, and AI/ML integration, which makes it easier for developers to create full-stack applications with AWS services.

Use Case: A mobile app developer wants to build a new application with features such as user authentication, file storage, and real-time data updates. They use AWS Amplify to quickly set up authentication, integrate with Amazon S3 for storage, and use AWS AppSync for real-time data synchronization, while reducing development time and effort.

AWS AppSync

AWS AppSync is a fully managed service for building real-time and offline-capable applications with GraphQL. It enables developers to define a flexible data schema and connect their applications to multiple data sources, including Amazon DynamoDB, Amazon RDS, and Lambda functions.

Use Case: A software development team is building a collaborative messaging application that requires real-time updates and offline capabilities. They use AWS AppSync to create a GraphQL API that connects to a backend data store, which allows users to send and receive messages in real-time and access the application offline.

Internet of Things (IoT)

IoT services provide developers and organizations with the tools and capabilities to build and deploy scalable, secure, and intelligent IoT solutions for various industries and use cases.

AWS IoT Core

AWS IoT Core is a managed cloud service that enables devices to connect securely to the AWS cloud and interact with other devices and applications. It provides features such as device authentication, message routing, and data processing, thereby allowing developers to build scalable and secure IoT applications.

Use Case: A smart home device manufacturer wants to create a connected thermostat that can monitor temperature and humidity levels and adjust settings remotely. They use AWS IoT Core to securely connect the thermostat to the AWS cloud, which allows users to control and monitor their devices using a mobile app or web interface.

Conclusion

In this chapter, we delved into a wide array of AWS services, spanning analytics, ML, IoT, front end and mobile computing, and customer engagement. Each of these services plays a crucial role in modern business operations and offers innovative solutions to address complex challenges and drive growth and efficiency.

From AWS Amplify empowering developers to build scalable cloud-powered applications to AWS IoT Core facilitating secure and seamless device connectivity, the breadth of services covered in this chapter underscores AWS's commitment to providing comprehensive solutions for diverse business needs.

Thus, by understanding how these services are applied in real-world scenarios across industries, readers can gain insights into the transformative potential of AWS technologies. Whether it is optimizing manufacturing processes with IoT-enabled predictive maintenance or enhancing customer experiences through personalized recommendations powered by ML, AWS services empower businesses to innovate and thrive in today's digital landscape.

As we conclude this chapter, readers are encouraged to not only grasp the technical aspects of these services but also explore their practical applications within their respective industries. Additionally, continued engagement with end-of-chapter problems will reinforce learning and foster deeper understanding.

In the upcoming chapter, we will shift our focus to cost management within the AWS ecosystem, while exploring various tools and services offered by AWS to track, analyze, and optimize costs. Stay tuned as we delve into the realm of cost economics and unveil strategies for maximizing value and managing expenses effectively.

Points to Remember

Analytics

- **Amazon Redshift:** Fully managed data warehouse service for analyzing large datasets
- **AWS Glue:** Fully managed Extract, Transform, and Load (ETL) service for preparing and transforming data
- **Amazon EMR:** Managed big data processing framework for processing and analyzing large datasets using Apache Hadoop, Spark, and other open-source tools
- **Amazon Kinesis:** Real-time data streaming and processing service for collecting, processing, and analyzing streaming data
- **Amazon OpenSearch Service:** Fully managed service for deploying, managing, and scaling Elasticsearch clusters for search, analytics, and log processing
- **Amazon QuickSight:** Business intelligence and data visualization service for creating interactive dashboards and reports
- **Amazon Athena:** Amazon Athena is a **serverless query service** that lets you analyze data stored in Amazon S3 using standard SQL, without needing to set up or manage any infrastructure

Machine Learning

- **Amazon SageMaker:** Fully managed machine learning service to build, train, and deploy machine learning models
- **Amazon Comprehend:** Natural language processing service for analyzing text to extract insights and relationships
- **Amazon Lex:** Managed service for building conversational interfaces using natural language understanding

- **Amazon Transcribe:** Automatic speech recognition service to convert speech to text
- **Amazon Rekognition:** Deep learning-based image and video analysis service for object and scene detection, facial recognition, and content moderation
- **Amazon Polly:** Text-to-speech service to convert text into lifelike speech
- **Amazon Textract:** Service for extracting text and data from scanned documents using machine learning
- **Amazon Translate:** Neural machine translation service for translating text between languages
- **Amazon Kendra:** Enterprise search service powered by machine learning for providing accurate and relevant search results
- **Amazon Bedrock:** Hypothetical service for managing machine learning pipelines and workflows
- **Amazon Q:** Amazon Q is a generative AI–powered assistant that helps developers, business users, and analysts get answers, write code, and generate insights through natural language

Other AWS Services

- **AWS Activate:** Program designed to help startups grow and scale their businesses by providing access to resources, expertise, and credits for AWS services
- **AWS Support:** Subscription-based service providing technical assistance, best practices guidance, and troubleshooting resources for AWS customers
- **Amazon AppStream 2.0:** Fully managed application streaming service for securely delivering desktop applications from the cloud to any device
- **Amazon WorkSpaces:** Managed Desktop-as-a-Service (DaaS) solution providing virtual desktop environments in the cloud
- **Amazon WorkSpaces Web:** Web-based client for accessing Amazon WorkSpaces virtual desktops directly from a web browser
- **AWS Amplify:** Set of tools and services for building scalable cloud-powered applications for web and mobile platforms
- **AWS AppSync:** Managed GraphQL service for building real-time and offline-capable applications with flexible data schema
- **AWS IoT Core:** Managed cloud service for securely connecting IoT devices to the AWS cloud and interacting with other devices and applications

Multiple Choice Questions

1. Which AWS service is used for building real-time and offline-capable applications with GraphQL?
   a. Amazon Redshift
   b. Amazon EMR
   c. Amazon AppStream 2.0
   d. AWS AppSync
2. Which AWS service provides a managed data warehousing solution for analyzing large datasets?
   a. Amazon SageMaker
   b. Amazon Redshift
   c. Amazon Transcribe
   d. Amazon QuickSight
3. Which AWS service is used for automatic speech recognition and converting speech to text?
   a. Amazon Transcribe
   b. Amazon Comprehend
   c. Amazon Polly
   d. Amazon Rekognition
4. Which AWS service is suitable for building conversational interfaces using natural language understanding?
   a. Amazon Polly
   b. Amazon Rekognition
   c. Amazon Lex
   d. Amazon Kendra
5. Which AWS service provides a fully managed machine learning service to build, train, and deploy ML models?
   a. Amazon Rekognition
   b. Amazon Personalize
   c. Amazon SageMaker
   d. Amazon Polly

6. Which AWS service provides a generative AI–powered assistant that helps developers, business users, and analysts get answers and insights using natural language?
    a. Amazon Lex
    b. Amazon Q
    c. Amazon Polly
    d. Amazon Transcribe
7. Which AWS service is used for building personalized recommendation systems?
    a. Amazon Forecast
    b. Amazon Personalize
    c. Amazon Comprehend
    d. Amazon Rekognition
8. Which AWS service enables developers to build conversational interfaces for applications?
    a. Amazon Lex
    b. Amazon Transcribe
    c. Amazon Polly
    d. Amazon Rekognition
9. Which AWS service is used for securely connecting IoT devices to the AWS cloud and interacting with other devices and applications?
    a. AWS IoT Core
    b. AWS Device Farm
    c. AWS AppSync
    d. Amazon WorkSpaces
10. A company wants to build, train, and deploy machine learning models at scale without managing infrastructure. Which AWS service should they use? (Select **two**)?
    a. Amazon SageMaker
    b. Amazon EC2
    c. Amazon SageMaker Canvas
    d. Amazon RDS
    e. Amazon DynamoDB

11. Which AWS service provides a fully managed data warehousing solution for preparing and transforming data?
    a. Amazon Redshift
    b. Amazon SageMaker
    c. AWS Glue
    d. AWS AppSync
12. Which AWS service enables real-time data streaming and processing for collecting, processing, and analyzing streaming data?
    a. Amazon QuickSight
    b. Amazon Kinesis
    c. Amazon MSK
    d. Amazon SageMaker
13. Which AWS service is suitable for extracting text and data from scanned documents using machine learning?
    a. Amazon Translate
    b. Amazon Textract
    c. Amazon Polly
    d. Amazon Transcribe
14. What AWS service provides a managed cloud service for securely connecting IoT devices to the AWS cloud?
    a. Amazon Pinpoint
    b. AWS IoT Core
    c. Amazon Rekognition
    d. Amazon Polly
15. Which AWS service is used for building conversational interfaces using natural language understanding?
    a. Amazon Lex
    b. Amazon Pinpoint
    c. Amazon Connect
    d. Amazon WorkSpaces
16. Which AWS service provides virtual desktop environments in the cloud?
    a. AWS AppStream 2.0
    b. Amazon WorkSpaces

   c. Amazon WorkSpaces Web
   d. AWS Device Farm

17. Which of the following AWS services are used for real-time data processing and analysis? (Select all that apply)
    a. Amazon Redshift
    b. AWS Glue
    c. Amazon Kinesis
    d. Amazon Pinpoint

18. Which of the following AWS services are suitable for building conversational interfaces? (Select all that apply)
    a. Amazon Lex
    b. Amazon Polly
    c. Amazon Connect
    d. Amazon Rekognition

19. A manufacturing company wants to implement predictive maintenance for its machinery to reduce downtime and maintenance costs. Which AWS service(s) should the company consider for this task?
    a. Amazon SageMaker
    b. AWS IoT Core
    c. Amazon Rekognition
    d. Amazon QuickSight

20. A media streaming company wants to analyze customer engagement and viewership patterns to improve content recommendations and advertising strategies. Which AWS service(s) should the company consider for this task?
    a. Amazon Pinpoint
    b. Amazon Redshift
    c. Amazon Personalize
    d. Amazon Connect

Answers

1. d
2. b
3. b

4. c
5. c
6. b
7. b
8. a
9. a
10. a, c
11. c
12. b
13. b
14. b
15. a
16. b
17. b, c
18. a, b
19. b
20. b, c

Reference

- https://docs.aws.amazon.com/index.html - Documents for each services can be accessed via this link.

CHAPTER 9
Billing and Pricing

Introduction

Welcome to this chapter, where we will delve into the critical aspect of billing and pricing in AWS. As you have journeyed through the various AWS services, you have gained a comprehensive understanding of their functionalities and applications. Now, it is time to explore how to effectively manage the costs associated with utilizing these services.

In this chapter, we will uncover the intricacies of AWS billing and pricing, which is essential for optimizing costs and maximizing the value of your AWS investment. We will start by examining the various pricing models offered by AWS such as on-demand instances, reserved instances, and spot instances. Understanding these models is crucial for making informed decisions about resource provisioning and cost allocation.

Next, we will explore the AWS Free Tier, which is a valuable resource for newcomers and organizations looking to experiment with AWS services at no cost. We will discuss its benefits and limitations and provide insights into how you can leverage it to your advantage for cost savings and experimentation.

However, effective cost management does not stop there. We will also dive into advanced tools and features like Cost Explorer and Budgets, which are designed to provide visibility into your AWS spending and help you set and manage your budget effectively. By leveraging these tools, you can gain insights into your usage patterns, identify cost optimization opportunities, and ensure compliance with your budgetary constraints.

By the end of this chapter, you will have a comprehensive understanding of AWS billing and pricing and will be equipped with the knowledge and tools needed to effectively manage your AWS costs. You will also be able to optimize your resource utilization and ensure budget compliance. So, let us dive in and unlock the secrets to successful cost management in AWS.

Structure

In this chapter, we will explore the following topics:

- Pricing and billing mechanisms in AWS ecosystem
- Cloud financial management services
- Brief introduction to cost calculator by AWS
- Identify best practices a company/individual must follow to maintain cost

Pricing and Billing Mechanisms in AWS

The pricing models and billing mechanisms used in AWS play a crucial role in determining the cost structure and financial aspects of utilizing cloud resources. We have explained some of them in this section.

- **On-Demand Instances**
    - On-demand instances provide users with the flexibility to pay for compute capacity by the hour or second, without engaging any long-term commitments or upfront payments.
    - This pricing model is ideal for applications with unpredictable workloads, short-term projects, or for users who want to avoid upfront costs and commitments.
    - **Benefits:** Flexibility; no long-term commitments; pay-as-you-go pricing
    - **Limitations:** Higher cost compared to reserved instances for steady-state workloads
    - **Use Cases:** Development and testing environments, applications with variable or unpredictable workloads
- **Reserved Instances (RIs)**
    - Reserved instances allow users to reserve EC2 computing capacity for a fixed term (typically one or three years) in exchange for a significant discount compared to on-demand pricing.
    - RIs offer cost savings for applications with steady-state or predictable workloads, while providing a lower effective hourly rate compared to on-demand instances.

  - Users can choose between standard RIs (offering capacity reservations within a specific availability zone) and convertible RIs (offering flexibility to change instance attributes during the term).
  - **Benefits**: Cost savings, predictable pricing, capacity reservation
  - **Limitations**: Upfront payment or commitment required, limited flexibility compared to on-demand instances
  - **Use Cases:** Production environments, applications with consistent workloads, steady-state workloads

- **Spot Instances**
  - Spot instances enable users to bid on unused EC2 capacity, which allows them to take advantage of spare capacity at significantly lower prices compared to on-demand pricing.
  - Spot instances are well-suited for fault-tolerant, flexible applications, batch processing, or workloads that can be interrupted or rescheduled without impact.
  - Users can specify a maximum price (bid) they are willing to pay for spoti and if the current spot price falls below the bid price, their instances will be provisioned.
  - **Benefits:** Cost savings, flexible pricing, access to excess capacity
  - **Limitations:** Instances can be reclaimed with short notice, pricing variability
  - **Use Cases:** Batch processing, data analysis, fault-tolerant applications, non-critical workloads

- **Savings Plans**

  Savings Plans provide flexible pricing models that help you save up to 72% compared to on-demand pricing.
  - **Compute Savings Plans:** Apply across Amazon EC2, AWS Fargate, and AWS Lambda usage that offer maximum flexibility
  - **EC2 Instance Savings Plans:** Apply to a chosen instance family in a specific region

These plans are ideal for customers with predictable workloads who want flexibility without the instance lock-in found in reserved instances.

- **AWS Free Tier**

  The **AWS Free Tier** allows new users to get hands-on experience with AWS services at little or no cost. It provides access to a selection of services such as Amazon EC2, Amazon S3, Amazon RDS, AWS Lambda, and more, which allows customers to explore the platform, build small projects, and experiment without immediate financial commitment.

The Free Tier is structured into **three categories**:

- **Always Free:** Benefits that never expire, such as 1 million AWS Lambda requests per month or 25 GB of storage with Amazon DynamoDB
- **12-Month Free Tier:** Offers valid for the first 12 months after account creation, such as 750 hours of EC2 `t2.micro` or `t3.micro` instances each month
- **Short-Term Trials:** Time-bound offers that allow free use of certain services for a limited period, typically to promote new features

While the Free Tier is a valuable way to get started, it comes with **limits and restrictions**. Usage is capped by monthly service quotas, certain features are only available in specific regions, and functionality is limited compared to paid tiers. Once limits are exceeded or the 12-month period ends, normal AWS rates apply.

By understanding these categories and restrictions, new users can take full advantage of the Free Tier to explore AWS effectively, while avoiding unexpected charges.

- **Volume Discounts:**
    - AWS offers volume discounts for customers who use large amounts of certain services, such as EC2, S3, and EBS.
    - Volume discounts are based on the usage volume and commitment level, while providing cost savings for customers with significant usage.
- **Pay-as-You-Go Pricing:**
    - With Pay-as-You-Go Pricing, users only pay for the resources they consume, with no long-term commitments or upfront payments required.
    - This pricing model is flexible and allows users to scale resources up or down based on demand and pay only for what they use.

Cloud Financial Management Services

Cloud Financial Management Services are tools and practices that help businesses handle their spending effectively in the cloud. They give insights into how much you are using and spending on cloud services, help you set budgets, and suggest ways to save money. It is like having a financial advisor for your cloud expenses, making sure you get the most value out of your investment while keeping costs in check. Let us look at services offered by AWS to manage your cloud expense.

AWS Budgets

AWS Budgets is a service that helps you manage your AWS spending by setting up budgets and tracking your actual costs against those budgets. It provides you with the ability to set limits. AWS Budgets can be used for a variety of purposes like managing cloud costs, monitoring resource

usage, and ensuring that you are staying within your AWS budget. AWS Budgets can be used to limit your spending, receive notifications when you exceed your budget limits, and take actions to reduce your costs. AWS Budgets can be used for a variety of purposes, such as managing cloud costs, monitoring resource usage, and ensuring that you are staying within your AWS budget.

Use case: AWS Budgets can be used by organizations of all sizes to manage their AWS spending. For example, you can use AWS Budgets to set a limit on your spending on a specific AWS service such as Amazon EC2 and receive notifications when your spending exceeds that limit. You can then take actions to reduce your usage of that service such as scaling down your EC2 instances or migrating to a different service.

AWS Cost and Usage Report (CUR)

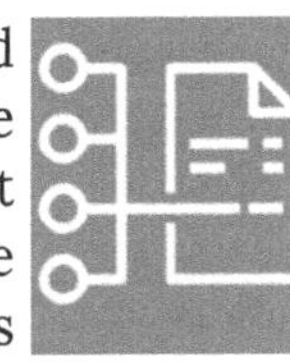

AWS Cost and Usage Report (CUR) is a service that provides you with detailed information about your AWS usage and costs. It provides you with a comprehensive view of your spending, including the type of resources you are using, the amount of usage, and the cost associated with each resource. CUR can be used to analyze your AWS usage, identify cost-saving opportunities, and track your AWS costs over time.

Use case: AWS Cost and Usage Report (CUR) can be used by organizations of all sizes to analyze their AWS usage and costs. It can be used to identify cost-saving opportunities, track resource usage, and monitor your AWS costs over time. For example, you can use AWS Cost and Usage Report (CUR) to identify which AWS services are consuming the most resources and take actions to reduce your usage of those services. You can also use AWS Cost and Usage Report (CUR) to identify cost-saving opportunities such as using reserved instances or purchasing a software subscription.

AWS Cost Explorer

AWS Cost Explorer is a service that provides you with a visual interface to explore and analyze your AWS costs. It provides you with the ability to filter your costs by region, service, or resource type, and generate custom reports to help you understand your AWS spending. AWS Cost Explorer can be used to identify cost-saving opportunities, track resource usage, and monitor your AWS costs.

Use case: AWS Cost Explorer can be used by organizations of all sizes to explore and analyze their AWS costs. It can be used to identify cost-saving opportunities, track resource usage, and monitor your AWS costs. For example, you can use AWS Cost Explorer to identify which AWS services are consuming the most resources and take actions to reduce your usage of those services. You can also use AWS Cost Explorer to identify cost-saving opportunities such as using reserved instances or purchasing a software subscription.

AWS Marketplace

AWS Marketplace is a service that provides you with access to a wide range of software and services that are available on AWS. It provides you with the ability to purchase and deploy these services directly from AWS, without the need to go through a third-party provider. AWS Marketplace can be used to find and purchase software and services that meet your specific needs, and to integrate these services into your AWS environment.

Use case: AWS Marketplace can be used by organizations of all sizes to find and purchase software and services that meet their specific needs. It can be used to find and purchase software and services that are compatible with your AWS environment, and to integrate these services into your existing applications and services. For example, you can use AWS Marketplace to find and purchase software that is designed to run on Amazon EC2 instances, or to find and purchase software that is designed to integrate with AWS services such as Amazon S3 or Amazon DynamoDB.

AWS Trusted Advisor

AWS Trusted Advisor is an online tool that provides real-time guidance to help you follow AWS best practices. It continuously scans your AWS environment and offers recommendations across categories such as cost optimization, performance, security, fault tolerance, and service limits. For billing and pricing, it highlights underutilized resources, idle instances, or opportunities to switch to savings plans and reserved instances.

Use Case: A company running multiple EC2 instances discovers through Trusted Advisor that several instances are underutilized and could be downsized or stopped to save money. By acting on these recommendations, the organization reduces monthly costs without impacting application performance.

AWS Organizations: Consolidated Billing

AWS Organizations allows businesses to centrally manage multiple AWS accounts under one umbrella. One of its key features is **consolidated billing**, which combines usage from all linked accounts into a single bill. This not only simplifies payment but also allows **reserved instances and savings plans to be shared across accounts**, while maximizing cost savings for the organization.

Use Case: A large enterprise operates separate AWS accounts for development, testing, and production teams. By enabling consolidated billing, the finance department receives a single, unified invoice and can apply savings plans purchased in one account across all accounts. This provides better visibility into total spending and ensures the business takes full advantage of AWS volume discounts.

AWS Pricing Calculator

The AWS Pricing Calculator is a powerful tool provided by Amazon Web Services (AWS) to help customers estimate their monthly AWS bill based on their usage patterns and selected AWS services. It enables users to quickly and accurately calculate the costs associated with running their workloads on AWS, while allowing them to plan and budget effectively.

Key Features

- **Simple Interface:** The Pricing Calculator offers a user-friendly interface that allows users to easily select and configure the AWS services they intend to use. It provides a comprehensive list of AWS services such as compute, storage, databases, networking, analytics, machine learning, and more.
- **Customizable Configurations:** Users can customize their configurations by specifying parameters such as instance types, storage options, data transfer volumes, and usage patterns. They can also adjust settings based on factors such as region, operating system, storage class, and desired performance characteristics.
- **Real-Time Pricing Estimates:** As users make changes to their configurations, the Pricing Calculator provides real-time pricing estimates for each selected service. This enables users to see how different choices impact their overall costs and make informed decisions accordingly.
- **Cost Breakdowns:** The Pricing Calculator provides detailed cost breakdowns for each selected service, including hourly rates, monthly costs, and any applicable discounts or savings plans. This allows users to understand the cost implications of their choices and identify areas for optimization.
- **Savings Plans Integration:** Users can incorporate AWS Savings Plans into their cost calculations to estimate potential savings based on their usage commitments. This helps users determine the most cost-effective purchasing options for their workloads.
- **Export and Share Estimates:** The Pricing Calculator allows users to export their cost estimates in various formats such as CSV or JSON for further analysis or sharing with stakeholders. This facilitates collaboration and decision-making within organizations.
- **Saved Configurations:** Users can save their configurations within the Pricing Calculator for future reference or comparison. This enables them to revisit and refine their cost estimates over time as their requirements evolve.

Overall, the AWS Pricing Calculator is an invaluable tool for organizations planning their AWS deployments. By providing detailed cost estimates, customizable configurations, and real-time insights, it empowers users to make informed decisions, optimize costs, and maximize the value of their AWS investments.

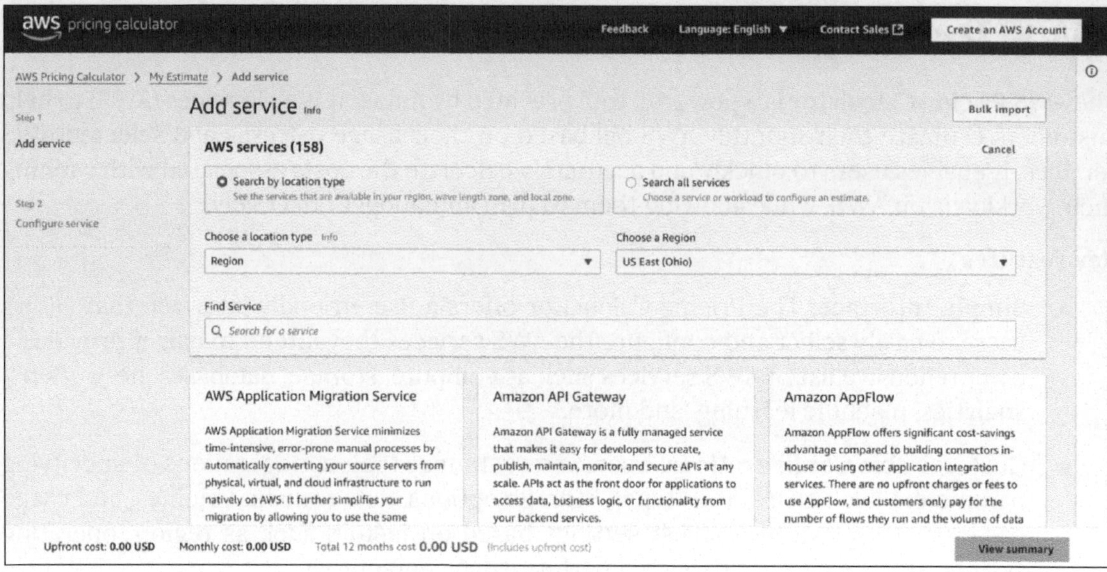

Figure 9.1: *Pricing Calculator*

Best Practices to Manage Costs on AWS

Understanding how to manage costs effectively on AWS is important for businesses using cloud services. This section will help you learn about different ways to save money while still retrieving good performance from your AWS resources. We will talk about things like picking the right size for your instances, using auto-scaling, and how to keep an eye on your spending.

- **Sustainability and Cost Optimization**

  Optimizing cloud costs is not just about financial savings; it also supports sustainability goals. Rightsizing workloads, turning off idle resources, and choosing energy-efficient regions help reduce carbon emissions while lowering bills. AWS publishes a *Customer Carbon Footprint Tool* to provide visibility into the environmental impact of your usage.

- **Tips and Strategies for Optimizing AWS Costs**
  - Regularly review and analyze your AWS usage and spending patterns to identify areas for optimization.
  - Utilize AWS Cost Explorer and AWS Budgets to gain insights into your spending and set budgetary constraints.
  - Consider utilizing AWS Trusted Advisor to receive recommendations on cost optimization opportunities and best practices.

- **Recommendations for Rightsizing Instances and Leveraging Auto-Scaling**
    - Rightsize your instances by selecting instance types and sizes that match your workload requirements to avoid over-provisioning. You can do it via the compute optimizer service as well.
    - Implement auto-scaling to dynamically adjust resources based on demand, while ensuring that you have the right amount of capacity to handle workload fluctuations.
    - Utilize AWS savings plans or reserved instances to commit to usage in advance and receive discounted pricing for predictable workloads.
- **Guidance on Monitoring and Managing Costs**
    - Set up AWS Budgets to track spending and receive alerts when approaching or exceeding budget thresholds.
    - Monitor resource utilization using AWS CloudWatch metrics and logs to identify underutilized resources or opportunities for consolidation. Configure alarms when usage hits a threshold.
    - Implement tagging strategies to categorize resources and allocate costs accurately, while enabling better cost attribution and accountability.
    - Regularly review and optimize storage usage, including deleting unused snapshots, archiving infrequently accessed data, and utilizing lifecycle policies to manage object storage efficiently.
    - Consider utilizing AWS Cost Anomaly Detection to detect unusual spending patterns and investigate potential cost anomalies.

To sum up, keeping costs down on AWS means being smart about how you use your resources. By following tips like choosing the right instance size and using auto-scaling, you can save money while still getting the most out of AWS. Remember to keep an eye on your spending and adjust as needed to stay within your budget.

Conclusion

With the conclusion of this chapter, we have covered a comprehensive overview of the services offered by AWS, spanning security, management, governance, application integration, analytics, machine learning, IoT, front-end web, and customer engagement. From understanding the fundamentals of each service to exploring key features, use cases, and best practices, readers have gained valuable insights into harnessing the power of AWS to meet their business needs.

As we prepare to transition to the next chapter, it is important to reflect on the breadth and depth of AWS offerings and the myriad possibilities they present for organizations looking to innovate, scale, and thrive in the cloud. Whether you are a seasoned cloud professional or just starting your journey with AWS, the knowledge and skills acquired in this chapter serve as a solid foundation for success in navigating the AWS ecosystem.

In the upcoming chapter, we will focus on exam preparation strategies, while equipping readers with tips and techniques to excel in the AWS Certified Cloud Practitioner exam. Additionally, we will provide two sample question papers to help reinforce concepts and assess readiness for the exam. Stay tuned for actionable insights and practice resources to help you ace the certification exam with confidence.

Points to Remember

- **Understanding Pricing Models:** Familiarize yourself with different pricing models like on-demand instances, reserved instances, and spot instances to choose the most cost-effective option for your workload.
- **Optimization Strategies:** Implement cost optimization strategies such as rightsizing instances, leveraging auto-scaling, and monitoring costs to maximize value and minimize expenses.
- **Free Tier Benefits:** Take advantage of the AWS Free Tier to explore and experiment with various services at no cost, but be mindful of usage limits and restrictions.
- **Budgeting and Monitoring:** Set budgets, use AWS Cost Explorer and Budgets to monitor spending, and configure alerts to ensure budget compliance and cost efficiency.
- **Continuous Improvement:** Regularly review and optimize your AWS usage, implement best practices for cost management, and stay updated on new features and offerings to drive continuous improvement in cost optimization efforts.

Multiple Choice Questions

1. Which of the following is NOT a pricing model offered by AWS?
    a. On-Demand Instances
    b. Reserved Instances
    c. Elastic Instances
    d. Spot Instances
2. What is one of the key benefits of utilizing Reserved Instances (RIs) on AWS?
    a. No upfront payment required
    b. Pay-as-you-go pricing model
    c. Predictable pricing and cost savings
    d. Flexibility to scale resources up or down based on demand

3. Which AWS service provides insights into AWS spending, and allows users to set budgetary constraints?
    a. AWS Trusted Advisor
    b. AWS Cost Explorer
    c. AWS Budgets
    d. AWS Billing Dashboard
4. What is the primary purpose of AWS Free Tier?
    a. To provide unlimited access to all AWS services
    b. To offer a limited-time trial for new customers
    c. To provide discounted pricing for long-term commitments
    d. To provide free support for AWS services
5. Which AWS tool allows users to receive recommendations on cost optimization opportunities?
    a. AWS Cost Explorer
    b. AWS Budgets
    c. AWS Trusted Advisor
    d. AWS Cost Anomaly Detection
6. What is one of the limitations of Spot Instances on AWS?
    a. Instances can be reclaimed with short notice.
    b. Instances offer fixed pricing with no variability.
    c. Instances always provide guaranteed availability.
    d. Instances are billed on a pay-as-you-go basis.
7. Which AWS service helps users track spending and receives alerts when approaching or exceeding budget thresholds?
    a. AWS Cost Explorer
    b. AWS Budgets
    c. AWS Trusted Advisor
    d. AWS Cost Anomaly Detection
8. How can users optimize costs when using AWS EC2 instances?
    a. By choosing the largest instance size available
    b. By utilizing auto-scaling to adjust resources based on demand
    c. By using Reserved Instances for unpredictable workloads
    d. By ignoring usage patterns and monitoring costs retrospectively

9. Which AWS pricing model allows users to bid on unused EC2 capacity, potentially accessing resources at lower rates?
    a. On-Demand Instances
    b. Reserved Instances
    c. Spot Instances
    d. Elastic Instances
10. What is the primary benefit of AWS Cost Explorer?
    a. Provides recommendations on cost optimization opportunities
    b. Allows users to set budgetary constraints
    c. Provides insights into AWS spending and usage patterns
    d. Enables users to monitor resource utilization and performance

Answers

1. c
2. c
3. c
4. b
5. c
6. a
7. b
8. b
9. c
10. c

References

- https://aws.amazon.com/pricing/
- https://aws.amazon.com/ec2/pricing/
- https://aws.amazon.com/free/
- https://aws.amazon.com/ec2/pricing/reserved-instances/
- https://aws.amazon.com/pricing/cost-optimization/
- https://docs.aws.amazon.com/awsaccountbilling/latest/aboutv2/billing-recommendations.html

CHAPTER 10
Preparing for Exam

Introduction

Welcome to the final chapter of our comprehensive guide! After journeying through nine chapters that addressed the fundamentals of cloud computing, diving deep into AWS services, exploring security models, and navigating billing and pricing structures, you have reached the final leg of your preparation journey.

In this chapter, we will focus on equipping you with effective strategies and tips to prepare for the AWS Certified Cloud Practitioner exam. Whether you are a seasoned IT professional or new to the cloud world, this chapter will provide invaluable guidance to maximize your chances of success.

As you embark on this final leg of your preparation, remember the foundational knowledge you have acquired throughout the book. You have gained insights into AWS services, learned about the shared responsibility model, and grasped the intricacies of billing and pricing in the cloud. Now, it is time to consolidate that knowledge and hone your exam readiness.

Throughout this chapter, we will share study strategies, highlight valuable resources, and provide expert tips to help you optimize your preparation efforts. From understanding exam objectives to navigating practice exams and mastering time management on exam day, we have got you covered for every step of the way.

So, let us dive in and explore the strategies and techniques that will propel you towards success on the AWS Certified Cloud Practitioner exam.

Structure

In this chapter, we will explore the following topics:

- Essential Study Strategies
- Importance of Practice Tests and Mock Exams
- Tips for the Exam Day
- Study Plan

Essential Study Strategies

This chapter will equip you with the tools to navigate this roadmap effectively. We will delve into the importance of understanding exam objectives, crafting a personalized study plan that fits your learning style, and leveraging a variety of resources to solidify your knowledge. Let us dive in and ensure that you are fully prepared to conquer the AWS Cloud Practitioner exam.

- **Understanding Exam Objectives:** Before diving into your study journey, it is crucial to have a clear understanding of the exam objectives outlined by AWS. These objectives serve as a roadmap for what you need to know to pass the exam. Take the time to review the exam guide provided by AWS, which outlines the domains, subdomains, and competencies covered in the exam. You can refer to *Chapter 1* of this book for detailed information on the exam objectives. This will help you grasp what you need to focus on for the AWS Certified Cloud Practitioner exam.

- **Creating a Personalized Study Plan:** With the exam objectives in mind, create a personalized study plan that aligns with your schedule, learning style, and existing knowledge. Break down the topics into manageable chunks and allocate dedicated time for studying each day or week. Consider your strengths and weaknesses and prioritize areas where you need more focus. A well-structured study plan will help you stay organized and track your progress effectively.

  Let us say that you are a developer with no cloud experience but have three years of work management experience and are studying for the exam.

  Therefore, you must plan to dedicate:

  - An hour hour per day during the weekdays (five hours per week)
  - Three hours on the weekends (a total of six hours)
  - Total Study Time Per Week: Eleven hours (maintain this consistency for about 1a month or two)

- **Leveraging Various Other Resources**
    - **Official AWS Documentation:** AWS provides comprehensive documentation for all its services like whitepapers, FAQs, and user guides. You can dive into the official documentation to gain in-depth insights into AWS services, best practices, and architectural patterns.
    - **Hands-on Practice:** Hands-on practice with AWS services is essential for reinforcing theoretical concepts and gaining practical experience. Utilize AWS Free Tier to experiment with different services, build sample projects, and troubleshoot issues firsthand. Consider setting up a sandbox environment where you can explore without impacting production workloads.

Importance of Practice Exams and Mock Tests

The AWS Certified Cloud Practitioner exam validates your foundational knowledge of the AWS cloud platform. While studying the core concepts is crucial, there is another vital step in your exam preparation journey: taking adequate **practice exams and mock tests**. These tools go beyond simply testing your knowledge. They simulate the real exam environment and help you refine your skills and build the confidence needed to succeed. We have listed the following points that state the importance of taking practice exams and mock tests:

- **Gauging Readiness for the Exam:** Practice exams and mock tests are invaluable tools for assessing your readiness for the AWS Certified Cloud Practitioner exam. By simulating the exam environment and format, these assessments help you gauge your knowledge, identify areas of strength and weakness, and determine your overall readiness to sit for the exam.
- **Identifying Areas for Improvement:** Taking practice exams and mock tests allows you to identify gaps in your understanding and areas where you need further study. Reviewing your performance and analyzing the questions you answered incorrectly can provide valuable insights into which topics require additional focus. Use this feedback to adjust your study plan and prioritize areas for improvement.
- **Building Confidence and Familiarity:** Familiarizing yourself with the format and structure of the exam through practice exams can help alleviate test anxiety and build confidence. As you become more comfortable with the types of questions asked and the time constraints, you will feel better prepared and more confident on exam day.
- **Learning the Method of Eliminating Wrong Answers:** Mock exams provide valuable practice in eliminating incorrect answer choices, which improve your ability to identify and select the correct answers. This strategy increases the probability of choosing the right answers during the actual exam.

In summary, incorporating essential study strategies such as understanding exam objectives, creating a personalized study plan, and leveraging a variety of resources along with taking regular practice exams and mock tests is the key to effectively preparing for the AWS Certified Cloud Practitioner exam and achieving success.

Tips for the Exam Day

Here are some important tips for the exam day to ensure that you do not encounter any hiccups during the exam:

- **Prepare Your Environment:** Find a quiet, distraction-free environment for the exam. Ensure that your internet connection is stable and your computer meets the system requirements provided by Pearson VUE. Pre-check your system configurations to avoid any technical issues during the exam.
- **Have the Required ID Ready:** The proctor will ask for identification before the exam begins. Ensure that your government ID has your signature, picture, and is an original document. You must have it readily accessible for verification.
- **Follow Proctor Instructions:** Listen carefully to the proctor's instructions before and during the exam. They will guide you through the check-in process, security measures, and exam guidelines.
- **Review Exam Details:** Once you have completed the check-in process, review the exam-related information provided by Pearson VUE. This includes exam duration, number of questions, and any specific instructions or rules.
- **Use Provided Resources:** During the exam, make use of any provided resources such as a virtual whiteboard or calculator. Familiarize yourself with these tools beforehand to use them effectively.
- **Stay Focused and Calm:** Maintain focus and stay calm throughout the exam. If you encounter any technical issues or have questions, communicate with the proctor immediately for assistance.
- **Read the Instructions Carefully:** Pay close attention to the exam instructions and format to understand how to navigate through the questions.
- **Manage Your Time Wisely:** Pace yourself during the exam to ensure that you have enough time to answer all questions. Prioritize questions based on difficulty and allocate time accordingly. You can also follow these steps:
    - **Answer Easy Questions First:** Start with the questions you find easier to tackle and then proceed to the more challenging ones. Do not spend too much time on any single question.

  - **Use Process of Elimination:** If you are unsure about an answer, use elimination to rule out incorrect options to improve your chances of selecting the correct one.
  - **Flag Questions for Review:** If you are unsure about an answer or need more time to think, flag the question for review and come back to it later.
- **Double-Check before Submitting:** Before submitting your exam, double-check your answers and review any flagged questions. Ensure you have not missed anything and that all responses are accurate. Since there is no negative marking, ensure that you have answered all the questions.
- **Stay Positive:** Approach the exam with a positive mindset and confidence in your preparation. Trust in your abilities and believe that you can successfully complete the exam.

Following these tips will help you navigate the online exam experience smoothly and effectively, while boosting your chances of achieving success on the AWS Certified Cloud Practitioner exam.

Study Plan

The following study plan is created assuming a developer with no cloud experience but has three years of work management experience, and is studying for the exam:

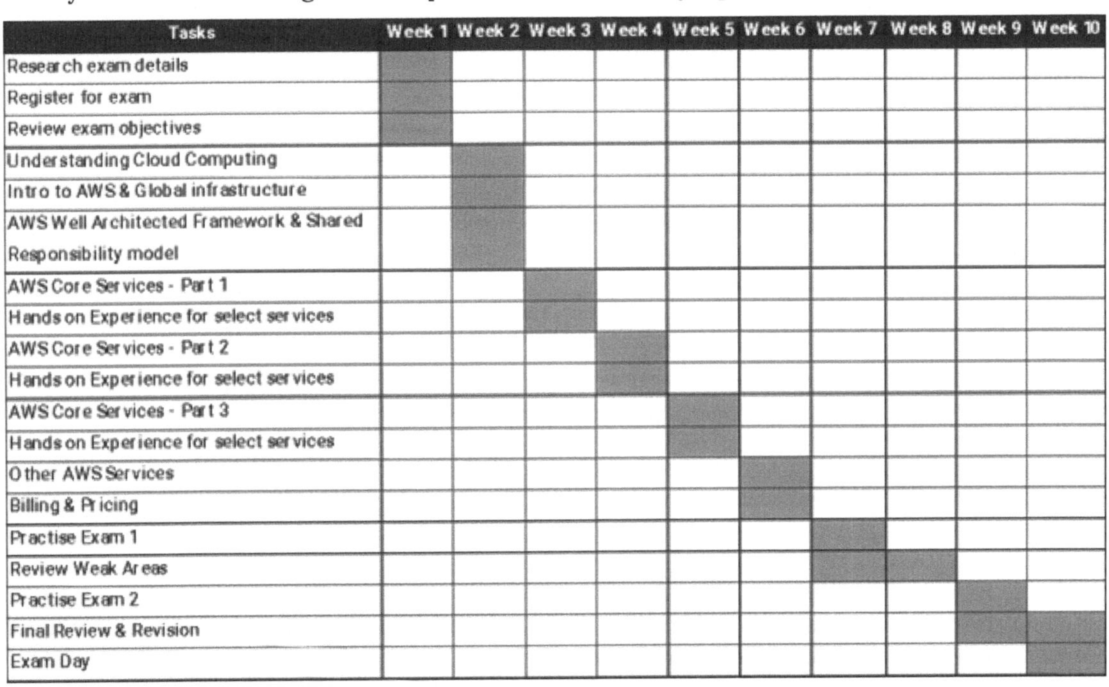

Figure 10.1: *Gantt Chart Indicating an Ideal Study Plan for Cloud Practitioner Exam*

This Gantt chart outlines a timeline spanning approximately two months leading up to the exam day. It includes tasks such as researching exam details, creating a study plan, studying core concepts, practicing exams, reviewing weak areas, and final revision. The chart also allocates time for relaxation and rest before the exam day. You can adjust the durations and start dates based on your individual study schedule and preferences.

Conclusion

In this chapter, we have explored essential strategies and tips to help you prepare effectively for the AWS Certified Cloud Practitioner exam. From understanding exam objectives to creating a personalized study plan, leveraging practice exams, and mastering time management on exam day, you have gained valuable insights to optimize your preparation journey.

By following the guidance outlined in this chapter, you can approach the exam with confidence and readiness. Remember to stay focused, maintain a positive mindset, and trust in your abilities. With diligent preparation and perseverance, you're well-equipped to excel on the exam and achieve AWS Certified Cloud Practitioner status.

As you embark on this final stage of your preparation, remember that consistency is the key. Stay committed to your study plan, review your learnings regularly, and make the most of available resources. Keep calm, stay focused, and believe in your capabilities.

We wish you the best of luck on your AWS Certified Cloud Practitioner exam journey. May you approach the exam with confidence, perform to the best of your abilities, and emerge victorious in your quest for the AWS certification.

Practice Exam 1

1. **A medium-sized enterprise is planning to migrate its on-premises infrastructure to AWS to take advantage of cloud scalability and flexibility. The enterprise aims to optimize costs while ensuring seamless migration and ongoing management of resources. Which of the following strategies should the enterprise adopt to achieve cost optimization in their AWS migration journey? (Select all that apply)**

    a. Utilize AWS Database Migration Service (DMS) for migrating databases to AWS with minimal downtime and cost.

    b. Implement AWS Direct Connect to establish a dedicated network connection between the on-premises data center and AWS to reduce data transfer costs.

    c. Choose Amazon RDS for managed database services to eliminate the overhead of database administration and maintenance.

    d. Utilize AWS Snowball for transferring large datasets offline to AWS to avoid high data transfer costs over the internet.

e. Opt for AWS Lambda for serverless computing to pay only for the compute time consumed without provisioning or managing servers.

2. **According to the AWS Shared Responsibility Model, who is responsible for managing user access and permissions within AWS services?**
    a. AWS
    b. Customer
    c. Both AWS and the customer
    d. AWS Partner Network (APN) members
3. **A company wants to build a serverless application that processes data from IoT devices and triggers automated actions. Which AWS service should they use to securely ingest and process IoT data?**
    a. Amazon SQS
    b. AWS IoT Core
    c. Amazon SNS
    d. Amazon Kinesis
4. **What is the primary benefit of using a cloud-based security solution like AWS IAM?**
    a. It is a more secure way to manage access to cloud resources.
    b. It allows for easier management of user identities.
    c. It is a more cost-effective way to manage security.
    d. It allows for better scalability of security measures.
5. **Which of the following AWS services offer a "free tier"? Select all that applies**
    a. Amazon Elastic Compute Cloud (EC2)
    b. Amazon Relational Database Service (RDS)
    c. Amazon Simple Storage Service (S3)
    d. Amazon CloudWatch
    e. AWS Lambda
6. **Which AWS service allows you to run code without provisioning or managing servers?**
    a. Amazon EC2
    b. AWS Lambda
    c. Amazon EKS
    d. Amazon ECS

7. **A company wants to automate the deployment and management of their containerized applications. Which AWS services should they use to orchestrate container deployments and manage containerized environments? (Select two.)**
   a. Amazon ECS
   b. Amazon EKS
   c. Amazon EC2
   d. AWS Lambda
8. **A company is required to comply with regulatory standards regarding data privacy and protection. They need to ensure that all data stored in Amazon RDS databases is encrypted both at rest and in transit. Which combination of AWS services and configurations should the company implement to meet these requirements? (Select all that apply.)**
   a. Enable encryption at rest for RDS instances using AWS KMS.
   b. Enable encryption in transit for RDS instances using SSL/TLS.
   c. Implement IAM policies to restrict access to RDS resources.
   d. Enable AWS CloudTrail logging for RDS API calls.
   e. Enable Amazon RDS Enhanced Monitoring.
9. **Which of the following AWS services provides a pay-per-use pricing model? (Select all that apply.)**
   a. Amazon Elastic Compute Cloud (EC2)
   b. Amazon Relational Database Service (RDS)
   c. Amazon Simple Storage Service (S3)
   d. Amazon CloudFront
10. **In the AWS Shared Responsibility Model, who is responsible for managing security groups and network Access Control Lists (ACLs)?**
    a. AWS
    b. Customer
    c. Both AWS and the Customer
    d. Third-Party Vendors
11. **A company wants to analyze customer sentiment in real-time from social media feeds and customer support interactions. Which AWS service can they use to perform natural language processing and sentiment analysis?**
    a. Amazon Comprehend
    b. Amazon Lex

c. Amazon Polly
d. Amazon Textract

12. **What is the primary benefit of using a cloud-based data encryption solution like AWS Key Management Service (KMS)? (Select two.)**
    a. It is a more cost-effective way to encrypt data.
    b. It allows for easier management of data encryption.
    c. It provides a more secure way to encrypt data.
    d. It allows for better scalability of data encryption measures.
13. **Which AWS service provides guidance on cost optimization, security best practices, and performance improvements?**
    a. AWS Config
    b. AWS Trusted Advisor
    c. AWS Control Tower
    d. AWS Cloud Formation
14. **What is the minimum duration for which you can reserve resources in AWS?**
    a. 1 hour
    b. 24 hours
    c. 1 Year
    d. 30 days
15. **What is the primary benefit of using a cloud-based backup and recovery solution like AWS Backup?**
    a. It is a more cost-effective way to store backups.
    b. It allows for easier management of backups.
    c. It is a more secure way to store backups.
    d. It allows for faster recovery of data in case of a disaster.
16. **Which AWS service provides a fully managed DDoS (Distributed Denial of Service) protection service that safeguards applications running on AWS from the impact of DDoS attacks?**
    a. AWS WAF (Web Application Firewall)
    b. Amazon GuardDuty
    c. AWS Shield
    d. AWS Security Hub

17. **What is the key benefit of using AWS Backup compared to traditional on-premises backup solutions?**
    a. Provides centralized backup across multiple AWS services
    b. Requires dedicated on-premises hardware
    c. Provides only local copies of backups
    d. Cannot integrate with compliance requirements

18. **An organization wants to analyze large volumes of data stored in Amazon S3 using SQL queries without managing servers. Which AWS service should they use?**
    a. Amazon Athena
    b. Amazon Redshift
    c. Amazon EMR
    d. Amazon DynamoDB

19. **Which of the following statements about AWS pricing is true?**
    a. All AWS services have a pay-per-use pricing model.
    b. Some AWS services have a subscription-based pricing model.
    c. AWS offers discounts when you commit to usage with reserved instances or savings plans.
    d. All AWS services have a free tier with unlimited usage.

20. **An organization is using Amazon EC2 instances to host its production environment. The operations team wants to ensure that the instances are regularly patched and updated to protect against security vulnerabilities. Which of the following options illustrates the Shared Responsibility Model in this scenario?**
    a. AWS is responsible for patching and updating the EC2 instances.
    b. The operations team is solely responsible for patching and updating the EC2 instances.
    c. Both AWS and the operations team share responsibility for patching and updating the EC2 instances.
    d. The responsibility for patching and updating the EC2 instances is outsourced to a managed service provider.

21. **A company wants to deploy a highly available and scalable relational database in AWS. Which AWS service should they use for this purpose?**
    a. Amazon RDS
    b. Amazon DynamoDB

c. Amazon S3

d. Amazon Redshift

22. **Which of the following is a benefit of using AWS Key Management Service (KMS)?**

    a. Automatic patching of security vulnerabilities in AWS services

    b. Secure and centrally managed storage of API keys and secret tokens

    c. Seamless integration with third-party identity providers

    d. Encryption of data stored in AWS services using customer-controlled keys

23. **An organization is planning to migrate their existing database to AWS and needs a managed database service that is compatible with their current database engine. Which AWS service should they use for this purpose?**

    a. Amazon RDS

    b. Amazon DynamoDB

    c. Amazon Redshift

    d. Amazon S3

24. **What is the primary benefit of using AWS Reserved Instances?**

    a. They provide significant discounts compared to on-demand pricing.

    b. They allow you to reserve EC2 instances only for a specific time slot.

    c. They provide a free tier for EC2 instances.

    d. They eliminate upfront costs.

25. **What is the primary benefit of using a cloud-based data warehousing solution such as AWS Redshift?**

    a. It provides a more cost-effective way to store and analyze data.

    b. It allows for easier management of data warehousing.

    c. It provides a more secure way to store and analyze data.

    d. It allows for faster querying of data.

26. **A startup is developing a web application using AWS services. The development team wants to ensure that the application code is secure and free from vulnerabilities. Which of the following options best reflects the Shared Responsibility Model in this scenario?**

    a. AWS is responsible for securing the application code.

    b. The development team is solely responsible for securing the application code.

c. Both AWS and the development team share responsibility for securing the application code.

d. The responsibility for securing the application code is outsourced to a third-party vendor.

27. An organization wants to ensure that their EC2 instances are automatically replaced in the event of a failure to maintain application availability. Which AWS service should they use for this purpose?

a. Amazon CloudFront

b. Amazon CloudWatch

c. Amazon Auto Scaling

d. Amazon Route 53

28. What is the name of the pricing model used by AWS for its on-demand instances?

a. Pay-per-use

b. Subscription-based

c. Metered

d. Spot pricing

29. What is the primary customer concern addressed in the AWS Shared Responsibility Model when migrating applications to the cloud?

a. Security

b. Compatibility

c. Scalability

d. Downtime

30. Which AWS service provides a fully managed database solution?

a. Amazon EC2

b. Amazon S3

c. Amazon RDS

d. Amazon VPC

31. What is the most cited benefit of using cloud-based infrastructure?

a. Scalability

b. Security

c. Cost-effectiveness

d. Reliability

32. Which AWS service provides a managed Kubernetes service?

a. Amazon EKS
b. Amazon ECS
c. Amazon RDS
d. Amazon S3

33. Which of the following pricing models does AWS Lambda use?

a. Pay only for the number of requests and compute time used
b. Subscription-based
c. Pay-per-VM-hour
d. Free, Unlimited use

34. Which AWS service allows you to create and manage users, groups, and permissions to securely control access to AWS services and resources?

a. Amazon GuardDuty
b. AWS IAM (Identity and Access Management)
c. AWS WAF (Web Application Firewall)
d. AWS Shield

35. What is the purpose of AWS CloudTrail?

a. Monitoring AWS resource utilization
b. Auditing API calls and activity
c. Automated backup and recovery
d. Network traffic analysis

36. Your team is designing a disaster recovery plan for your AWS environment. Which of the following AWS services can help achieve this goal? (Select TWO)

a. Amazon Redshift
b. AWS Backup
c. AWS Direct Connect
d. Amazon S3

37. What is the purpose of an IAM role in AWS?

a. To manage security groups for EC2 instances
b. To define network Access Control Lists (ACLs) for VPCs
c. To delegate permissions to entities that you trust
d. To automatically provision EC2 instances based on demand

38. Which AWS service enables publish/subscribe messaging between distributed applications?

a. Amazon SNS

b. Amazon SQS

c. Amazon CloudFront

d. Amazon Glacier

39. What is the purpose of a cloud Service Level Agreement (SLA)?

a. To define the level of service provided by a cloud service provider

b. To define the level of security provided by a cloud service provider

c. To define the level of compliance provided by a cloud service provider

d. To define the level of support provided by a cloud service provider

40. What is the difference between a public cloud and a private cloud?

a. A public cloud is owned by a third-party provider, while a private cloud is owned by the organization using it.

b. A public cloud is owned by the organization using it, while a private cloud is owned by a third-party provider.

c. A public cloud is available to the general public, while a private cloud is only available to a specific organization.

d. A public cloud is only available to a specific organization, while a private cloud is available to the general public.

41. Which AWS service is used for hosting static websites?

a. Amazon S3

b. Amazon EC2

c. Amazon RDS

d. Amazon Redshift

42. Which of the following best describes an IAM group in AWS?

a. A collection of IAM policies that define permissions for users

b. A logical firewall to control traffic to EC2 instances

c. A container for users with similar permissions

d. A service for monitoring AWS resource configurations

43. **Which AWS service provides the ability to enable Multi-Factor Authentication (MFA) for user accounts?**
    a. Amazon GuardDuty
    b. AWS IAM (Identity and Access Management)
    c. AWS Inspector
    d. AWS Trusted Advisor
44. **Which AWS service is used for managing and securing network traffic?**
    a. Amazon Route 53
    b. Amazon VPC
    c. Amazon CloudFront
    d. Amazon RDS
45. **Which AWS service provides a managed CI/CD pipeline for automating software builds and deployments?**
    a. AWS CodePipeline
    b. Amazon CloudWatch
    c. AWS CloudFormation
    d. Amazon Inspector
46. **What is the benefit of using a cloud-based Identity and Access Management (IAM) solution?**
    a. It provides greater security and compliance.
    b. It provides easier management of user identities and access.
    c. It provides greater scalability and flexibility.
    d. It provides easier integration with other cloud services.
47. **Which AWS service allows developers to build and deploy full-stack web and mobile apps quickly, without managing infrastructure?**
    a. AWS Amplify
    b. Amazon EKS
    c. AWS Lambda
    d. Amazon CloudFront
48. **Which AWS service provides a fully managed disaster recovery solution for quickly recovering applications to AWS?**
    a. AWS Backup
    b. AWS Elastic Disaster Recovery

   c. Amazon RDS
   d. Amazon CloudFront

49. What is the purpose of AWS Direct Connect?

   a. Content Delivery Network
   b. High-Speed Internet Access
   c. Private Network Connectivity to AWS
   d. Managed Database Service

50. Which strategies can help achieve cost savings in AWS? (Select TWO)?

   a. Purchase savings plans or reserved instances.
   b. Use AWS Lambda for infrequent tasks.
   c. Implement multi-region redundancy for all services.
   d. Choose on-demand instances for all workloads.

51. A company wants to ensure compliance with industry regulations by encrypting data at rest in their Amazon S3 buckets. Which AWS service can they use to accomplish this?

   a. AWS CloudTrail
   b. AWS Key Management Service (KMS)
   c. AWS Config
   d. AWS Firewall Manager

52. Which AWS service allows customers to define and enforce network security rules for their VPCs (Virtual Private Clouds)?

   a. AWS WAF (Web Application Firewall)
   b. Amazon GuardDuty
   c. AWS IAM (Identity and Access Management)
   d. AWS Network ACLs (Access Control Lists)

53. Which AWS service is used for content delivery and edge caching?

   a. Amazon RDS
   b. Amazon DynamoDB
   c. Amazon CloudFront
   d. Amazon Route 53

54. **Which AWS service provides continuous security monitoring and threat detection for AWS accounts and workloads?**
    a. AWS Config
    b. AWS GuardDuty
    c. AWS Inspector
    d. AWS Security Hub

55. **A company wants to ensure that data transferred between its on-premises data center and AWS is encrypted and that AWS services used comply with relevant regulatory requirements. Which AWS service should they use?**
    a. AWS Certificate Manager (ACM)
    b. AWS Direct Connect
    c. AWS VPN (Virtual Private Network)
    d. AWS CloudHSM (Hardware Security Module)

56. **A company wants to monitor the performance and health of their AWS resources in real-time and receive alerts when thresholds are exceeded. Which AWS service should they use for this purpose?**
    a. Amazon CloudFront
    b. Amazon CloudWatch
    c. Amazon CloudTrail
    d. Amazon Inspector

57. **Which AWS service aggregates findings from multiple security services to help assess and remediate risks??**
    a. Amazon GuardDuty
    b. Amazon Security Hub
    c. AWS WAF (Web Application Firewall)
    d. AWS Shield

58. **Your company is considering migrating its infrastructure to AWS. Which of the following factors should be considered to ensure scalability and high availability? (Select TWO)**
    a. Elastic Load Balancing
    b. Amazon RDS (Relational Database Service)
    c. Auto Scaling Groups
    d. AWS Lambda functions

59. A company is migrating its infrastructure to AWS and wants to ensure that all data stored in Amazon S3 buckets is encrypted at rest. Additionally, they need to ensure that access to sensitive data is restricted based on predefined policies. Which combination of AWS services and actions should the company implement to meet these requirements? (Select all that apply.)

   a. Enable Server-Side Encryption with AWS KMS-managed keys (SSE-KMS) for the S3 buckets.

   b. Enable Server-Side Encryption with Amazon S3-managed keys (SSE-S3) for the S3 buckets.

   c. Implement bucket policies to restrict access to specific IAM roles or users.

   d. Use AWS Config to monitor compliance with encryption requirements.

   e. Enable Amazon S3 Access Points to manage access at the bucket level.

60. Which AWS service helps developers analyze and debug distributed applications by tracing requests end-to-end?

   a. Amazon CloudWatch

   b. AWS X-Ray

   c. AWS Config

   d. AWS Inspector

61. Which AWS service is used for scalable and elastic computing capacity?

   a. Amazon S3

   b. Amazon EC2

   c. Amazon RDS

   d. Amazon SQS

62. An organization needs to monitor and analyze network traffic within its AWS environment to detect potential security threats and intrusions. They also want the ability to automate response actions based on predefined rules. Which combination of AWS services should the organization use to fulfill these requirements? (Select all that apply.)

   a. Amazon VPC (Virtual Private Cloud)

   b. AWS CloudTrail

   c. Amazon GuardDuty

   d. AWS Network Firewall

   e. AWS Lambda

63. **Which AWS service provides business intelligence dashboards and data visualization?**
    a. Amazon QuickSight
    b. Amazon Athena
    c. Amazon Redshift
    d. AWS Glue

64. **What is a key benefit of a cloud-native threat detection solution like Amazon GuardDuty compared to traditional on-premises tools?**
    a. Provides continuous monitoring without requiring infrastructure management
    b. Requires customers to install and manage agents on all servers
    c. Offers less scalability than on-premises tools
    d. Cannot integrate with AWS services

65. **What is the primary benefit of using a cloud-based big data processing solution like AWS Glue?**
    a. It allows for easier management of big data processing.
    b. It provides a more cost-effective way to process big data.
    c. It provides a more secure way to process big data.
    d. It allows for faster processing of big data.

Practice Exam 2

1. **What is the primary benefit of using AWS Glue?**
    a. It provides a serverless service for preparing and transforming data.
    b. It provides a more cost-effective way to run applications.
    c. It allows for better scalability of applications.
    d. It provides a managed relational database service.

2. **A company is planning to migrate its infrastructure to AWS. The IT team is concerned about who will be responsible for securing the underlying infrastructure. Which of the following options best describes the Shared Responsibility Model in this scenario?**
    a. The company is solely responsible for securing the underlying infrastructure.
    b. AWS is solely responsible for securing the underlying infrastructure.

c. Both the company and AWS share responsibility for securing the underlying infrastructure.

d. The responsibility for securing the underlying infrastructure depends on the AWS region chosen.

3. An organization needs to process large volumes of data streams in real-time and run analytics. Which AWS service should they use?

a. Amazon RDS

b. Amazon S3

c. Amazon EMR

d. Amazon Kinesis

4. A small startup is planning to deploy its web application on AWS. They are concerned about managing their costs effectively while ensuring scalability and reliability. They are considering various AWS services for their infrastructure. Which of the following options should the startup consider to optimize their costs while meeting their requirements? (Select all that apply.)

a. Utilize AWS Free Tier services for eligible services during the initial phase.

b. Implement AWS Cost Explorer to analyze usage patterns and identify cost-saving opportunities.

c. Choose Amazon EC2 Reserved Instances for predictable workloads to benefit from significant cost savings.

d. Leverage AWS Trusted Advisor to receive real-time guidance on cost optimization and performance improvement.

e. Implement AWS Budgets to set custom cost and usage budgets to track spending and receive alerts when thresholds are exceeded.

5. What is the responsibility of AWS in the shared responsibility model?

a. Physical security of data centers

b. Patching and updating of operating systems

c. Managing access control policies

d. Data encryption and decryption

6. Which of the following is a security best practice for managing access to AWS resources?

a. Sharing AWS root account credentials with trusted partners

b. Creating IAM users with administrative privileges for all employees

c. Using temporary security credentials and roles to grant access

d. Storing IAM user credentials in plaintext files on local computers

7. **A company wants to deploy a serverless application that automatically scales based on demand and only charges for actual usage. Which AWS service should they use for this purpose?**
    a. Amazon S3
    b. Amazon EC2
    c. AWS Lambda
    d. Amazon RDS
8. **A company wants to ensure that all instances launched within its AWS account comply with security best practices and corporate policies. They need to automatically enforce security configurations and remediate non-compliant instances. Which combination of AWS services should the company use to achieve these requirements? (Select all that apply)**
    a. AWS Config
    b. AWS Systems Manager (SSM)
    c. AWS Trusted Advisor
    d. AWS Security Hub
    e. AWS Inspector
9. **Which AWS services offer discounted pricing options for long-term commitments (Reserved Instances or Savings Plans)?**
    a. Amazon Elastic Compute Cloud (EC2)
    b. Amazon Relational Database Service (RDS)
    c. Amazon Simple Storage Service (S3)
    d. Amazon Elastic Container Service (ECS)
10. **Which cloud deployment model allows for the greatest level of control and customization?**
    a. Public Cloud
    b. Private Cloud
    c. Hybrid Cloud
    d. Community Cloud
11. **What is the primary benefit of using a cloud-based monitoring and logging solution such as AWS CloudWatch?**
    a. It allows for easier monitoring of cloud resources.
    b. It provides a more cost-effective way to monitor resources.

c. It provides a more secure way to monitor resources.

d. It allows for better scalability of monitoring capabilities.

12. Which AWS service provides centralized management of workforce user access across multiple AWS accounts?

a. AWS Identity Center

b. AWS Shield

c. AWS Security Hub

d. AWS WAF (Web Application Firewall)

13. Your company wants to ensure resilience for a web app on AWS. Which services help achieve this? (Select TWO)

a. Amazon RDS (Relational Database Service) Multi AZ

b. Elastic Load Balancing

c. Multi-AZ deployment for Amazon EC2 instances

d. Amazon Direct Connect

14. What is the name of the service that allows you to purchase and manage third-party software licenses on AWS?

a. AWS Marketplace

b. AWS License Manager

c. AWS Software Hub

d. AWS AppStore

15. Which AWS service helps route traffic to healthy endpoints for high availability and fault tolerance?

a. Amazon S3

b. Amazon EC2

c. Amazon Route 53

d. Amazon RDS

16. A company is hosting a web application on AWS and wants to protect it from DDoS attacks. They also need to ensure high availability and minimal latency for their users. Which combination of AWS services should the company use to achieve these requirements? (Select all that apply)

a. AWS Shield Standard

b. AWS WAF (Web Application Firewall)

c. AWS CloudFront

   d. AWS Route 53 with DNS Shield
   e. AWS Shield Advanced

17. **What is a key difference between AWS Backup and traditional backup solutions?**
   a. AWS Backup is fully managed in the cloud.
   b. Traditional backups offer unlimited global scalability.
   c. AWS Backup requires customer-managed storage hardware.
   d. Traditional solutions integrate automatically with cloud services.

18. **Which AWS service lets you query structured and unstructured data in S3 using standard SQL without managing servers?**
   a. Amazon Redshift
   b. Amazon EMR
   c. Amazon Athena
   d. Amazon DynamoDB

19. **What is the maximum amount you can save by using AWS Reserved Instances?**
   a. 5%
   b. 10%
   c. 72%
   d. 30%

20. **What is a benefit of using Amazon S3?**
   a. High-Performance Computing
   b. Long-Term Data Archival
   c. Real-Time Data Analytics
   d. Virtually Unlimited Storage with High Durability

21. **What does the AWS Shared Responsibility Model define?**
   a. The division of responsibilities between AWS and its customers for security and compliance
   b. The pricing structure for AWS services
   c. The geographic distribution of AWS data centers
   d. The types of services offered by AWS

22. **What is the primary function of AWS CloudWatch?**
   a. Monitoring AWS resource utilization
   b. Auditing API calls and activity

c. Automating deployment and management
d. Managing network traffic

23. What is the difference between AWS Database Migration Service (DMS) and AWS DataSync?

a. DMS is used to migrate and replicate databases to AWS.
b. DMS is used to sync files, DataSync is for relational databases.
c. DataSync migrates apps, while DMS syncs apps.
d. Both services serve the same purpose.

24. Which AWS services are included in the Free Tier with limited usage? (Select all that apply)

a. Amazon Elastic Compute Cloud (EC2)
b. Amazon Relational Database Service (RDS)
c. Amazon Simple Storage Service (S3)
d. Amazon CloudWatch
e. AWS Lambda

25. A company is looking to host a static website with minimal cost. Which AWS service is the most cost-effective option for hosting static websites?

a. Amazon EC2
b. Amazon RDS
c. Amazon S3
d. Amazon DynamoDB

26. Your organization wants to migrate its data center to AWS. Which of the following concepts should be considered during the migration process? (Select TWO)

a. Elasticity and Scalability
b. Traditional Infrastructure Limitations
c. Capital Expenditure (CapEx) Model
d. Pay-As-You-Go Pricing Model

27. What is a key benefit of using AWS Lambda?

a. Real-Time Data Analytics
b. Fully Managed Container Orchestration
c. Serverless Compute Service
d. Long-Term Data Archival

28. Which of the following AWS services offer a "reservation" pricing model?

a. Amazon Elastic Compute Cloud (EC2)
b. Amazon Relational Database Service (RDS)
c. Amazon Simple Storage Service (S3)
d. Amazon Elastic Block Store (EBS)

29. Which best describes Software as a Service (SaaS)?

a. Provides fully managed applications to end users
b. Provides tools and frameworks for developers
c. Provides only infrastructure resources
d. Provides hardware in customer data centers

30. What is the benefit of using AWS CloudFront?

a. Long-Term Data Archival
b. Content Delivery and Edge Caching
c. Real-Time Data Analytics
d. Object Storage

31. You are responsible for ensuring security in your organization's AWS environment. Which of the following security best practices should be implemented? (Select TWO)

a. Using strong passwords for IAM users
b. Sharing AWS access keys publicly on GitHub
c. Regularly reviewing IAM policies
d. Disabling multi-factor authentication (MFA)

32. What is the primary benefit of using a cloud-based monitoring and logging solution such as AWS CloudWatch?

a. It allows for easier monitoring of cloud resources.
b. It provides a more cost-effective way to monitor resources.
c. It provides a more secure way to monitor resources.
d. It allows for better scalability of monitoring capabilities.

33. What lets you sell your unused Standard Reserved Instances?

a. AWS Reserved Instances
b. AWS Credits
c. AWS Refunds
d. AWS Exchange

34. Which AWS service provides a central view of security alerts and compliance status across AWS accounts?

a. AWS Config

b. AWS Security Hub

c. AWS Trusted Advisor

d. AWS Certificate Manager (ACM)

35. Which AWS service is best suited for delivering live and on-demand video globally with low latency?

a. Amazon S3

b. Amazon CloudFront

c. Amazon Kinesis

d. Amazon Elastic Transcoder

36. A company is using Amazon S3 to store sensitive customer data. The IT security team wants to ensure that access to the S3 buckets is properly configured and monitored. Which of the following options best represents the Shared Responsibility Model in this scenario?

a. AWS is responsible for configuring access controls for S3 buckets.

b. The company is solely responsible for configuring access controls for S3 buckets.

c. Both AWS and the company share responsibility for configuring access controls for S3 buckets.

d. The responsibility for configuring access controls for S3 buckets is delegated to an external consultant.

37. What is the difference between a cloud-native application and a traditional application?

a. A cloud-native application is designed to take advantage of cloud services, a traditional application is not.

b. A cloud-native application is designed to run on-premises, a traditional application is not.

c. A cloud-native application is designed to run on a cloud platform, a traditional application is not.

d. A cloud-native application is designed to run on a traditional platform, a traditional application is not.

38. What is the primary purpose of AWS Lambda?

a. Container Orchestration

b. Serverless Compute Service

c. Database Management
d. Object Storage

39. **Which AWS service continuously monitors for malicious activity and unauthorized behavior in AWS accounts?**
    a. AWS Certificate Manager (ACM)
    b. AWS GuardDuty
    c. AWS Inspector
    d. AWS Certificate Manager Private Certificate Authority (ACM PCA)

40. **Which cloud deployment model allows for the greatest level of control and customization?**
    a. Public Cloud
    b. Private Cloud
    c. Hybrid Cloud
    d. Community Cloud

41. **What is the purpose of a cloud security assessment?**
    a. To identify vulnerabilities
    b. To evaluate compliance
    c. To assess risk
    d. To evaluate the effectiveness of security controls

42. **What AWS service is used for collecting, analyzing, and visualizing log data in near realtime?**
    a. Amazon CloudWatch
    b. Amazon CloudTrail
    c. Amazon OpenSearch Service
    d. Amazon Athena

43. **What is the purpose of a cloud-based data governance framework?**
    a. To provide a set of guidelines and best practices for data management and use
    b. To provide a set of tools and technologies for data management and use
    c. To provide a set of regulations and compliance requirements for data management and use
    d. To provide a set of standards and certifications for data management and use

44. Which AWS service is used for real-time data streaming and processing?

a. Amazon Redshift

b. Amazon Kinesis

c. Amazon EMR

d. Amazon RDS

45. According to the AWS Shared Responsibility Model, which of the following is AWS responsible for?

a. Protecting cuistomer data

b. Encrypting data in transit

c. Ensuring physical security of AWS data centers

d. Managing the configuration of customer applications

46. Which AWS service provides automated security assessments to help improve the security and compliance posture of AWS resources?

a. AWS Config

b. AWS Inspector

c. AWS Trusted Advisor

d. Amazon Macie

47. Which AWS service is used for orchestrating and automating workflows across services?

a. Amazon SQS

b. AWS Step Functions

c. Amazon SNS

d. Amazon CloudWatch

48. What is the primary benefit of using a cloud-based patch management solution like AWS Systems Manager (SSM)?

a. It provides a more cost-effective way to manage patches.

b. It allows for easier management of patches.

c. It provides a more secure way to manage patches.

d. It allows for better scalability of patch management measures.

49. What is the purpose of Amazon VPC?

a. Object Storage

b. Virtual Private Cloud Networking

  c. Real-Time Data Processing
  d. Database Management

50. **Which of the following is a responsibility of AWS according to the Shared Responsibility Model?**
    a. Implementing application-level security
    b. Encrypting customer data
    c. Securing the underlying infrastructure of AWS services
    d. Configuring access controls for customer resources

51. **Which AWS service provides secure, encrypted connectivity between an on-premises data center and AWS?**
    a. AWS VPN
    b. AWS Direct Connect
    c. Amazon VPC
    d. AWS Shield

52. **Which AWS service helps track resource compliance with internal policies and industry standards?**
    a. AWS Config
    b. AWS GuardDuty
    c. AWS Certification Manager
    d. Amazon Inspector

53. **Which AWS service is best suited for petabyte-scale data warehousing and fast querying?**
    a. Amazon S3
    b. Amazon Redshift
    c. Amazon RDS
    d. Amazon DynamoDB

54. **What is a characteristic of Amazon EC2 instances?**
    a. Fully Managed Service
    b. Serverless Architecture
    c. Pre-Configured Databases
    d. Virtual Computing Environments

55. What is the difference between a cloud-based backup and a cloud-based archive?

a. A cloud-based backup is used to restore data, while a cloud-based archive is used to store data for long-term retention.

b. A cloud-based backup is used to store data for long-term retention, while a cloud-based archive is used to restore data.

c. A cloud-based backup is used to backup data, while a cloud-based archive is used to backup data.

d. A cloud-based backup is used to backup data, while a cloud-based archive is used to store data for long-term retention.

56. Which AWS service provides intelligent threat detection by analyzing AWS account activity?

a. Amazon GuardDuty

b. AWS Config

c. AWS Inspector

d. AWS Security Hub

57. What is the purpose of a cloud security framework?

a. To provide a set of guidelines and best practices for cloud security

b. To provide a set of tools and technologies for cloud security

c. To provide a set of regulations and compliance requirements for cloud security

d. To provide a set of standards and certifications for cloud security

58. An organization needs to securely connect their on-premises data center to resources in AWS without going over the public internet. Which AWS service should they use for this purpose?

a. Amazon VPC

b. AWS Direct Connect

c. Amazon Route 53

d. AWS VPN

59. In AWS, what is the primary purpose of a security group?

a. To manage IAM policies for user access

b. To define firewall rules that control inbound and outbound traffic to instances

c. To encrypt data stored in Amazon S3 buckets

d. To monitor and detect security threats in real-time

60. **When designing an AWS architecture, which of the following are the pillars of the Well-Architected Framework? (Select TWO)**
    a. Cost Optimization
    b. Performance Efficiency
    c. Operational Agility
    d. Disaster Recovery Planning
61. **What is the primary benefit of using a cloud-based network security solution like AWS Network ACLs?**
    a. It provides a more cost-effective way to manage network security.
    b. It allows for easier management of network security.
    c. It provides a more secure way to manage network security.
    d. It allows for better scalability of network security measures.
62. **An organization needs to ensure data privacy and compliance with regulations when storing sensitive customer information in the cloud. Which AWS service provides encryption and key management capabilities to achieve this?**
    a. Amazon CloudFront
    b. AWS KMS
    c. AWS Secrets Manager
    d. Amazon GuardDuty
63. **What is the benefit of using a cloud-based Customer Relationship Management (CRM) solution?**
    a. It provides greater scalability and flexibility.
    b. It provides easier integration with other cloud services.
    c. It provides greater collaboration and communication between sales, marketing, and customer service teams.
    d. It provides easier management of customer data and interactions.
64. **Which AWS service allows centralized patching of EC2 instances and on-premises servers?**
    a. AWS System Manager
    b. AWS Config
    c. AWS Inspector
    d. Amazon Macie

65. What is the difference between Infrastructure as a Service (IaaS) and Platform as a Service (PaaS)?

a. IaaS provides virtualized compute, storage, and networking resources; PaaS provides a managed environment for application development.

b. IaaS provides software, PaaS provides hardware.

c. IaaS provides databases, PaaS provides analytics.

d. IaaS provides user applications, PaaS provides operating systems.

Answers: Practice Exam 1

1. a, b, c, d, e
2. b
3. b
4. a
5. a, b, c, d, e
6. b
7. a, b
8. a, b, c
9. a, b, c, d
10. b
11. a
12. b, d
13. b
14. c
15. d
16. c
17. a
18. a
19. c
20. b
21. a
22. d
23. a
24. a
25. d
26. b
27. c
28. a
29. a
30. c
31. a
32. a
33. a
34. b
35. b
36. b, d
37. c
38. a
39. a
40. c
41. a
42. c
43. b
44. b
45. a
46. b
47. a
48. b
49. c
50. a, b
51. b
52. d
53. c
54. b
55. c
56. b
57. b
58. a, c
59. a, b, c, d
60. b
61. b
62. c, d, e
63. a
64. a
65. a

Answers: Practice Exam 2

1. a
2. b
3. d
4. a, b, c, d, e
5. a
6. c
7. c
8. a, b, c, d
9. a, b
10. b
11. a
12. a
13. a, b
14. a
15. c
16. a, b, c, e
17. a
18. c
19. c
20. d
21. a
22. a
23. a
24. a, b, c, d, e
25. c
26. a, d
27. c
28. a, b
29. a
30. b
31. a, c
32. a
33. a
34. b
35. b
36. b
37. a
38. b
39. b
40. b
41. a
42. c,
43. a
44. b
45. c
46. b
47. b
48. b
49. b
50. c
51. a
52. a
53. b
54. d
55. a
56. a
57. a
58. b
59. b
60. a, b
61. c
62. b
63. c
64. a
65. a

CHAPTER 11
AWS Hands-On Guide for Beginners

Introduction

Congratulations! You have conquered the foundational knowledge needed to navigate the vast world of AWS. By now, you are familiar with core services, security best practices, and the overall architecture of the AWS cloud. But there is nothing quite like getting a hang of practical applications through hands-on practice.

This chapter will be your launch pad for hands-on experimentation. We will be guiding you through a series of exercises utilizing some of the most popular AWS services. Remember those key concepts you learned in the previous chapters? Here is your chance to see them come to life in a real-world cloud environment.

By following these step-by-step exercises, you will gain practical experience with:

1. Creating an AWS environment
2. Creating an IAM role, group, and users
3. Launching and managing virtual machines (EC2)
4. Storing and retrieving data in the cloud (S3)
5. Working with SQL databases (Aurora Postgres)

These exercises are designed to be completed within the free tier limitations of AWS, so you can experiment without incurring any charges. They will not turn you into a certified AWS expert overnight, but they will provide a solid foundation for further exploration and solidify your understanding of the theoretical concepts you have mastered.

So, grab your metaphorical toolkit and get ready to put your AWS knowledge to the test!

Let us begin with how to create an AWS Account:

1. Go to the AWS website (https://aws.amazon.com) and click "`Create an AWS Account`".

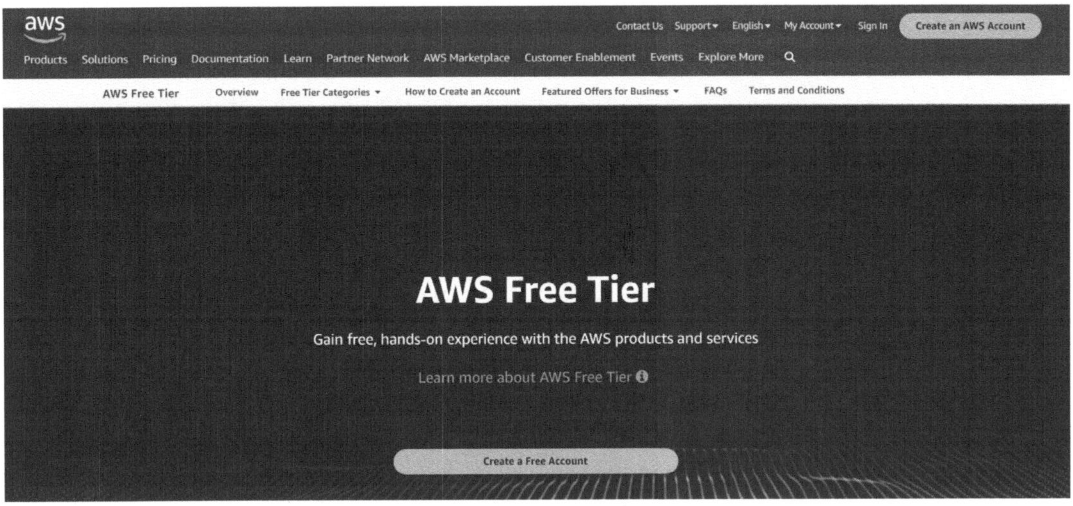

Figure 11.1: *Homepage for Creating an AWS Account*

2. Enter your email address, choose a password, and enter your country or region from the dropdown menu.
3. Click "`Verify Email Address`" and follow the instructions to verify your email address.
4. Once your email address is verified, you will be taken to the AWS Account page.
5. Enter your account details such as your name, company name, and phone number.
6. Choose a pricing plan that suits your needs. You can start with the free tier if you are just starting out.
7. Read and accept the AWS Terms of Service and Privacy Notice.
8. Click "`Create Account`".
9. You will receive an email with your AWS account credentials such as your access key ID and secret access key.
10. You can now start using AWS services, such as Amazon S3, Amazon EC2, and Amazon DynamoDB.

IAM Console:

Now that we have created the account let us understand how to create an IAM role, user group, and policy.

1. Open the IAM console from your AWS homepage.

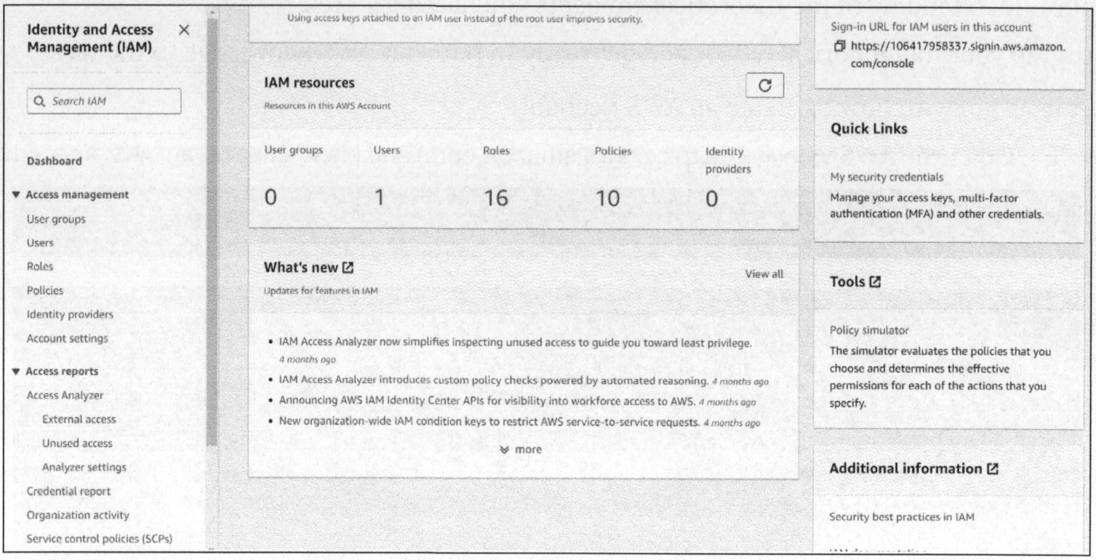

Figure 11.2: *Homepage for IAM Console*

2. In the navigation pane, choose "**`Roles`**".
3. Choose "**`Create role`**".
4. Under "**`Select type of trusted entity`**", choose **`AWS service`**.
5. Under "**`Choose a use case`**", choose **`Lambda`**.
6. Under "**`Select your use case`**", choose **`Lambda`** function.

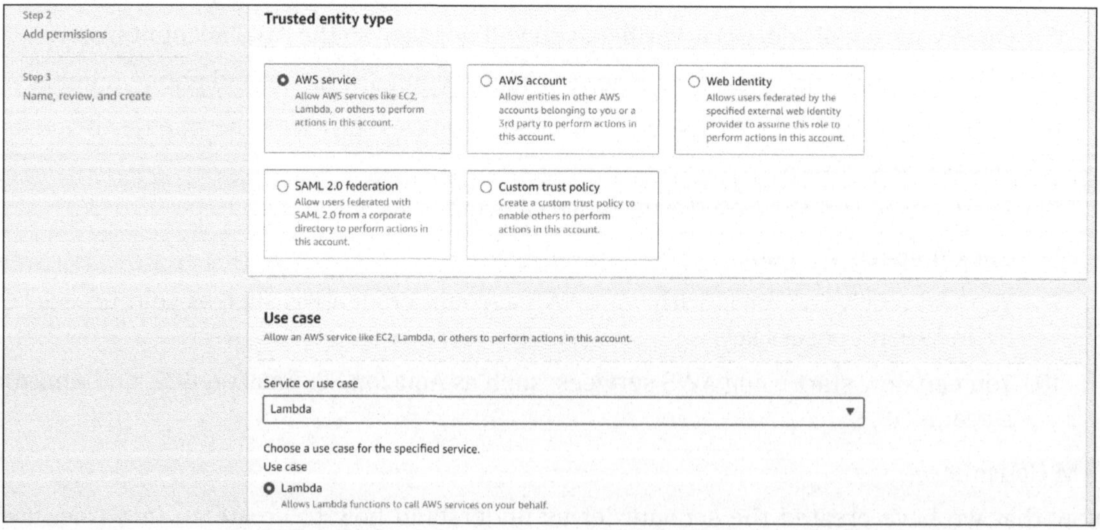

Figure 11.3: *Choosing Trusted Entity and Lambda Function*

7. Choose "**`Next: Permissions`**".
8. Search for and select the policy named **`AmazonDynamoDBFullAccess`**.

Figure 11.4: *Adding Permission to the IAM Role*

9. Choose "**`Next: Tags`**".
10. Choose "**`Next: Review`**".
11. Enter a name for the role, like **`AmazonDynamoDBFullAccessRole`**.
12. Choose "**`Create role`**".

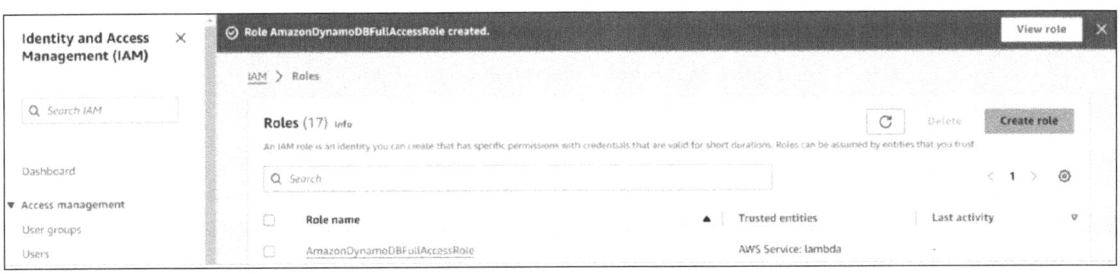

Figure 11.5: *Creation of IAM Role*

13. In the navigation pane, choose "**`User Groups`**".
14. Choose "**`Create group`**".

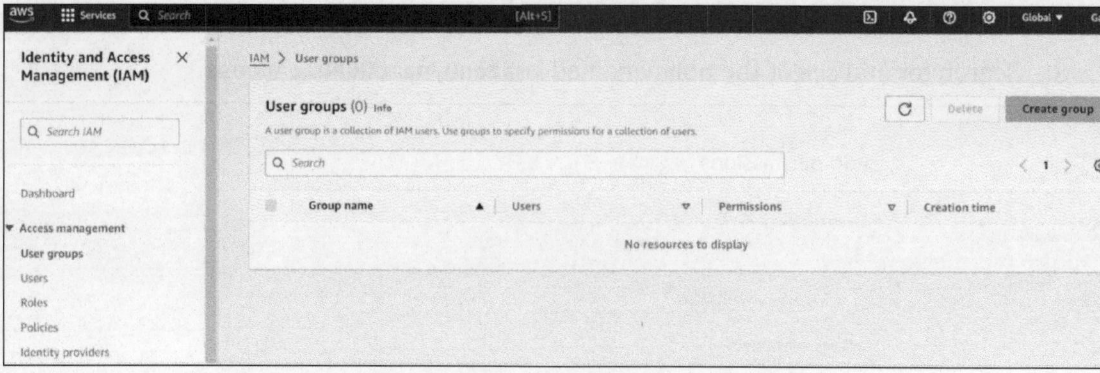

Figure 11.6: *Creating a User Group*

15. Enter a name for the group, such as **`AmazonDynamoDBFullAccessUsers`**.
16. Choose "**`Create group`**".

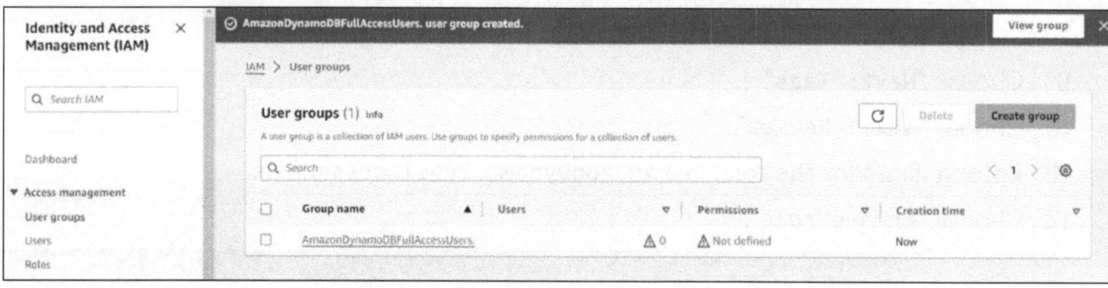

Figure 11.7: *Final Creation of a User Group*

17. In the navigation pane that follows, choose "**`Roles`**".
18. Choose the role you created earlier, such as **`AmazonDynamoDBFullAccessRole`**.

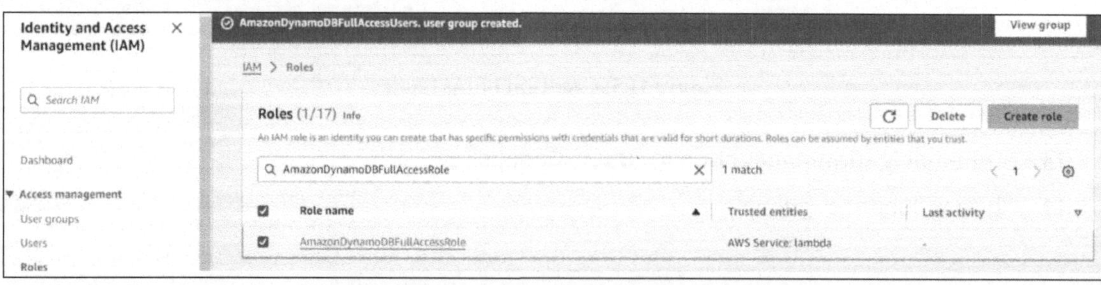

Figure 11.8: *Attaching Role to User Group*

19. Choose "**`Attach policies`**".
20. Search for and select the policy named **`AmazonDynamoDBFullAccess`**.

21. Choose "**`Attach policy`**".

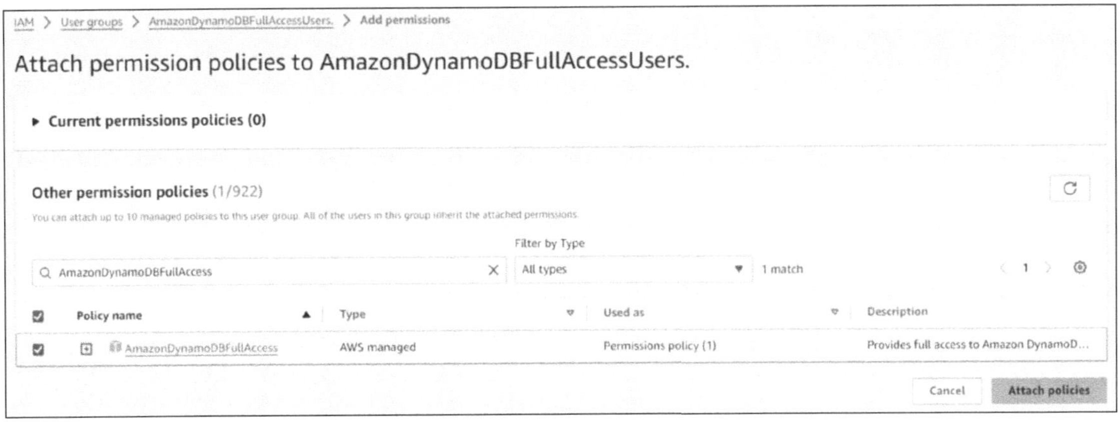

Figure 11.9: *Attaching Policy to the User Groups*

22. In the navigation pane, choose "**`Users`**".
23. Choose "**`Create user`**".

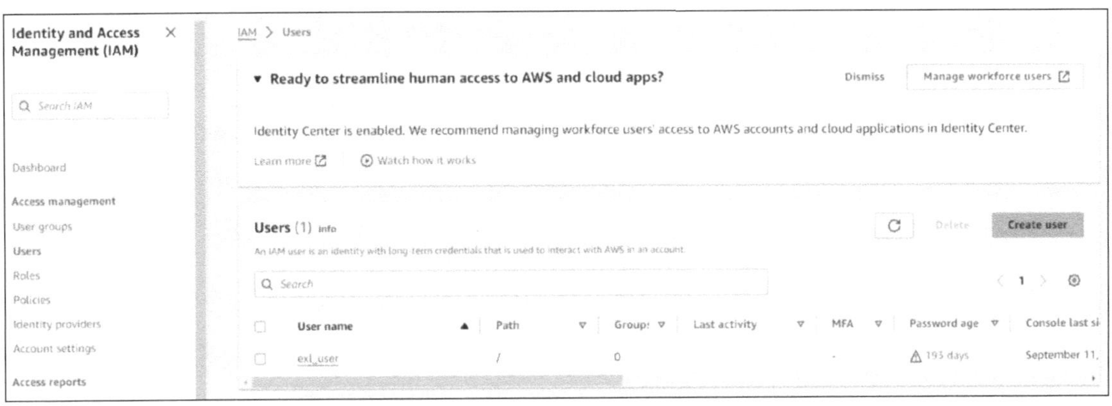

Figure 11.10: *Initial Steps to Creating an IAM User*

24. Enter a name for the user, such as {**`USERNAME-1`**}. In this exercise, we are not providing the user the front end console access.

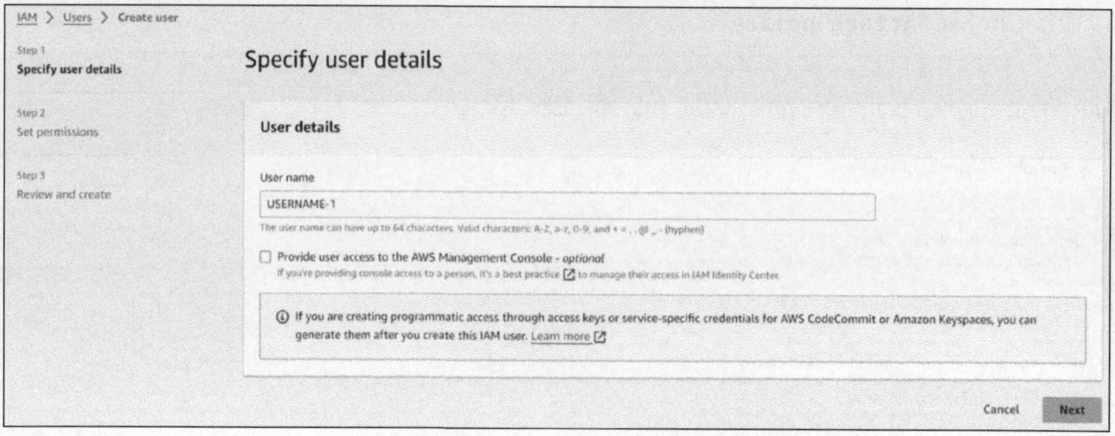

Figure 11.11: *Initializing User Details*

25. Choose "**`Create user`**".
26. Attach the user to the group you created earlier, such as **`AmazonDynamoDBFullAccessUsers`**.
27. Choose the group, like **`AmazonDynamoDBFullAccessUsers`**.
28. Choose "**`Attach users`**".
29. Choose the user you created earlier, such as **`AmazonDynamoDBFullAccessUser`**.

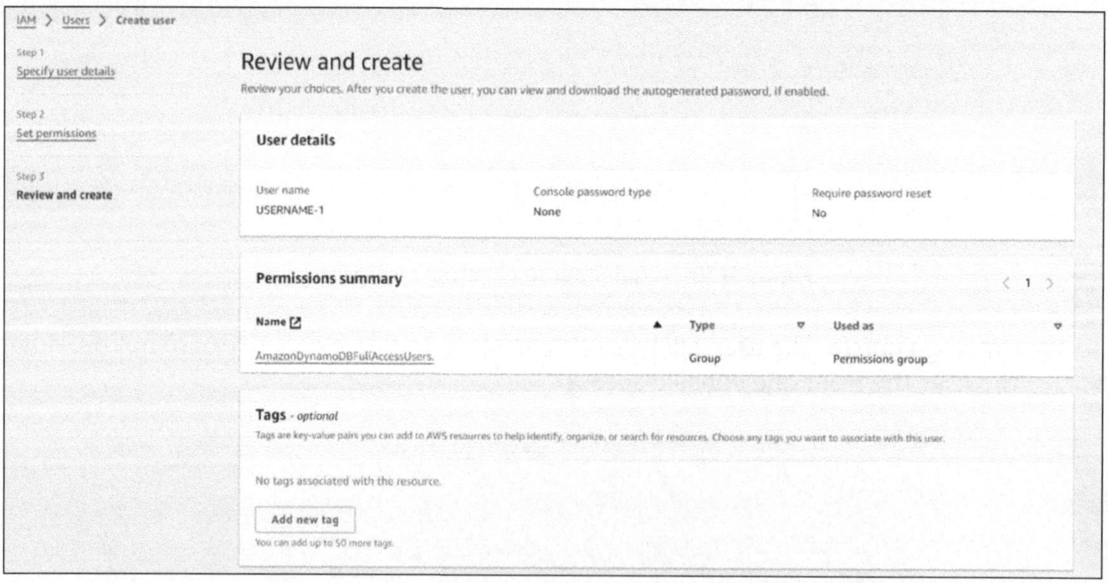

Figure 11.12: *Attaching Appropriate Role and UserG to the IAM User*

30. Choose "**`Attach user`**".

You have now created an IAM role, a user group, and have attached an inline policy. The role grants the user full access to Amazon DynamoDB and the user group allows the user to be assigned to roles. The inline policy grants the user full access to Amazon DynamoDB.

Note: *Full access is not recommended, as the preceding example is meant for hands-on learning.*

Creating an S3 Bucket:

Now that we have defined IAM role and users, let us explore the creation of S3 bucket. Here is a step-by-step guide to creating an S3 bucket, uploading a file, deleting a file, and enabling encryption on S3:

1. Open the Amazon S3 console from Search bar of AWS Console. Click "`Create bucket`" to create a new S3 bucket.

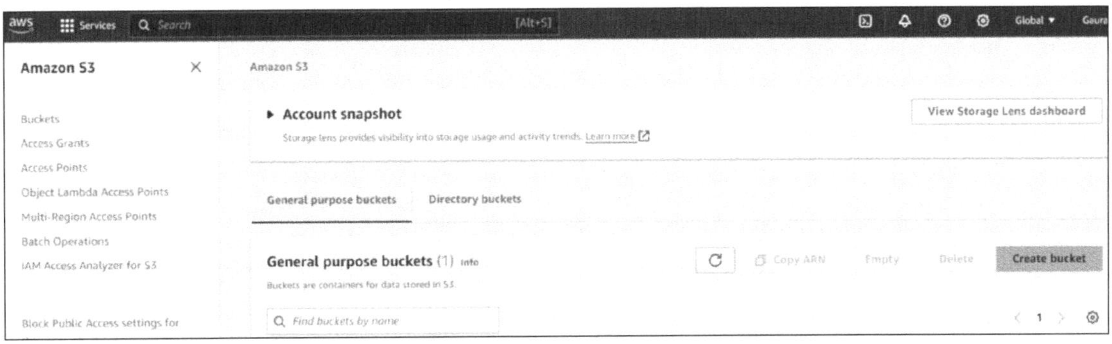

Figure 11.13: *Initial Screenshot of the S3 Bucket Creation*

2. Enter a bucket name and choose a region for your bucket.

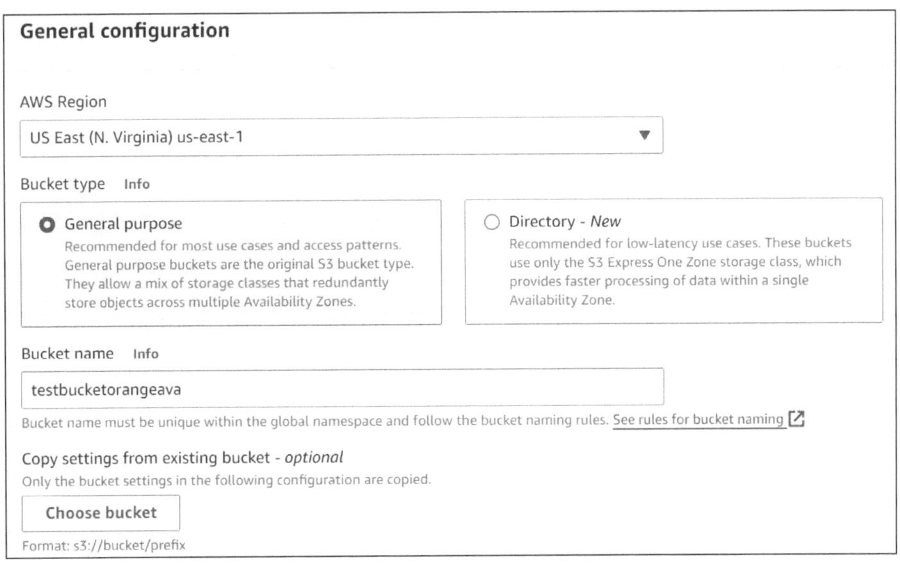

Figure 11.14: *Entering Information to Create S3 Bucket*

3. Click "**`Create bucket`**" to create the bucket.
4. Navigate to the bucket that you just created.
5. Click "**`Upload`**" to upload a file to the bucket.
6. Select the file that you want to upload and click "**`Open`**".
7. Enter a file name for the uploaded file and click "**`Upload`**".

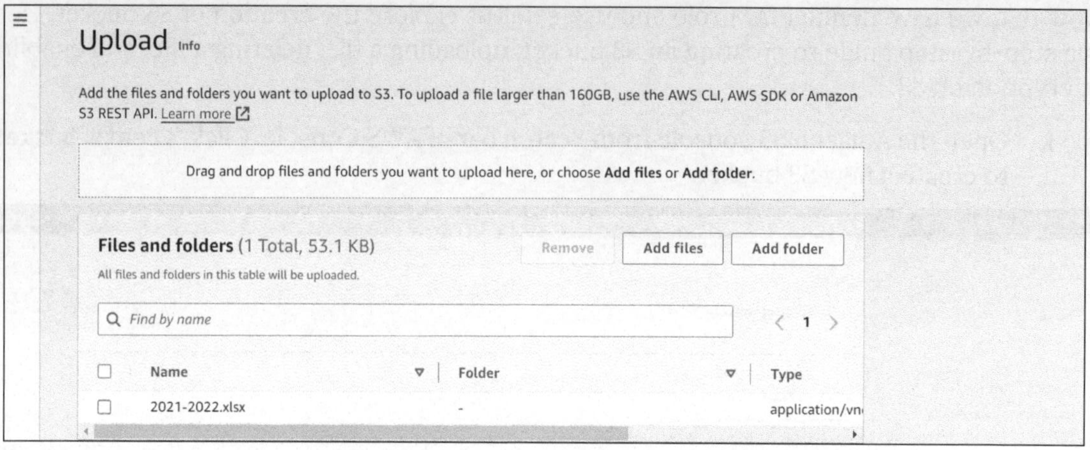

Figure 11.15: *Uploading a File to S3 Bucket*

8. Once the file is uploaded, you can view it in the bucket by clicking the file name.
9. To delete a file from the bucket, select the file that you want to delete and click the "**`Delete`**" button.
10. Confirm the deletion by clicking "**`Yes, delete`**".
11. To enable encryption on the bucket, click "**`Properties`**" tab and scroll down to the "**`Encryption`**" section.

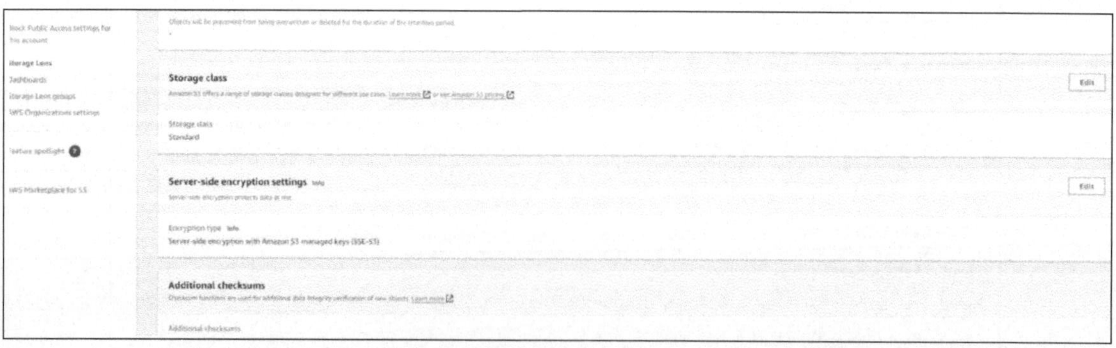

Figure 11.16: *Enabling Encryption of Files Stored in S3 Bucket*

12. Click "**`Enable encryption`**".

13. Choose the encryption algorithm that you want to use (for example, AES-256) and click "**Save**".
14. Wait for the encryption to be enabled on the bucket.

That is it! You have successfully created an S3 bucket, uploaded a file, deleted a file, and enabled encryption on S3.

Launching an EC2 Instance:

Let us now explore one of the most used AWS services EC2 instance. Here is a step-by-step guide to launching an EC2 instance:

1. Open the Amazon EC2 console from search bar within the AWS Console.

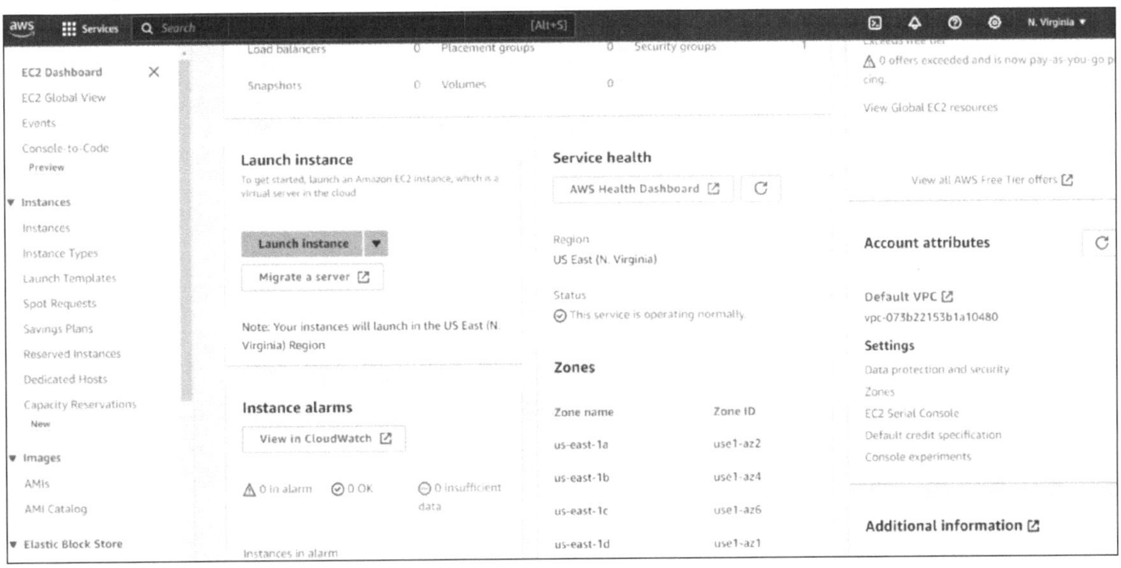

Figure 11.17: *Landing Screen of the EC2 Page in AWS Console*

2. In the navigation pane, choose "**`Instances`**".
3. Choose "**`Launch instance`**".
4. Under Name and tags, you can enter a name for your instance and optionally add tags.
5. Under "**`Application and OS Images (Amazon Machine Image)`**", choose an Operating System (OS) for your instance and an AMI.
6. Under "**`Instance type`**", choose the type of instance that you need. For this tutorial, we will choose **`t2.micro`**.

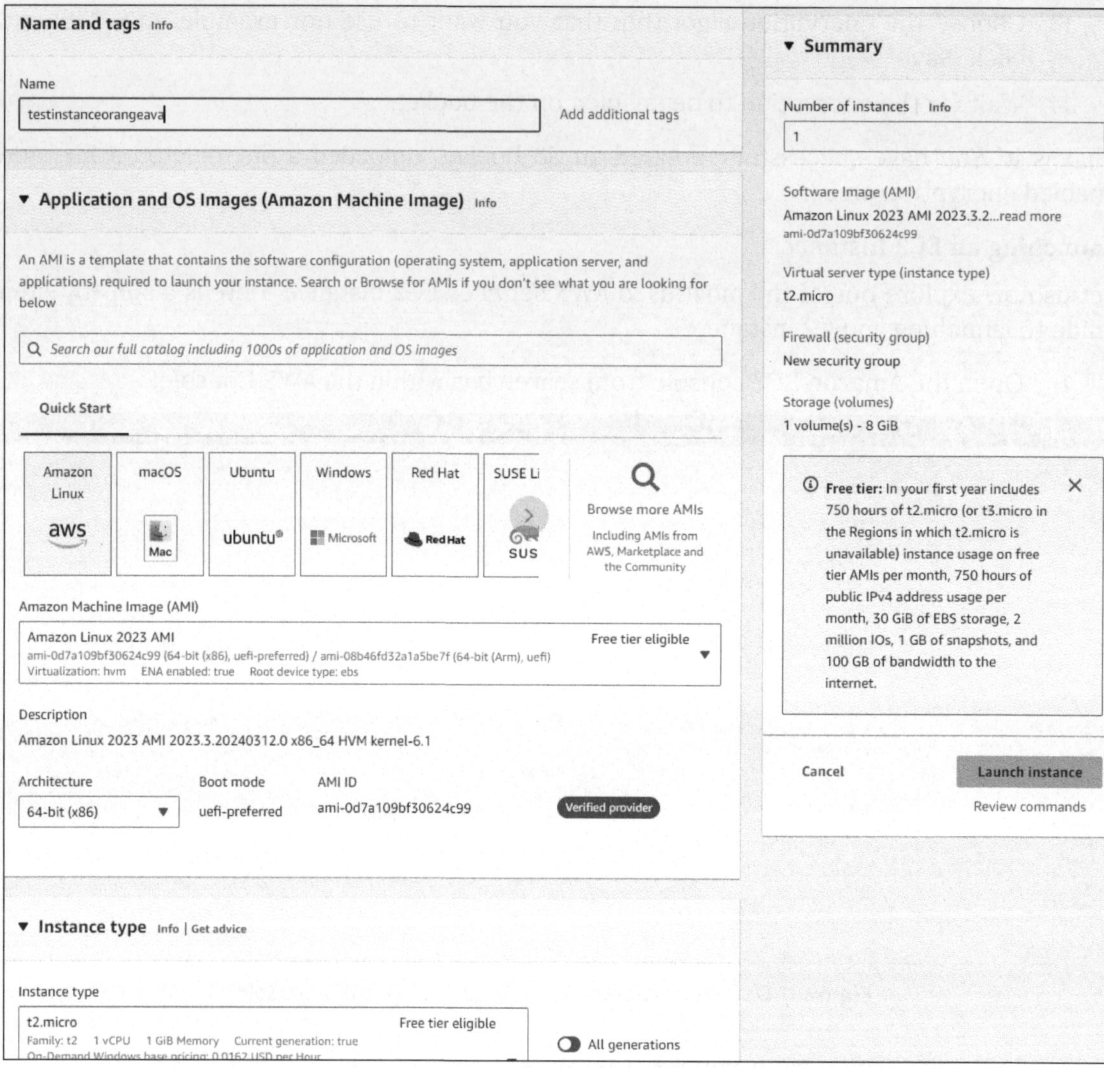

Figure 11.18: *Selecting an Operating System for EC2 Instance-Windows OS*

7. Under "**`Key pair (login)`**", choose an existing key pair or create a new one.
8. Under "**`Network settings`**", choose a VPC and subnet.
9. Under Security groups, choose a security group that allows inbound traffic from the internet.

Note: *SSH from the internet is not a recommended best practice and should be locked down to a specific IP address.*

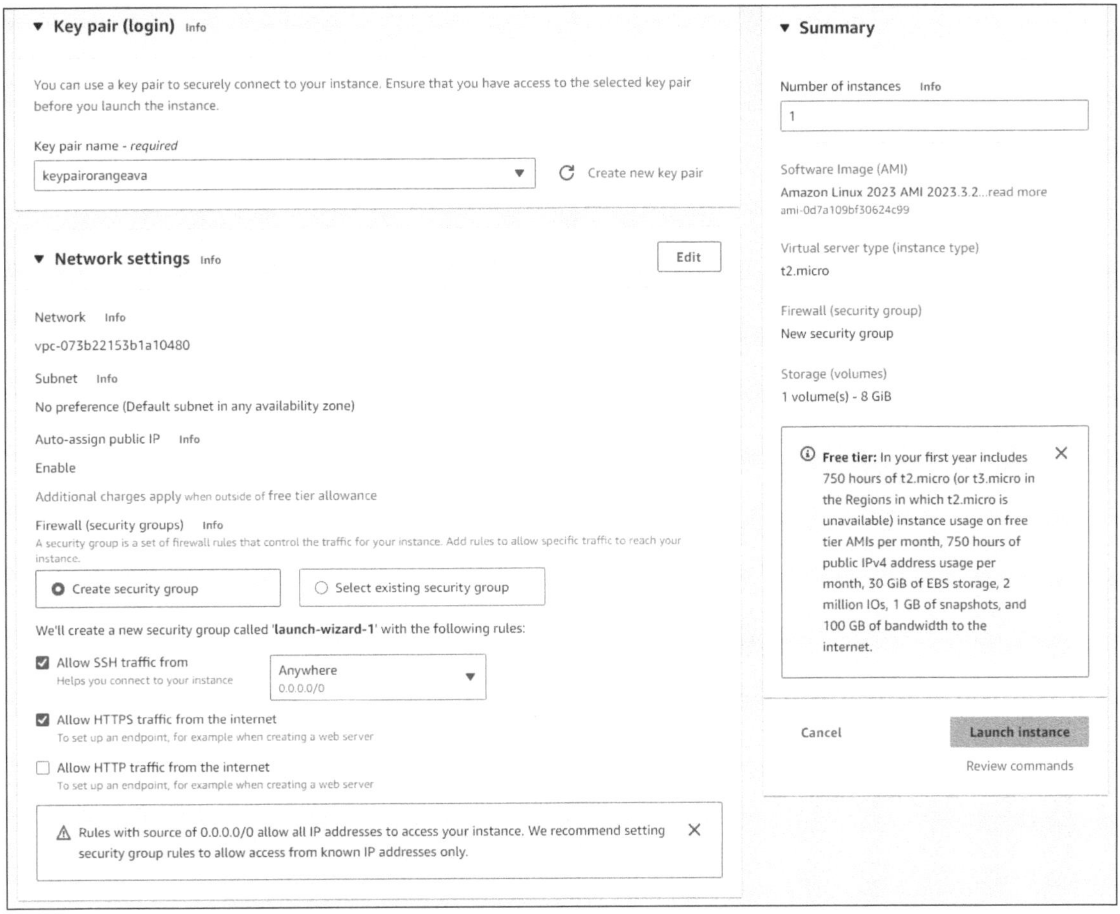

Figure 11.19: *Providing Configuration Details for Creating an EC2*

10. Under Advanced details, you can specify additional settings such as the instance placement, EBS volumes, and IAM roles.
11. Review your settings and choose Launch instance.
12. Amazon EC2 will launch your instance and provide you with an instance ID. You can use this instance ID to connect to your instance and manage it.

Accessing an EC2 Instance:

1. Open the launched instance in the EC2 console and then select "**`Connect`**" option on the instance.

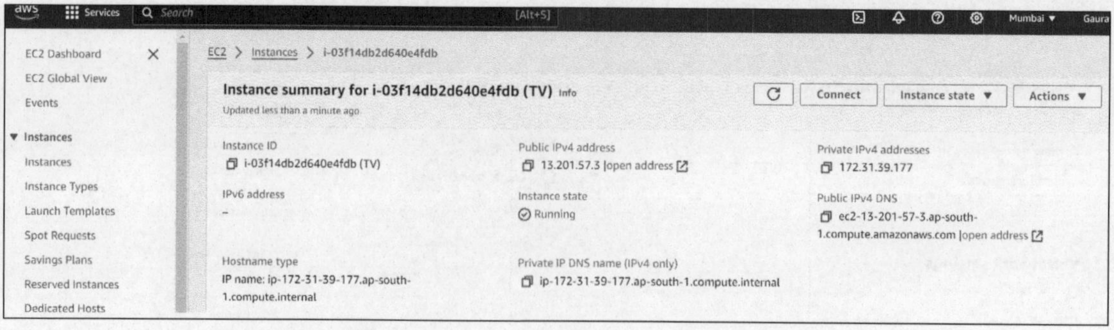

***Figure 11.20:** Selecting the Connect Button on the Instance Created*

2. In the Connect to instance page, select the option "**`RDP Client`**", download the remote desktop file and also use "**`Get Password`**" option to get the initial password to connect to EC2 instance.

   Note: *You would need to input the PEM file created during the key pair creation to retrieve password.*

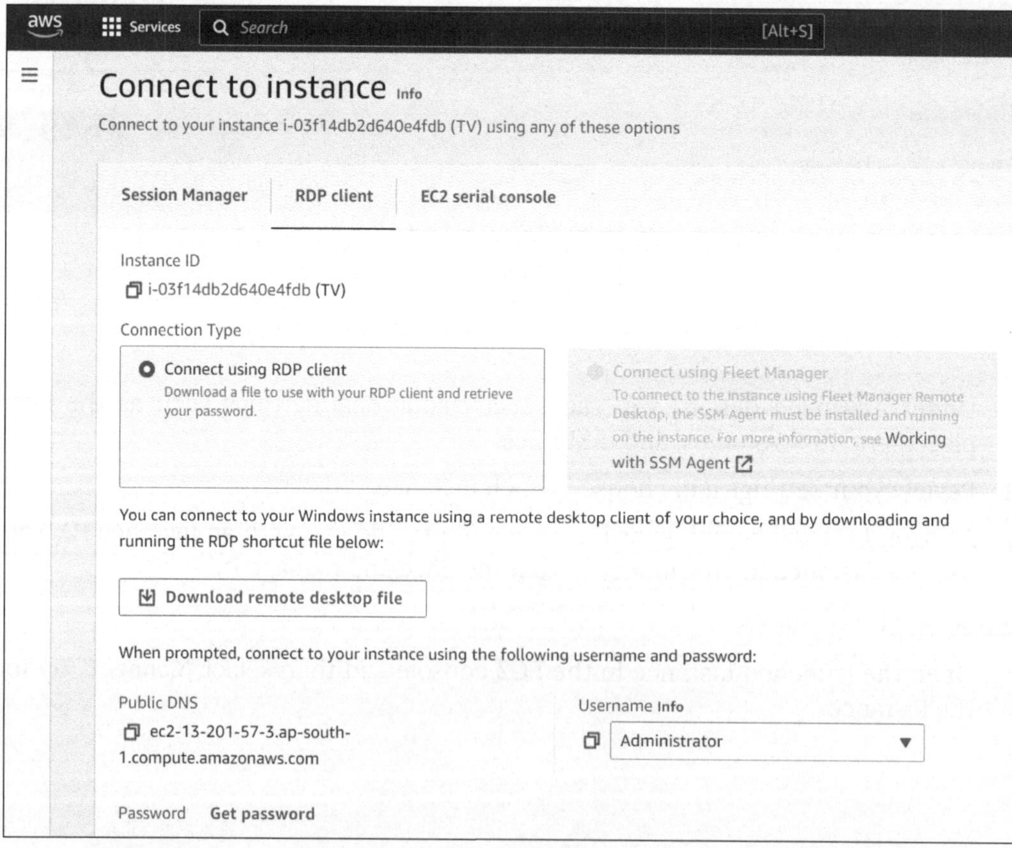

***Figure 11.21:** Connecting to the EC2 Instance through Remote Desktop Client*

You will now be able to use your very own EC2 instance. Explore the Windows system you have created.

Starting Your Own RDS Instance:

Let us now explore how to creating an Aurora RDS instance; here is the step by step guide to create it:

1. **Navigate to the RDS Service:** Search for "**`RDS`**" (Relational Database Service) in the search bar or navigate to the "**`Services`**" section and choose "**`Database`**" followed by "**`RDS`**".
2. **Create Database:** Click "**`Create database`**".

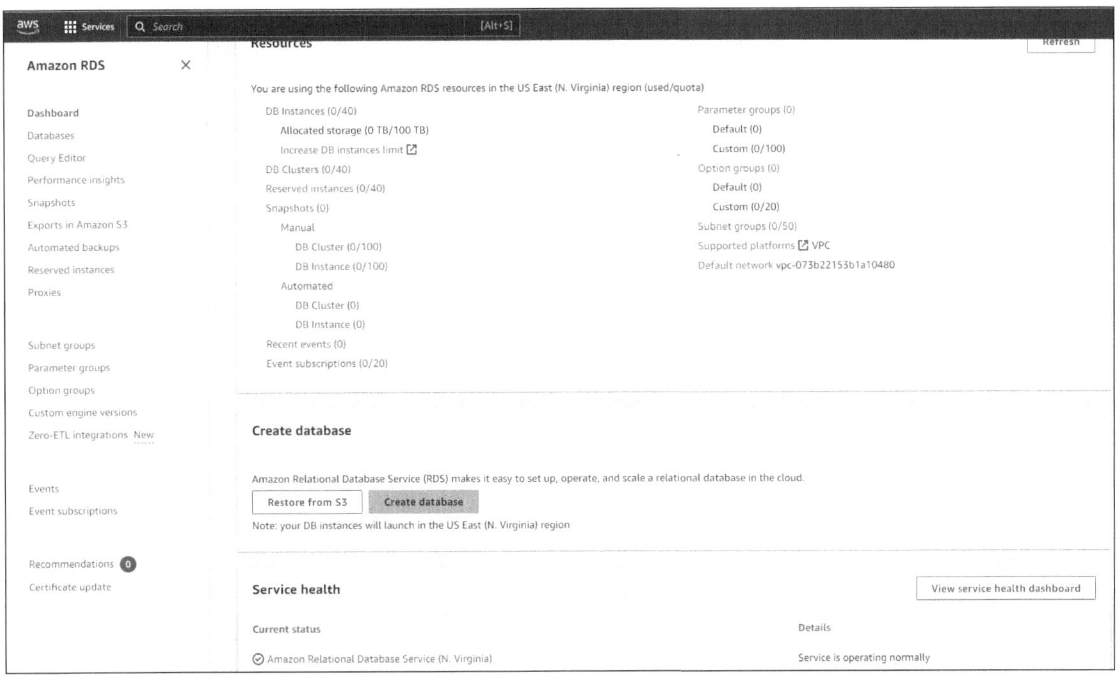

Figure 11.22: *Screenshot of RDS Homepage in AWS Console*

3. **Select Engine:**
   a. In the "**`Create database`**" section, choose "**`Aurora PostgreSQL`**" from the "**`Engine`**" dropdown menu.

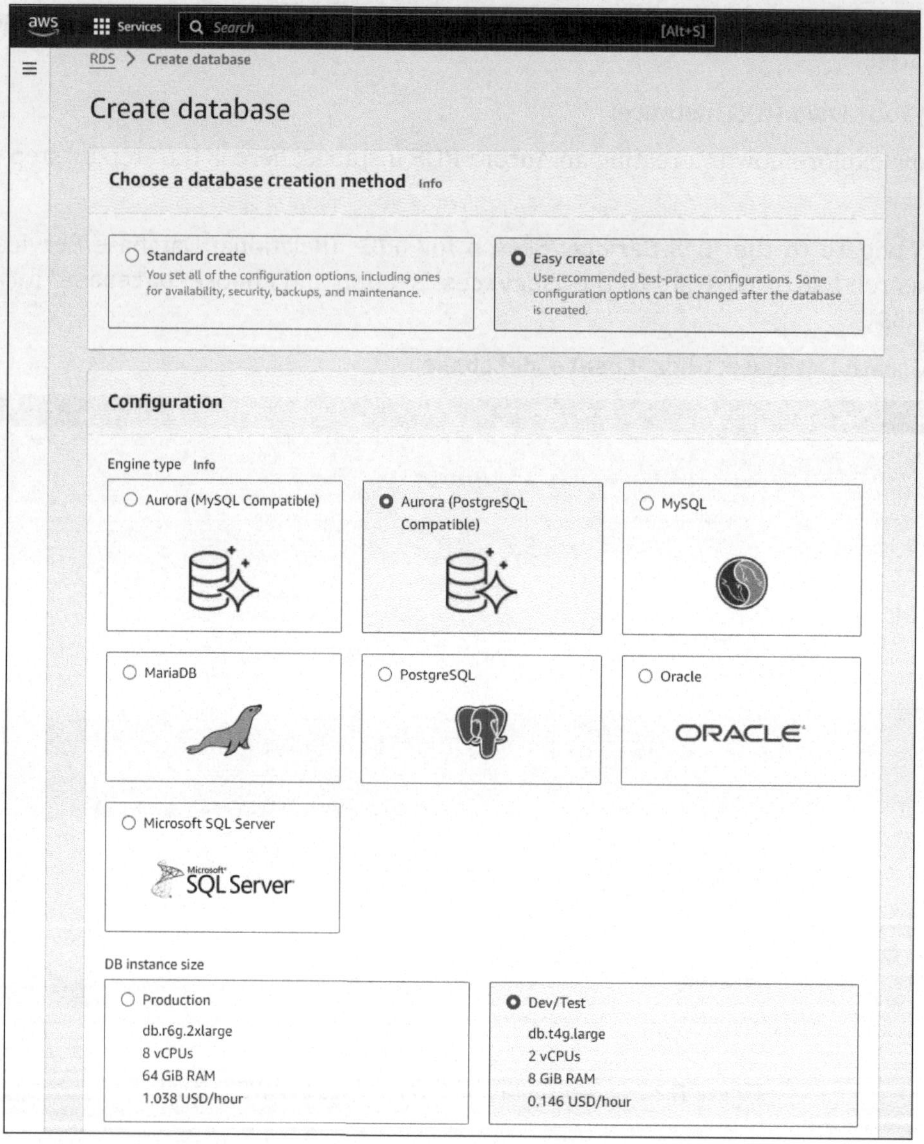

***Figure 11.23:** Selection of an Appropriate RDS Instance*

For training purpose, you can choose database creation method as "`Easy Create`"; in-case you want a control on each aspect of database, then choose "`Standard Create`" option and follow the steps mentioned here for configuration.

4. **Version:**
   a. Select the desired PostgreSQL version you want to use for your cluster. Popular options include versions 11, 12, 13, or 14. Choose based on your application requirements and compatibility needs.

5. **Settings:**
    a. **Cluster Identifier:** Provide a unique name for your Aurora PostgreSQL cluster.
    b. **Instance Class:** Select the instance class for your cluster›s writer (primary) instance. This defines the compute power, memory, and storage capacity. Consider your workload and performance needs when choosing an instance class. Free tier eligible options are available for testing purposes.
    c. **Number of Aurora Replicas:** Choose the number of read replicas for your cluster. Replicas provide high availability and allow scaling read operations. You can start with one replica for testing and adjust later.
    d. **Storage Type:** Select the storage type (General Purpose SSD or Provisioned IOPS SSD) based on your performance and cost requirements. General Purpose SSD is a good starting point for most workloads.
    e. **Storage Size:** Specify the initial storage size for your database cluster. You can scale storage up later as needed.
6. **Connectivity:**
    a. **VPC:** Choose the VPC (Virtual Private Cloud) where you want to deploy your cluster. If you don›t have a VPC, you can create a new one during this process.
    b. **Subnet Group:** Select a subnet group within your chosen VPC that has appropriate network access for your database cluster.
    c. **Security Group:** Create a new security group or choose an existing one that allows inbound traffic on port 5432 (default PostgreSQL port) from your application or tools that will access the database. Remember to configure security groups appropriately for production environments to restrict access for security reasons.
7. **Database Details:**
    a. **Master Username:** Specify a username for the master user account that will be used to access the database cluster.
    b. **Master Password:** Create a strong password for the master user account. Keep this password secure.
    c. **Database Name:** Provide a name for the initial database within your cluster.
8. **Availability and Durability:**
    a. **Availability Zone (AZ):** Choose an Availability Zone (AZ) for your cluster's writer instance. Consider using multiple AZs for high availability in production environments. The free tier allows launching in a single AZ.

9. **Database Options:**
   a. This section allows you to configure additional settings such as database parameters, backups, and encryption. You can explore these options based on your specific needs. Most can be left with default settings for initial setup.
10. **Review and Create:**
   a. Review all the configurations you have chosen.
   b. Click "`Create database`" to launch your Aurora PostgreSQL cluster.

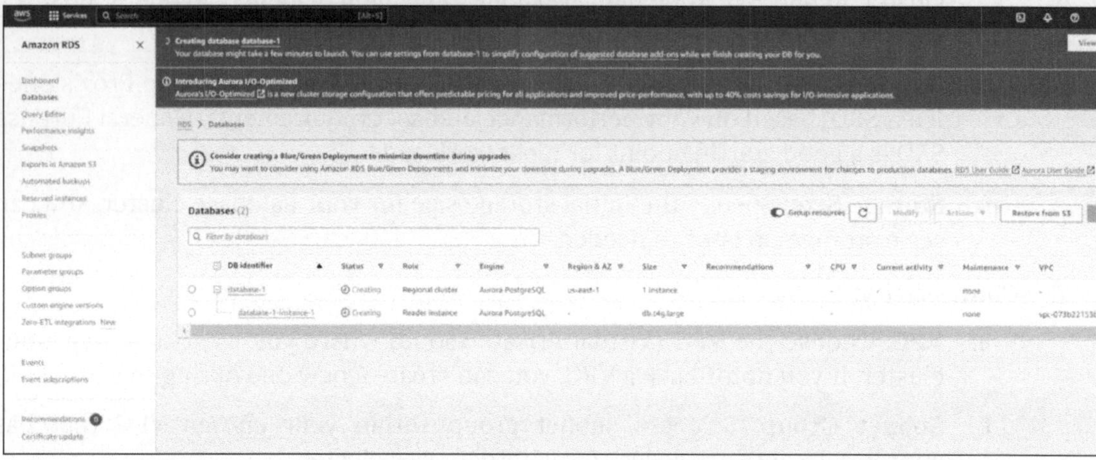

Figure 11.24: *Screenshot of a Created RDS Instance*

After Launch:

- It might take a few minutes for your cluster to be created and become available.
- You can find details about your cluster, including the endpoint address, in the RDS console.

Connecting to Your Aurora PostgreSQL Cluster:

- Use a PostgreSQL client tool such as pgAdmin or the command-line psql utility to connect to your Aurora PostgreSQL cluster endpoint using the master username, password, and endpoint address.
- You can then create additional databases, users, and tables within your Aurora PostgreSQL cluster.

Conclusion

Congratulations! You have reached the end of this comprehensive guide to becoming an AWS Cloud Practitioner. Throughout this book, we have explored the fundamental concepts, core services, security best practices, and billing models that underpin the vast and powerful AWS cloud platform. We have also equipped you with hands-on experience by guiding you through the creation and utilization of key AWS services like EC2 instances, S3 buckets, and Aurora databases.

By now, you should have a solid understanding of the value proposition of AWS and the confidence to navigate the AWS Management Console to deploy and manage basic cloud resources. Remember, the cloud computing landscape is constantly evolving, with new features and services emerging all the time. AWS provides a wealth of documentation and learning resources to help you stay up-to-date and continue expanding your knowledge. As you gain experience and delve deeper into specific cloud computing domains, numerous specialized AWS certifications are available to validate your expertise and propel your cloud career forward.

This book has served as a springboard for your AWS journey. We encourage you to leverage the knowledge you have gained, explore the ever-expanding world of AWS services, and keep building your cloud expertise. Remember, the power of the cloud is in your hands—go forth and innovate!

Index

A

D

E

F

N

O

P

T

V

W

X